It is art that makes life, makes interest, makes importance and I know of no substitute whatever for the force and beauty of its process

-Henry James

THE WAX ONION

DIEDIKER

The Art of SEAN DIEDIKER

written by
Julia Moris-Hartley

This book is issued in conjunction the 2010 unveiling of artist Sean Diediker's "The Wax Onion"- A Diediker Art Collaborative

ISBN 978-0-615-36727-9

Dimensions of paintings are in inches: height precedes width.

Library of Congress Cataloging-in-Publication Data:
A catalogue record for this book is available from the Library of Congress

Diediker, Sean, 1974-
The Wax Onion : The art of Sean Diediker / by Moris-Hartley, Julia & Diediker, Sean
"issued in conjunction the 2010 unveiling of artist Sean Diediker's "The Wax Onion"- A Diediker Art Collaborative "

Library of Congress Control Number: 2010905403

Book Design: Sean Diediker
PR Coordinator: Casey Brinkley
Senior Editor: Kinsi Jene Suttner
Editor: Kathy Brinkley

Photographers:
Joe Maurer Photography, Australia
E M I image Photography (studio shots), USA
Savchuk Photography, London
David Hawkinson, USA
PhotoCraft, USA

First Edition Printed 2010
Q-Tip Publishing
Printed in China

www.diediker.com

In Loving Memory

Valentina Moris
&
Dennis Hibshman

THE WAX ONION

What is the Wax Onion?

THE WAX ONION

The Wax Onion Art Collaborative is a project initiated by Sean Diediker that invites participants from anywhere in the world to comment on his artwork as it is being made. The dynamic is simple: Diediker starts with a completely chance driven abstraction. Then he posts it to his Facebook group called the Wax Onion and asks "What do you see?" After considering their responses, Diediker divines inspiration, extracts suggested images, and completes the work. "For participants, it might be like looking at clouds and eventually seeing Osama Bin Laden riding a mechanical bull, wearing a feather boa while blowing bubbles," jokes Diediker, who revels in the comments made on the Wax Onion.

The Wax Onion invites anyone and everyone to answer. There are no such things as right or wrong answers. Anyone can participate in this collaborative effort: the group is open for joining and each response is treated with respect as a valid interpretation, regardless of the participants' knowledge of artistic composition, use of color, or technique.

Robert Finch, a naturalist and essayist, has said, "True belonging is born of relationships not only to one another but to a place of shared responsibilities and benefits... The more [man] aligns himself to some varied and interdependent whole, the less he is subject to sudden and wholesale bereavement by chance. His heart rests at the bottom of things; anchored there, he may cast about and never be at sea." **Welcome to the Wax Onion**.

What do you see?

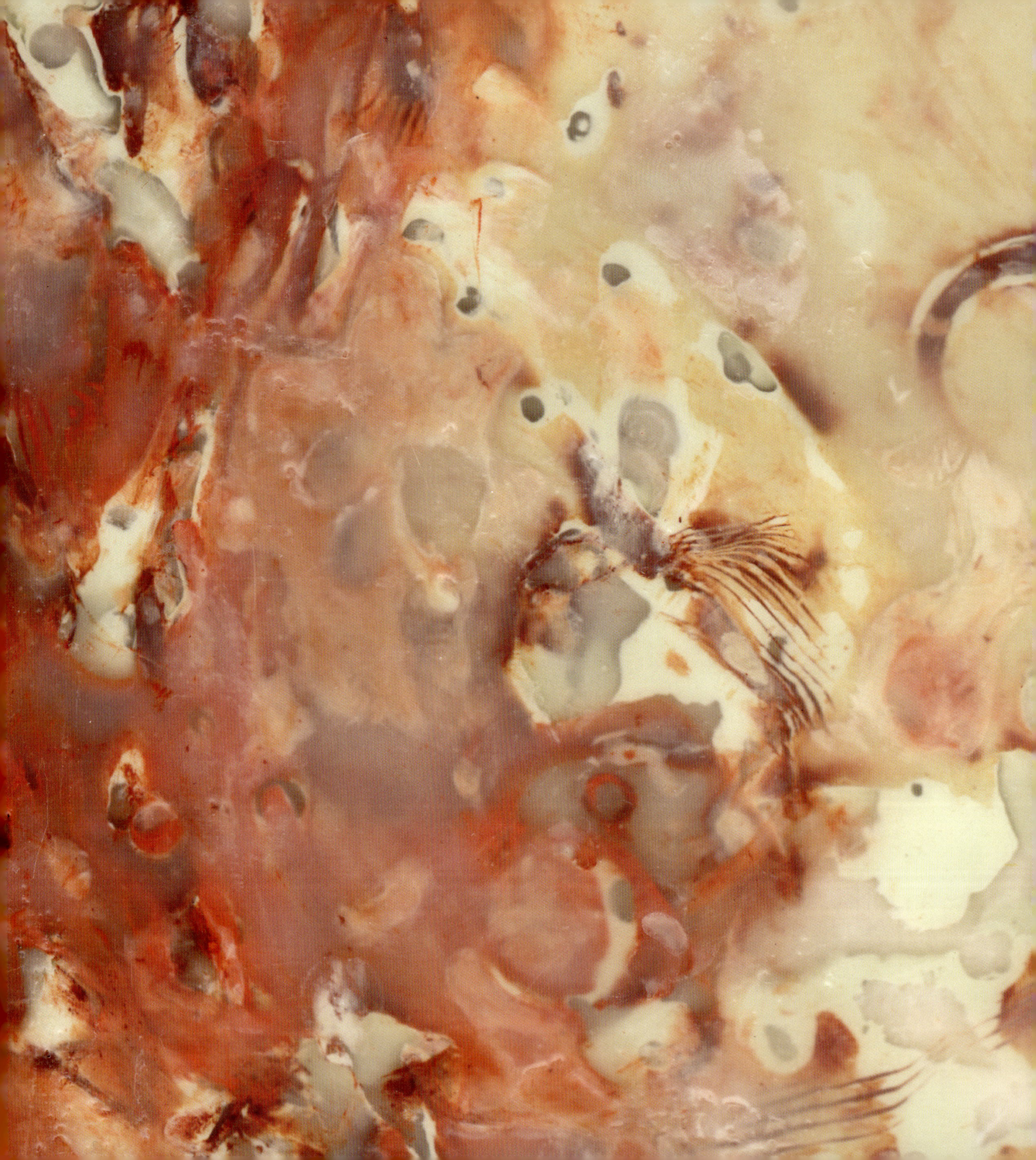

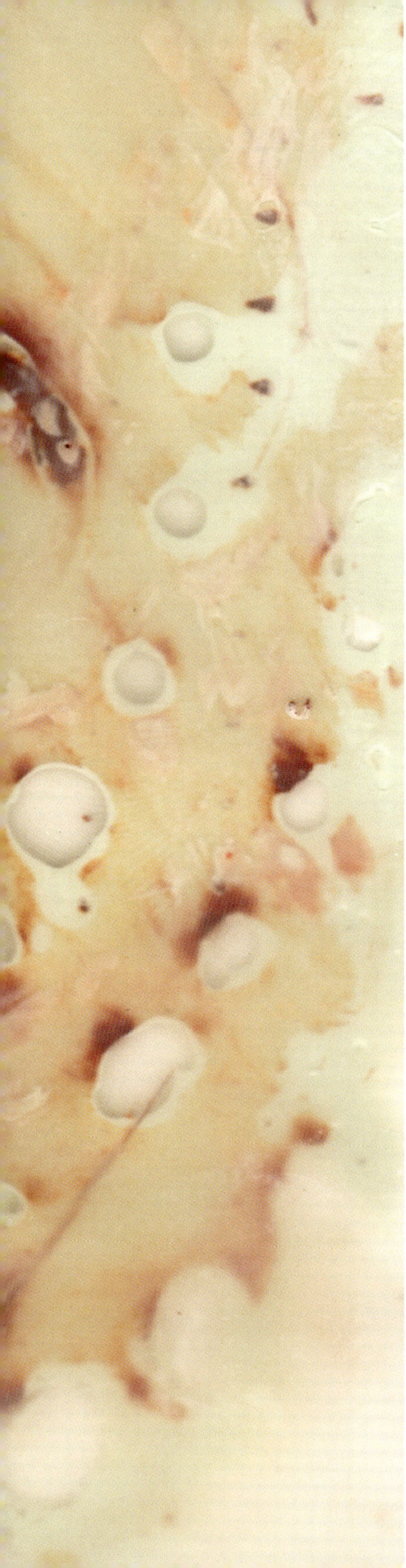

Contents

CHAPTER 1

FACEBOOK AND SOCIAL MEDIA

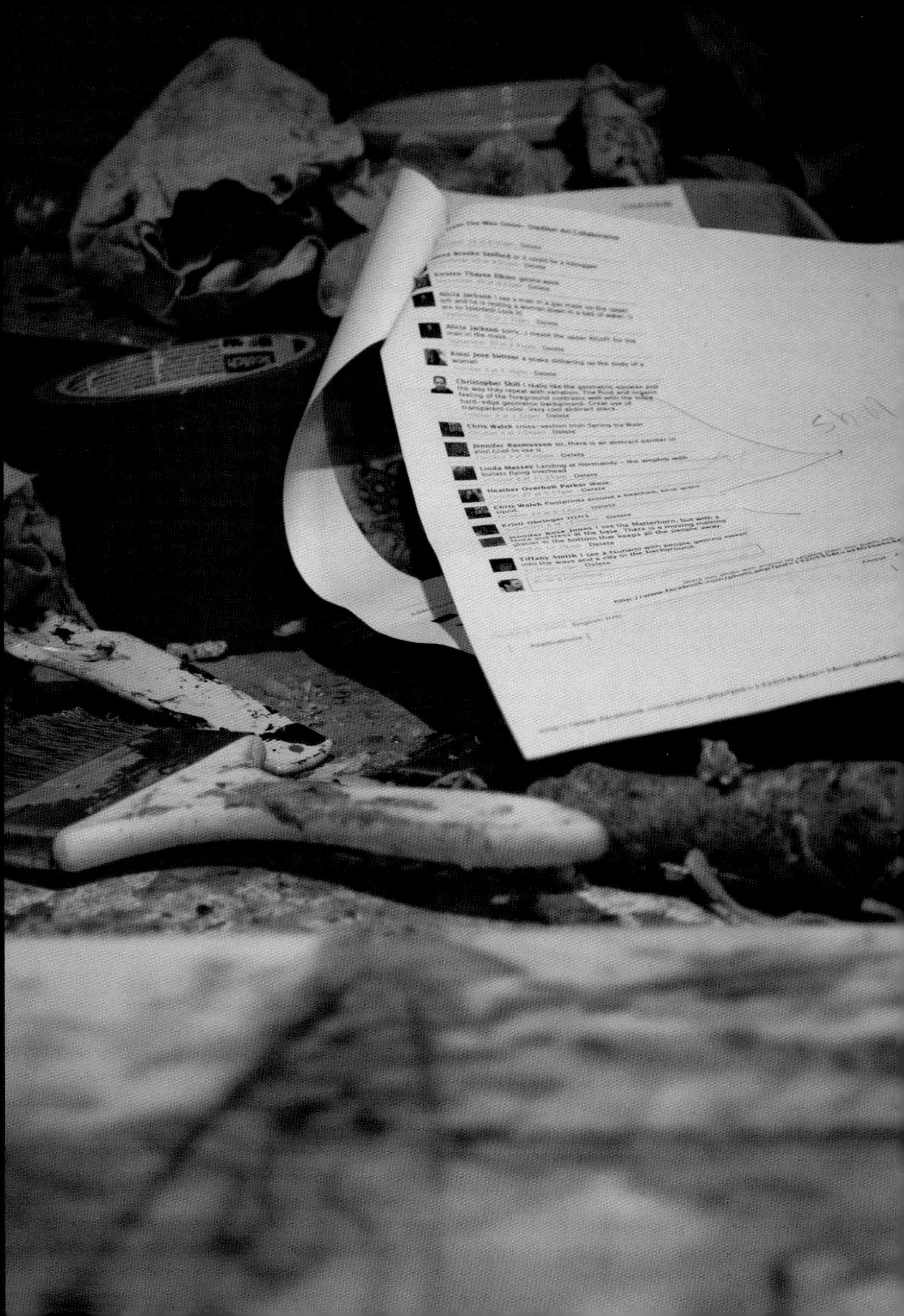
Christopher Skill I really like the geometric squares and the way they repeat with variation. The fluid and organic feeling of the foreground contrasts well with the more hard-edge geometric background. Great use of transparent color. Very cool abstract piece.
Chris Walsh cross-section Irish Spring Icy Blast
Jennifer Rasmusson so..there is an abstract painter in you! Glad to see it.
Linda Massey Landing at Normandy - the amphib with bullets flying overhead
Heather Overholt Parker Wave.
Chris Walsh Footprints around a beached, blue giant squid.
Kristi Obringer H1N1
Jennifer Rose Jones I see the Matterhorn, but with a fence and trees at the base. There is a moving melting glacier at the bottom that keeps all the people away.
Tiffany Smith I see a tsunami with people getting swept into the wave and a city in the background.
http://www.facebook.com/photo.php
Skill

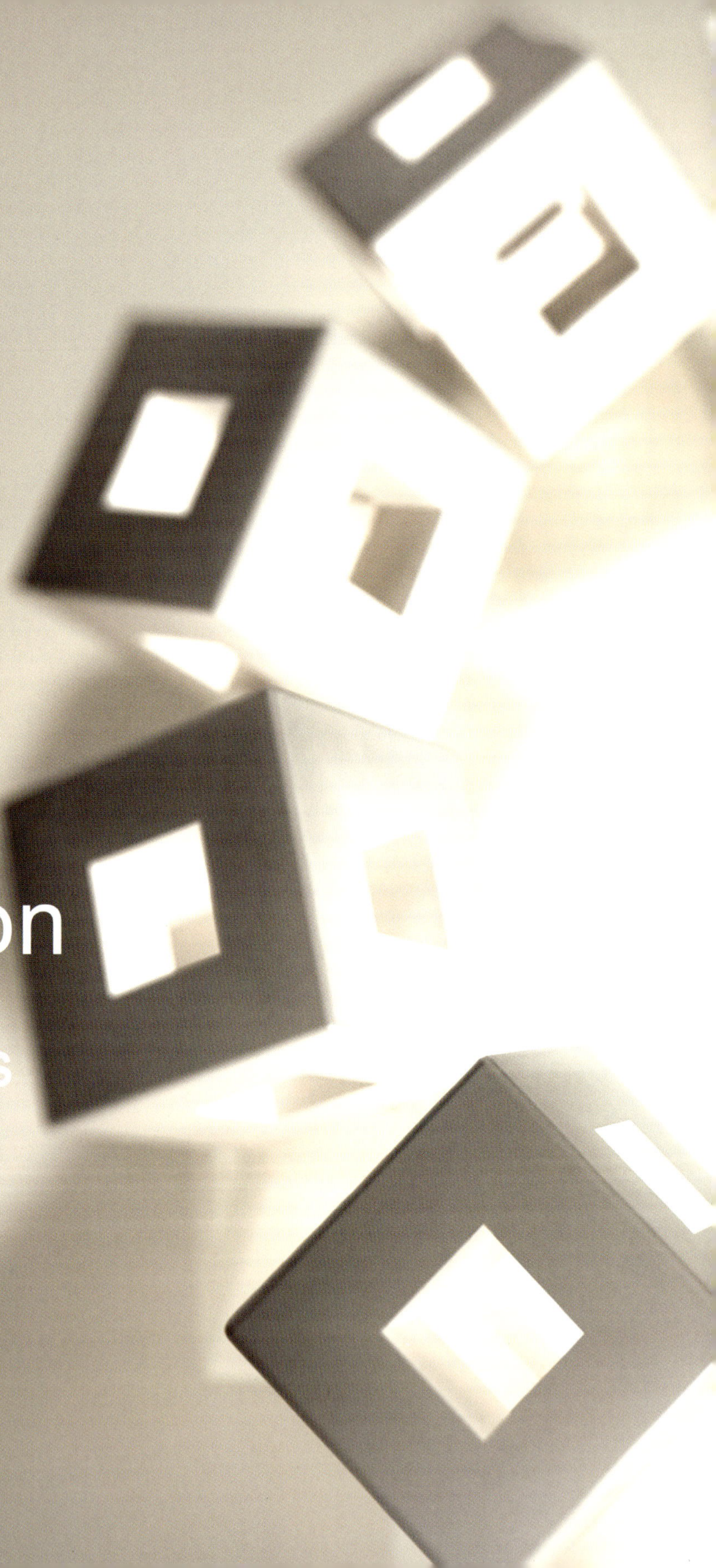

The Wax Onion

Collaborative allows for global collective thought on a single work

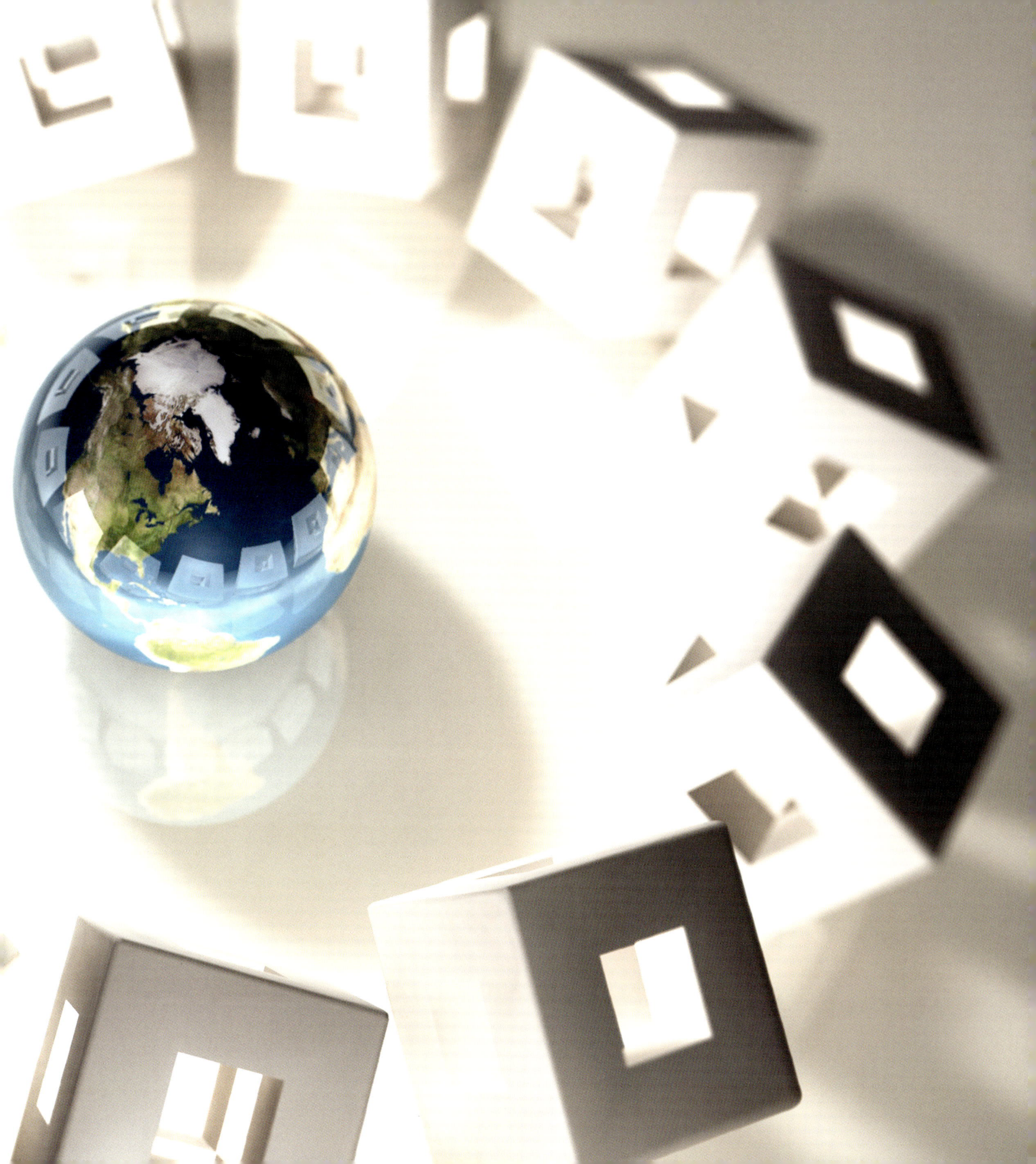

Facebook and Social Media

In Facebook's streamlined, text-based environment, images leap off the page, and the comments posted to these images appear almost as allegories through which the larger community "hears" comments from around the world. As an artist, Diediker's innate sense of creativity allowed him to recognize the untapped artistic opportunities inherent to the rapidly growing world of social networks, particularly Facebook. When Diediker created a Facebook group called the Wax Onion, he placed his finger on the pulse of a tremendous new era in art.

Diediker uses his Wax Onion Facebook group to help him "build" new things and make them great, with the help of over a thousand respondents around the world. When Diediker established the Wax Onion group on Facebook, inviting anyone to join, he essentially opened the doors of his studio to a richly diverse group of respondents representing the global community. "The Wax Onion Collaborative allows for global collective thought on a single work, which hasn't been logistically available until the advent of online communities," says Diediker. "With the aid of the internet and Facebook, I can gather perspective on imagery from all corners of the globe and incorporate it in the studio."

Members of the Wax Onion group share an interest in commenting on and influencing how art is made. The respondents cut across a wide range of socioeconomic and geographic strata, a characteristic that is also relatively new to history. The group includes artists, working professionals, students, stay-at-home parents... In other words, the group represents anyone interested in answering Diediker's one simple question: "What do you see?"

To Diediker's good fortune, participation in social media is a natural extension of his interest in people as a whole. In 2005, Diediker told Southwest Art: "People have always been a great interest in my life. I enjoy observing the stimulus and reaction in different human situations. Personal relationships have greatly influenced my work." In the setting of a social network, particularly in Facebook, it is easy to feel as if one is part of an intimate group, whether among "friends" or "fans." This online environment, then, is a powerful tool for divining inspiration from a large group of people, who reflect an infinite pool of global stimulus and expansively diverse reactions.

Sioux Elder 2009
Encaustic on clayboard
8 x 8 in.

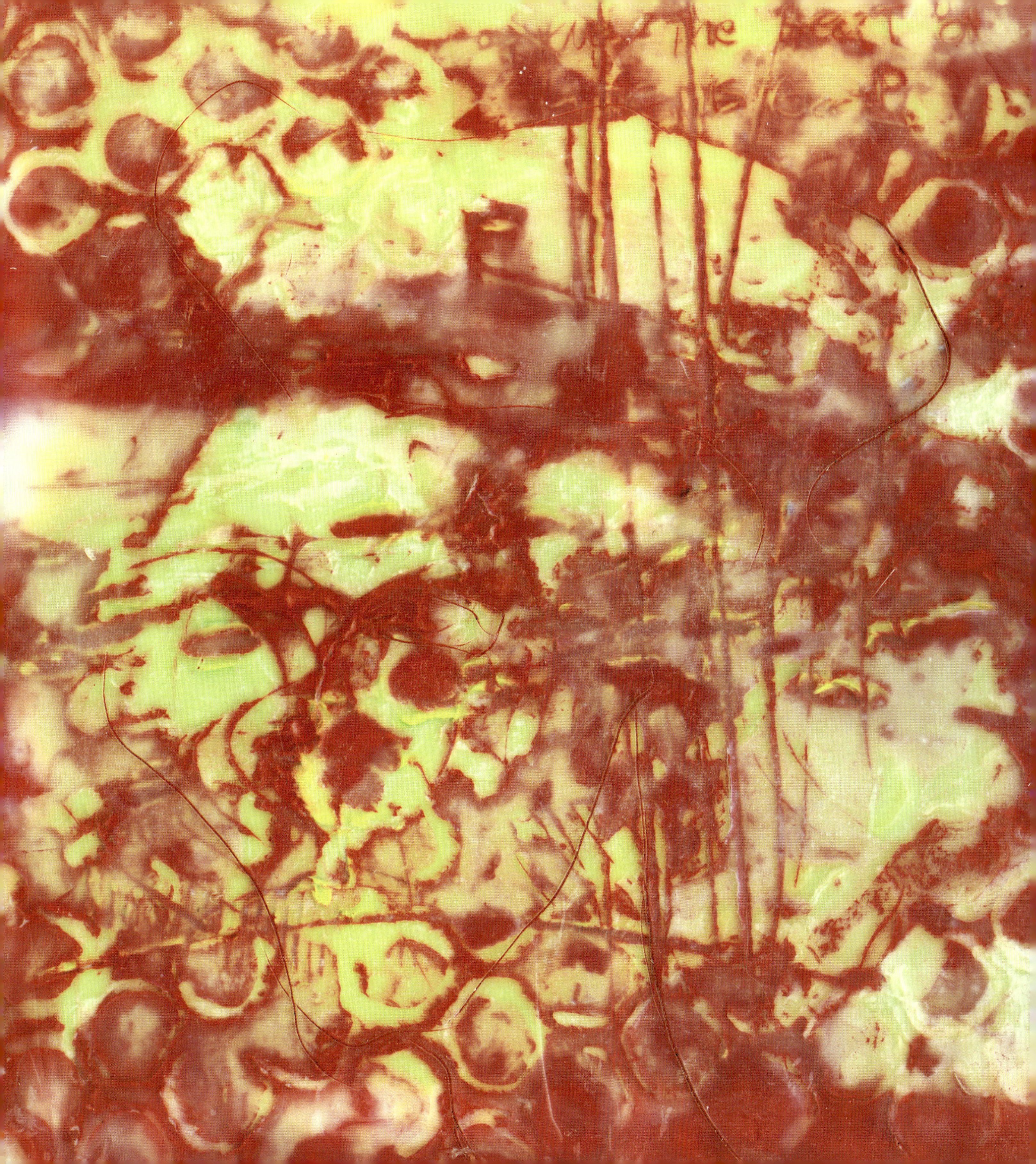

Facebook and Social Media

Diediker believes that references to time and place should influence and be reflected in an artist's work. "You might say that my work is directly affected by where I'm living," says Diediker. "The people, city, landscape – the things I see everyday. Environment should affect an artist's work. If not, then you're just painting decorations." In this light, the Wax Onion group amplifies Diediker's environmental influences, reflecting the day-to-day observations of people throughout the world. What respondents experience on a daily basis, what they see in the world outside their windows, how the events of their lives inform their responses to Diediker's unfinished work... all of these factors generate stimulus, reflecting hundreds of different human situations and shaping the completion of an encaustic piece by an extraordinary degree.

The artist's benefits from this type of shared interaction are evident: Diediker draws inspiration and insight from a wide sampling of extemporaneous interpretations of his unfinished work. He then completes his work by marrying his vision of the finished piece with influences from the group comments that struck him as most profound or apropos. Each encaustic piece is unique in its inception and completion. It seems natural, then, that some comments will show a deeper strain of insight than others, depending on how individual users connect with individual pieces as independent works of art influenced by the larger context of their daily lives and experiences. The reward reveals itself throughout the creative process and especially upon completion. By the time Diediker finishes each piece, it stands alone as an individual entity reflective of a wide and radiantly diverse range of interpretations, and as part of a series of work that reflects a wide and radiantly diverse sense of contemporary life.

How then do users benefit from participation in the Wax Onion collaboration? While not submitting to reductive thinking, Facebook's homepage presents a brief but very compelling invitation: "It's free and anyone can join." Inclusion is an appealing element of social networks. As the world population continues to grow, globalization and the increased use of technology tend to reduce face-to-face communication and splinter societies geographically. Facebook serves perhaps as a remedy to the isolation of modern living, offering users the next best thing to being part of a close-knit family. While geographic proximity among friends and family becomes rarer and rarer, technological proximity ameliorates the resulting isolation. In Facebook, users "see" and "talk" with others in communities of their making. Facebook enables inclusion. All users benefit from this.

What do you see?

Tony Schacher likes this.

Heather James I like this
September 18, 2009 at 6:16pm · Delete

Kent Miller haha. that is exactly what I saw.
September 18, 2009 at 6:18pm · Delete

Ray Muccillo Hm, I'm actually getting the River Styx from this, above the monkey is the shore with a body standing where the white is at the top, the figure in the middle rising from the stream of fire, souls or what have you, is the ferry man on a run to gather new arrivals.
September 19, 2009 at 8:29am · Delete

Wendy Johnson Roberts I think this looks like a man on a raft holding up a flag with a monkey head on it, meanwhile, he is chased down a river of lava by two dinosaur fossils. Only their heads are sticking out (like crocodiles).
September 21, 2009 at 6:51am · Delete

Melissa Beaman While I can't help but see the small monkey face and creature fishing from the wooden raft, I more-so see the bodice of a woman, yellow strapless dress, arms reaching up, beautiful bust and waist...the dark rust makes me wonder if she was murdered or spilled something really messy down the front of her dress.
September 21, 2009 at 12:55pm · Delete

Aubrey Pugmire This one is my favorite!!
October 30, 2009 at 4:20am · Delete

James M. Feezor looks like a kangaroo to me.
November 26, 2009 at 5:15pm · Delete

Quinn Peterson alligators on the prowl
February 2 at 5:51pm · Delete

Added September 14, 2009 · Comment · Like

Sean Diediker what do you see here? feel free to pluck it off facebook, rotate in any direction..even make photoshop notes
September 15, 2009 at 6:38am · Delete

Wendy Bader An animal standing up on its back legs, with the sun and lava and everything melting all at once.
September 15, 2009 at 8:17am · Delete

Kinsi Jene Suttner I see something indian like. Maybe droopy bunnies are being thrown through the air too.
September 15, 2009 at 8:37am · Delete

Mark Fernandez Spin the painting 180 degrees:

I see a woman's torso wearing a bikini top. Work some of the random designs from the wax into a tatoo design. Or the figure is swimming and is underwater
... See More
September 15, 2009 at 2:48pm · Delete

Fim Abbas A woman walking on a wave, a dolphin or some sort of sea creature is leaping up above her, at the height of it's arc.
September 16, 2009 at 3:16am · Delete

Ray Muccillo I said this in the other shot of this, but really the more I look at it, I see the ferryman poling his raft across the River Styx to get someone on the upper shore.
September 19, 2009 at 8:31am · Delete

Linda Massey Turn just 90 degrees clockwise: I see a reflection of a man and woman. Is he loving her - or is he killing her??? Guess it could depend on your mood.
September 20, 2009 at 11:32am · Delete

Atali Rebecca Staffler An american puritain advertisment against women immoral dressing.
November 7, 2009 at 7:14pm · Delete

Atali Rebecca Staffler There is the torso of a woman wearing a sleavless top and arms up (can see armpit on the right) in from of an americain banner. The bottom of the advertisment represents fire as if (in the ad.) the picture of that women had been put in fire to express the non acceptable dressing style.
November 7, 2009 at 7:15pm · Delete

Rose Datoc Dall hot momma kangaroo...
December 1, 2009 at 5:03pm · Delete

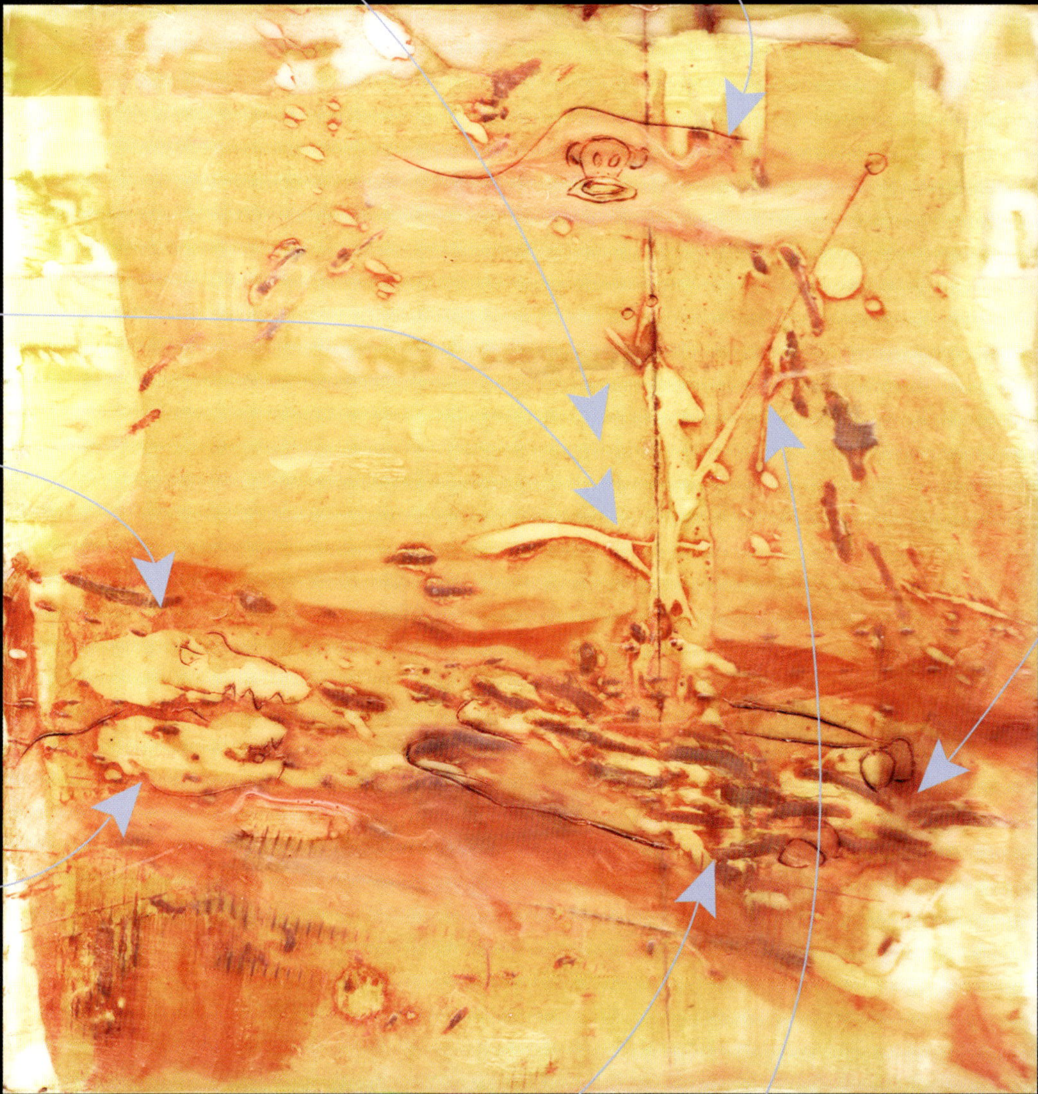

River monkey King in high heels flying the banner of his people followed by two Crocs 2009
Encaustic on clayboard
8 x 8 in.

3 people like this.

View previous comments 50 of 51

Aubrey Chandler The inside of a beehive with a little opossum peaking in from the outside. He's towards the top, a tad to the left..heeheehee :)
November 25, 2009 at 6:47am · Delete

Sri Whipple or tailings from kennecot copper?
November 25, 2009 at 6:47am · Delete

Justin Taylor insane clown posse
November 25, 2009 at 6:54am · Delete

Bryan P Jacobs I see a close-up of Mark Twain smoking a pipe in front of a crowd of faces
November 25, 2009 at 7:08am · Delete

Vanessa Harvard I see a lady crying... Feeling sorry for what she did. She has a tiger mask on her face and some snakes in her hair.
November 25, 2009 at 7:12am · Delete

Casey Waldron An an ancient sacrificial table of logs burning the remains...
November 25, 2009 at 7:17am · Delete

Chelsey Hillman Browning A lioness, a sad woman and a kite
November 25, 2009 at 7:25am · Delete

Stacy Moore Howard I see a peacock.
November 25, 2009 at 7:25am · Delete

Adam R. Hope I see Phoenix in blue laying down in the top left corner.
November 25, 2009 at 7:26am · Delete

Susan Wythe various birds flying from their catacombs
November 25, 2009 at 7:54am · Delete

Larry Ogan exploding peacock
November 25, 2009 at 8:00am · Delete

Doug Reeder Hindu priest flying a kite over a giant serpent
November 25, 2009 at 8:03am · Delete

Wade Stubblefield I see an explosion. massive explosion. like planetary. eh maybe like a sun.
November 25, 2009 at 8:32am · Delete

Ingrid Martis honeycomb
November 25, 2009 at 8:56am · Delete

SallyAnne Rutherford turn it 90 derees to r - I see a dog's face
November 25, 2009 at 9:03am · Delete

Jenevieve Hubbard A melted beehive, hair, petri dish, death, decay, rebirth.
November 25, 2009 at 9:26am · Delete

Sherrie Posternak an irradiated person running away from a giant burning beehive
November 25, 2009 at 9:37am · Delete

Debbie Borow I see a profile of an Egyptian priest....interesting!
November 25, 2009 at 9:44am · Delete

Chris Shurian Richard Nixon "I am not a thief"
November 25, 2009 at 9:48am · Delete

Erica Bookstaber A cougar about to destroy a fourth of July picnic
November 25, 2009 at 10:34am · Delete

Kay Fallon An aliens hand reaching for the flying message
November 25, 2009 at 10:41am · Delete

Sarah Thompson A war between two beehive colonies. (So much for my peaceful persona!)
November 25, 2009 at 11:06am · Delete

Marcella Nemec a little man in the bottom right corner, flying a kite, standing on some logs
November 25, 2009 at 11:12am · Delete

Marcella Nemec I also see an egyptian priest.....
November 25, 2009 at 11:12am · Delete

Atali Rebecca Staffler A modern dancer on the left
November 25, 2009 at 12:03pm · Delete

Vanessa Harvard Ethan sees a girl running for the gem of life. Spikes and arrows are flying towards her. A beehive is trying to help her.
November 25, 2009 at 2:31pm · Delete

Katrina Maurer I see a big tiger but within that a tiger falling a water buffalo
November 25, 2009 at 3:25pm · Delete

Dan Oldham I see a sad woman crying a ton of tears and flying a kite.
November 25, 2009 at 3:45pm · Delete

Marc Trombella war..opposing forces exchanging mortar fire
November 25, 2009 at 3:52pm · Delete

Andrea L. Deming A man reflecting on his childhood: Giraffes, kites, and coco puffs.
November 25, 2009 at 3:56pm · Delete

Philip Sherlock Odend'hal einstein with a mohamad karzi type kepkie pup hat watching two kids flying a kite in a dust storm
November 25, 2009 at 8:37pm · Delete

Kirsten Thayne Elkins magical monday
November 26, 2009 at 1:46am · Delete

Tuck Neilson A clown with a puddle of tears below him
November 26, 2009 at 2:21am · Delete

Aubrey Pugmire Seahorse
November 26, 2009 at 4:35am · Delete

Cynthia Wood Stott an angel with a crown of honeycomb
November 26, 2009 at 5:47am · Delete

Maha Madanat-Bahnam A huge bee and honeycomb ...
November 26, 2009 at 12:34pm · Delete

James M. Feezor looks like an MRI of a queen with her crown askew
November 26, 2009 at 4:51pm · Delete

Elizabeth Howard A Sea Dog shocked at flying higher than a Santa's Elf soaring a kite
November 27, 2009 at 5:41am · Delete

Michaelangelo Krum i would call this 'today is monday somehow'
November 27, 2009 at 4:14pm · Delete

Whitney Phillips a boy getting taken away by balloons
November 28, 2009 at 5:51pm · Delete

Rose Datoc Dall Lion and Frankenstein.... (profiles of each facing left)
December 1, 2009 at 4:39pm · Delete

Amber Sanders Call Perseverance over Strife.... Powerful
December 14, 2009 at 6:52am · Delete

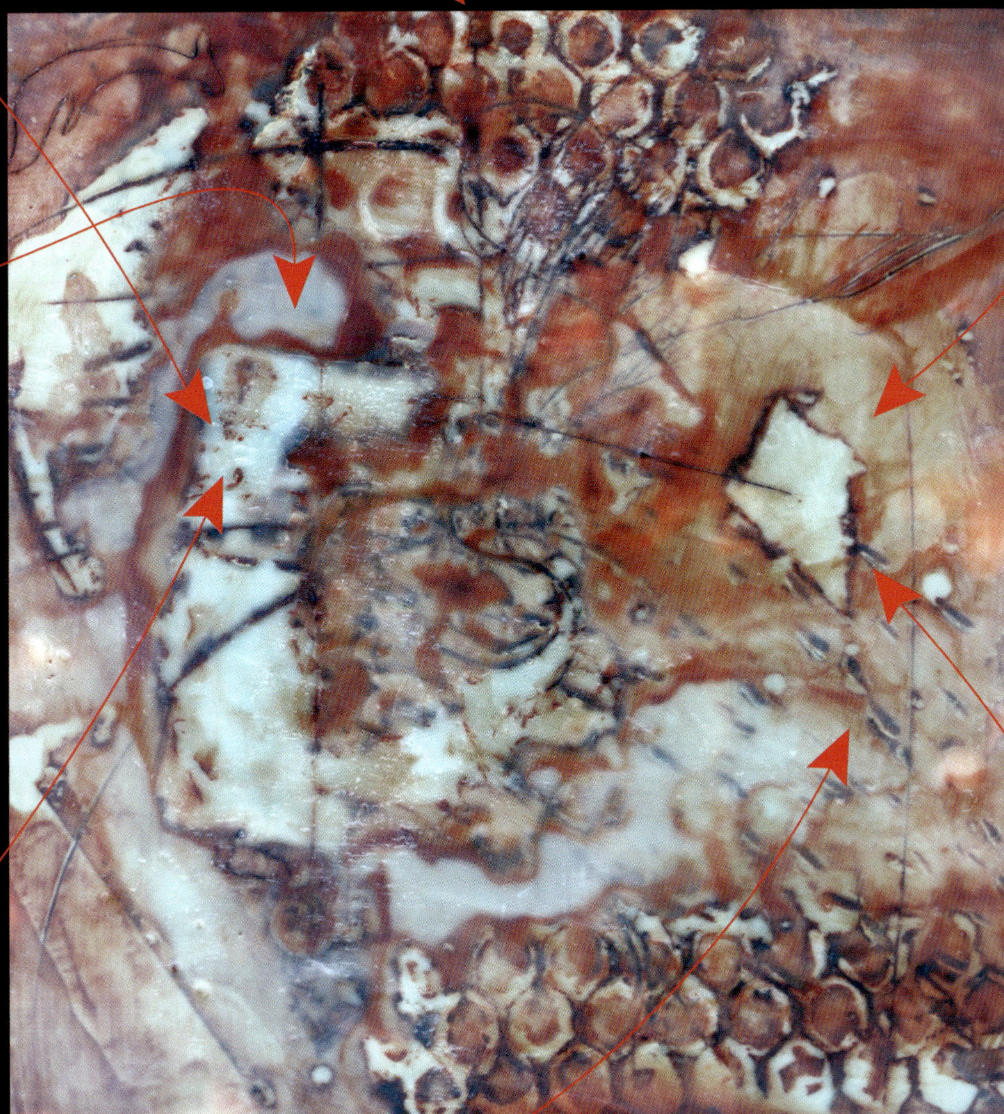

Crying Nun and Phoenix flying white kite
between two battling bee armies 2009
Encaustic on clayboard
12 x 12 in.

JFK thinking… 7 of 10 "smart bombs" initially dropped in plan "A-Strike" missed there targets by a kilometer or more

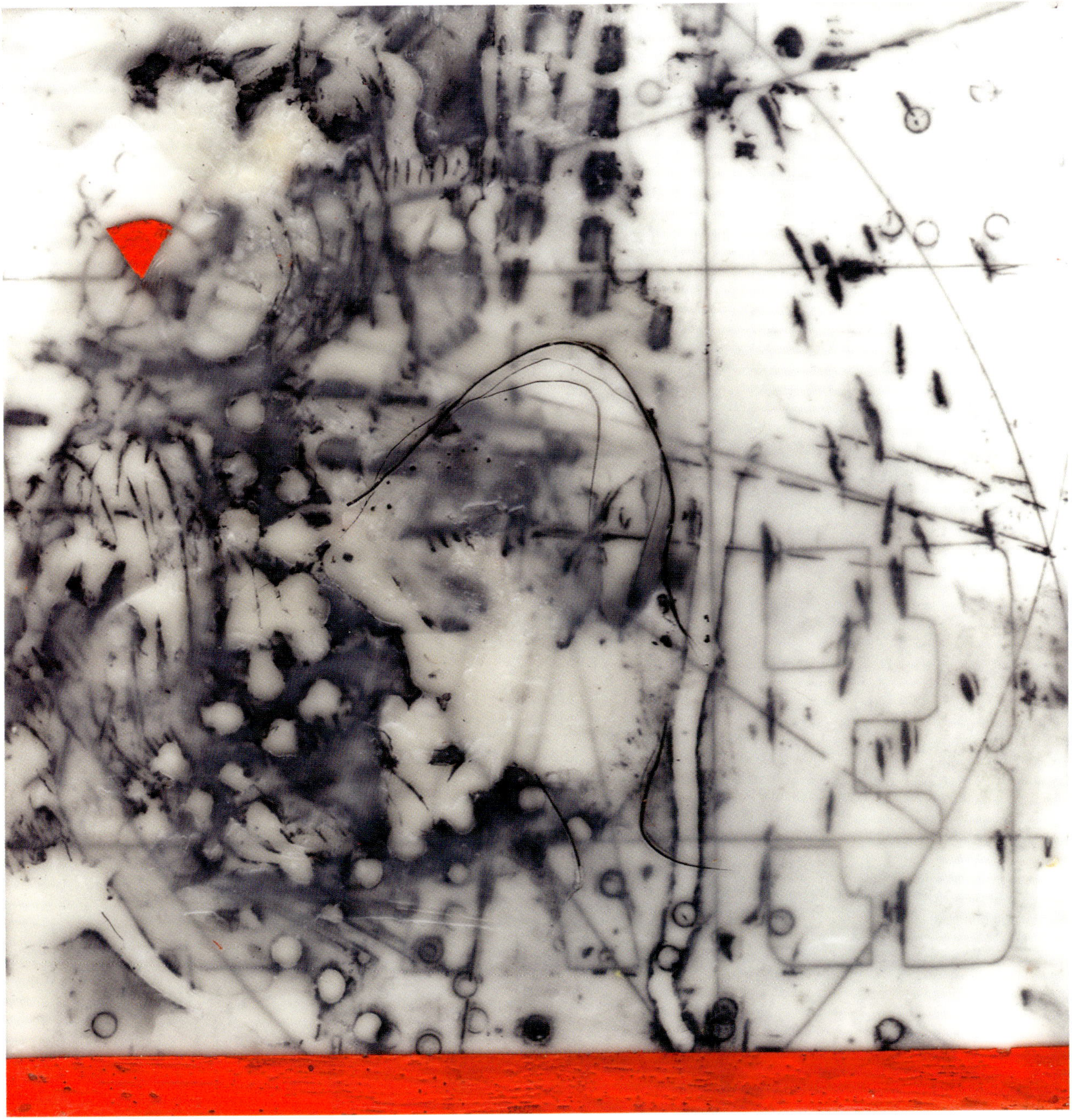

JFK thinking... 7 of 10 "smart bombs" initially dropped in plan "A-Strike" missed their targets by a kilometer or more 2010
Encaustic on clayboard
8 x 8 in.

Clown in white dress upset by low battery warning

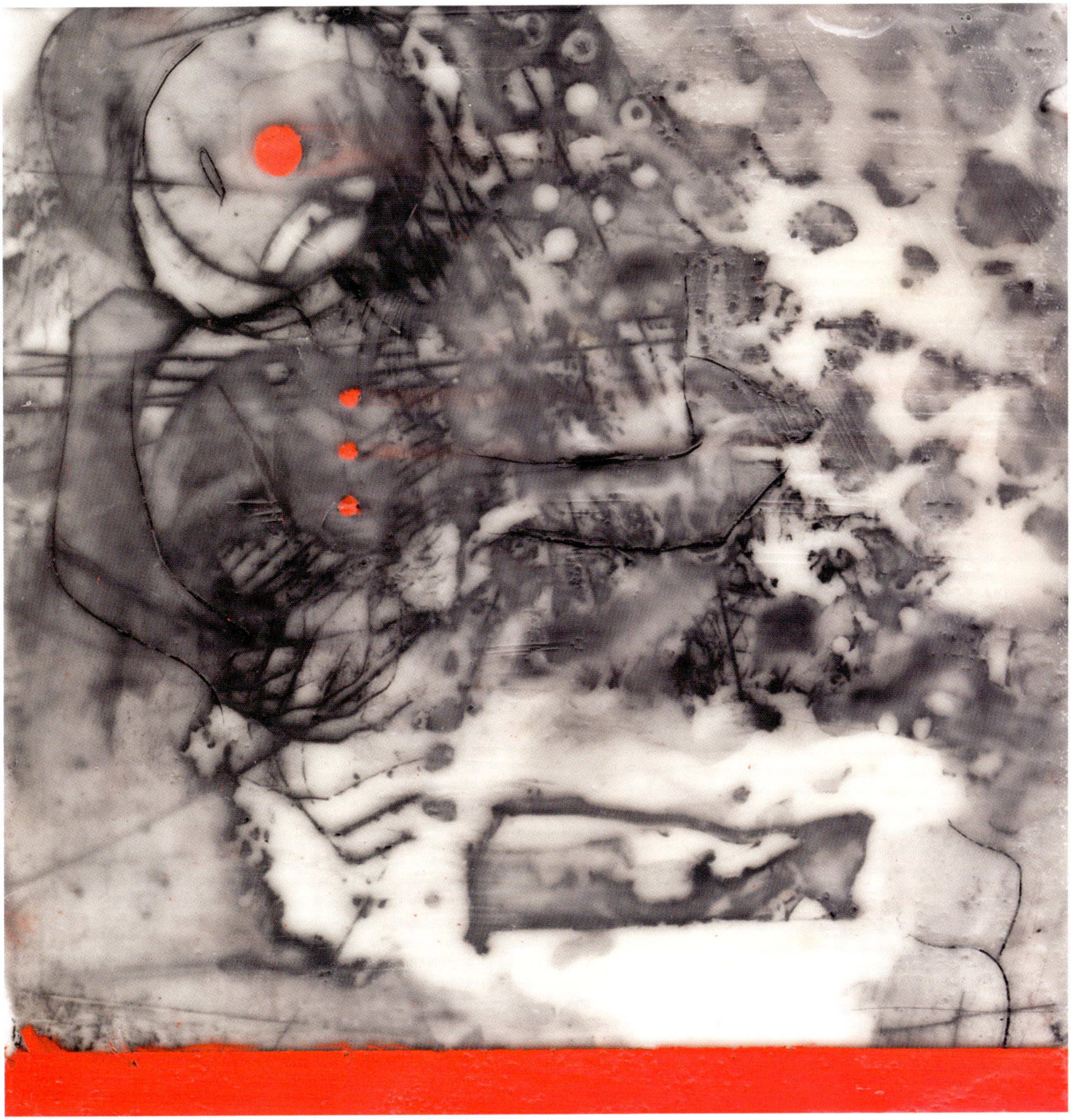

Clown in white dress upset by low battery warning 2009
Encaustic on clayboard
8 x 8 in.

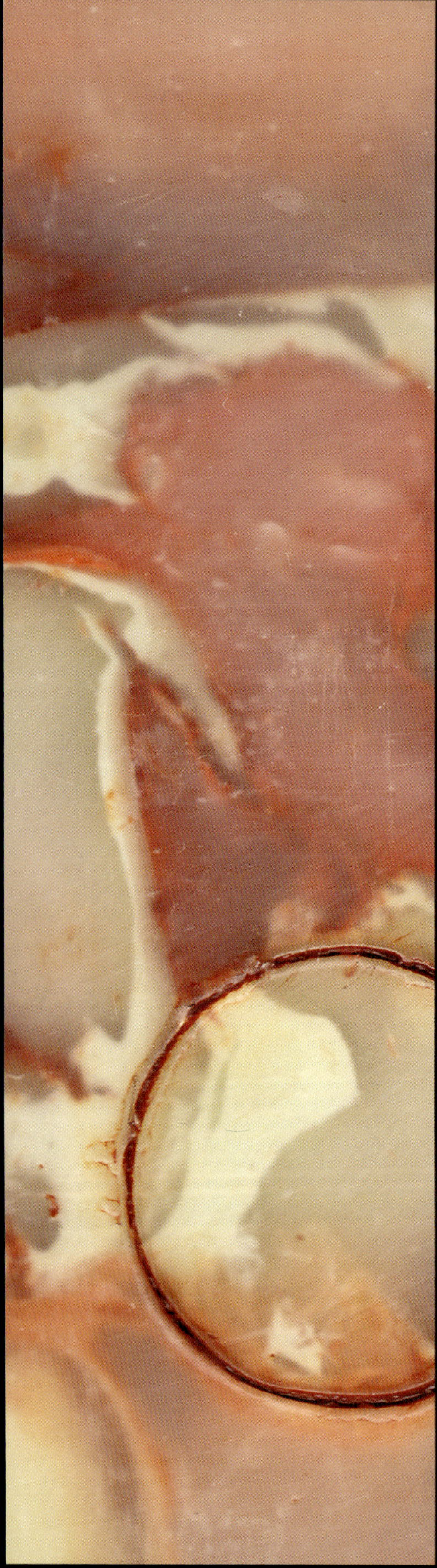

John Lennon thinking in the key of G

John Lennon thinking in the key of G
2010
Encaustic on clayboard
8 x 8 in.

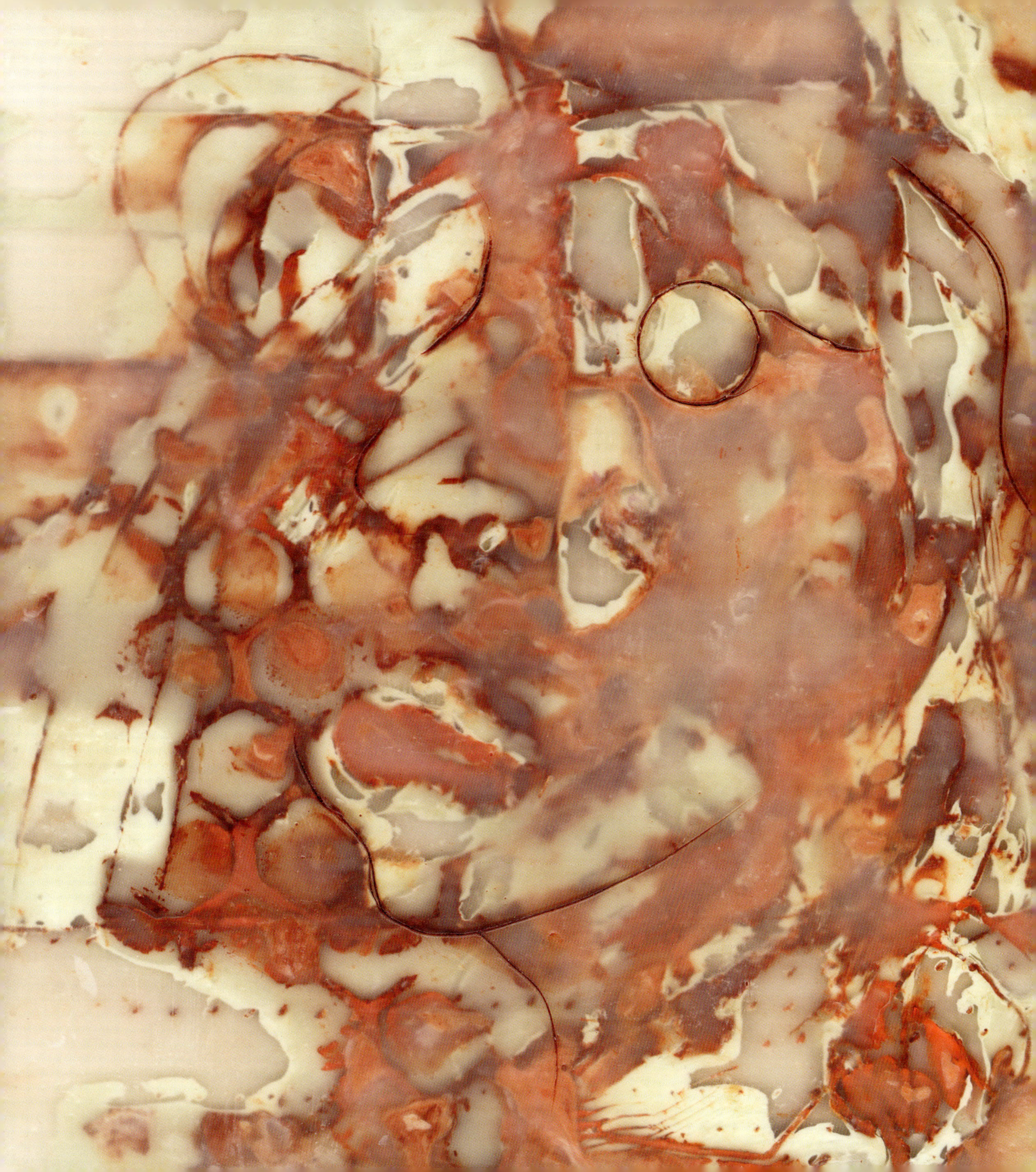

Facebook and Social Media

In the Wax Onion, a community that relies on inclusion and participation, respondents benefit from an exchange of ideas that ultimately impacts how art is seen and made. Facebook enables the Wax Onion global public to suggest the imagery in each piece, using social and cultural context, even daily experience, as "lenses" through which the art is interpreted. Individual voices are "heard," and a sense of connection is forged among respondents. There is tremendous benefit in being heard and being part of a larger movement to create something beautiful and enduring. There is also great benefit in sharing one's natural associational tendencies – participants enrich their own lives by broadening their perspectives and "seeing" things through the "eyes" of others.

"We are constantly in contemplation of how we view ourselves and how others view us," Diediker notes. This may inform some of the quality or verity of the responses posted within the Wax Onion group. But the majority of respondents genuinely seem to enjoy the collaborative element of the Wax Onion project. There is something poignant and even intimate in sharing one's ideas so openly.

The comments made on each piece are fascinating in their own right. The Wax Onion comments vary widely, and they reflect the world that the participants know and live each day. Although some of the group members tend to comment in a consistent manner, part of the Wax Onion's success and whimsical charm rests in the surprising juxtapositions and perspectives posted to each encaustic plate.

Diediker comments minimally in the Wax Onion forum, allowing the Wax Onion members to participate in true collaborative capacity. His primary interjections are to gently remind participants to respond to the imagery rather than try to name the piece. There is an interesting tendency for some users to want to give a title to the work in their comments. This tendency highlights the sense of ownership that results from participation in a larger project.

These Pieces are Collective Journals of Humanity as it Exists Today

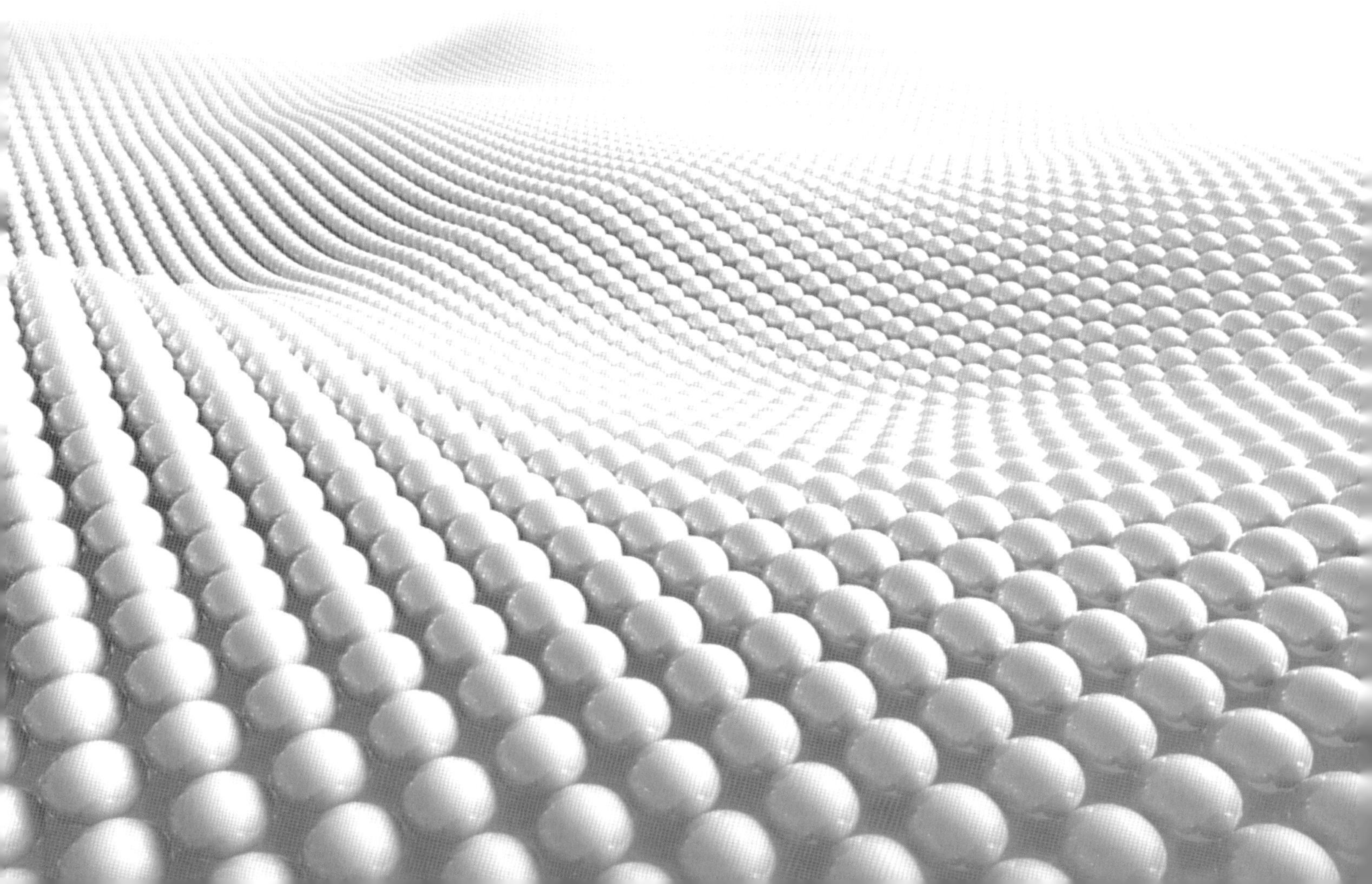

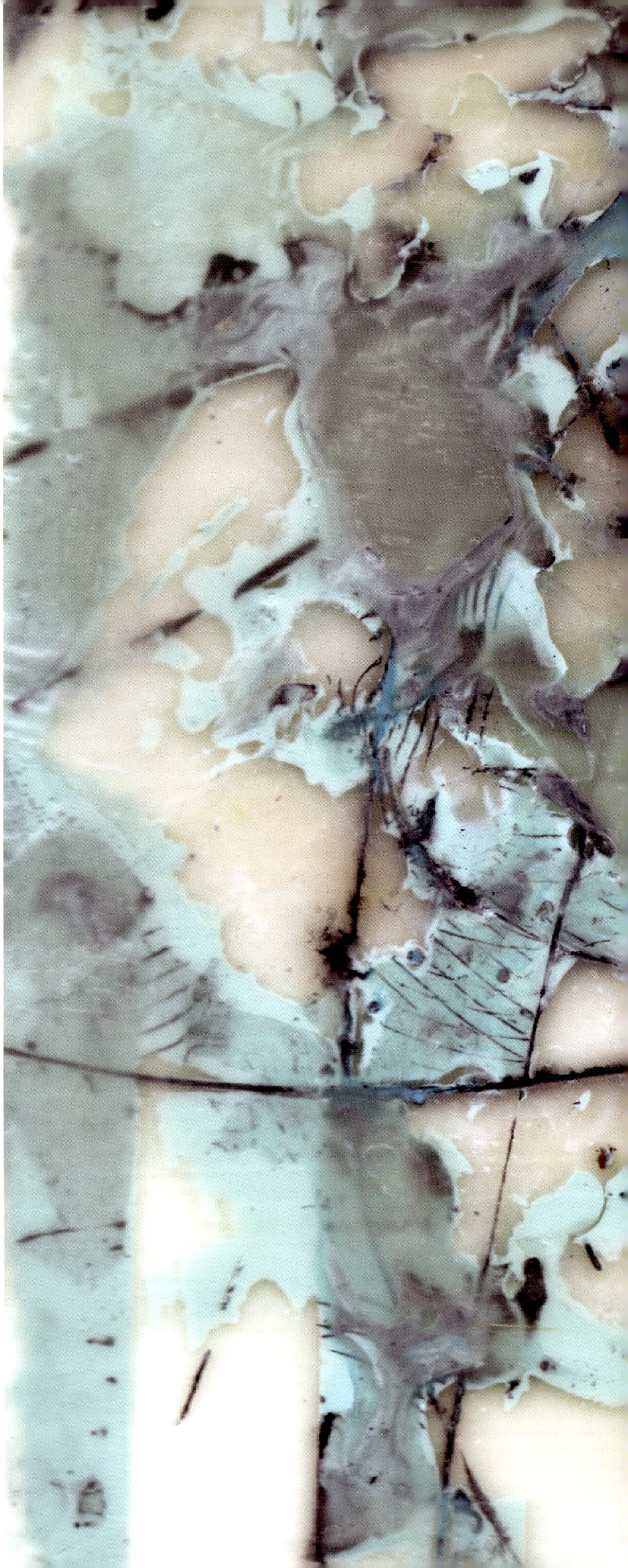

Everest 2010
Encaustic on clayboard
8 x 8 in.

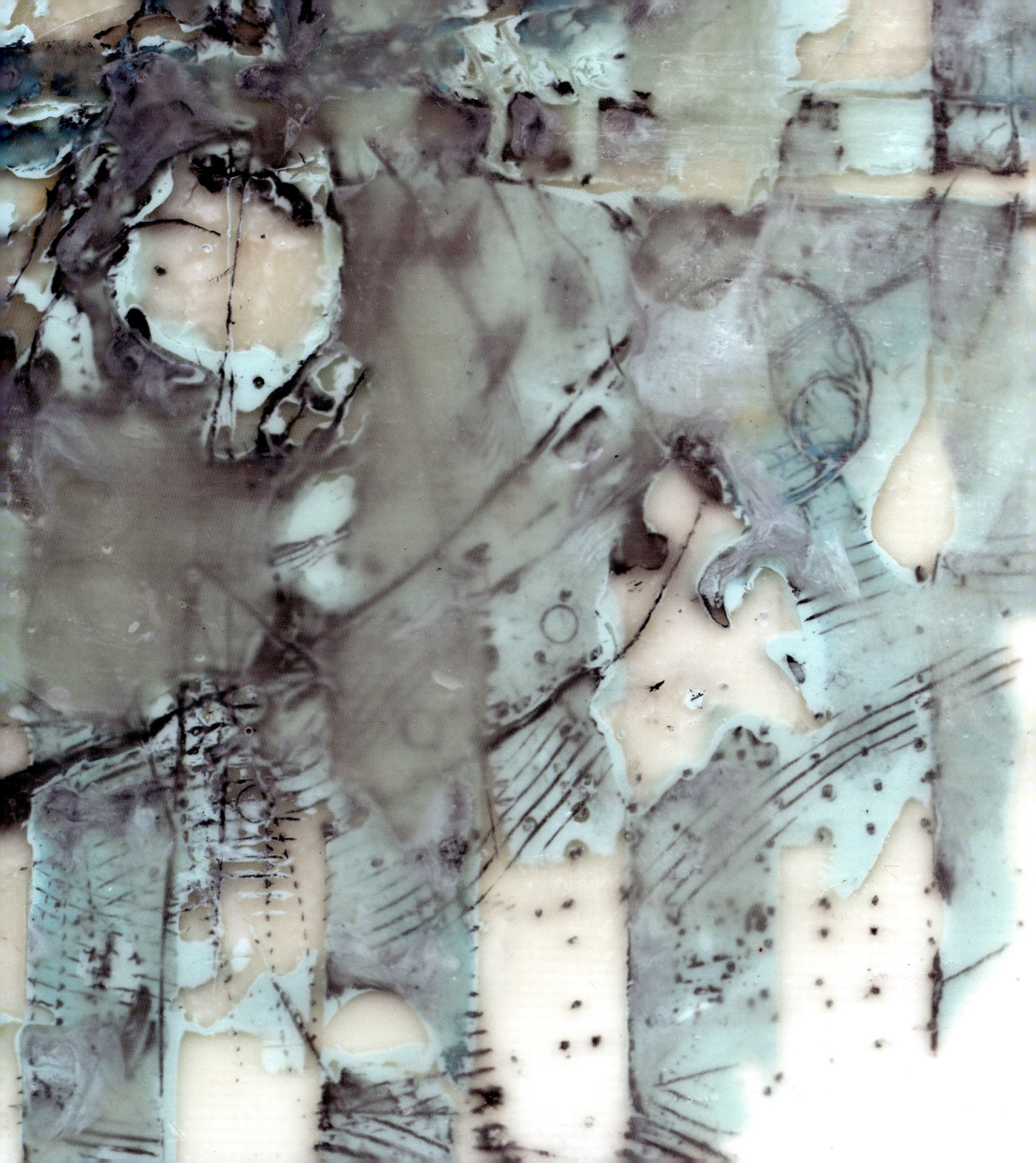

Facebook and Social Media

The Wax Onion Collaborative project was born quite coincidentally. When Diediker first joined Facebook, he posted one of his encaustic plates on his personal profile. The response from his friends was overwhelming. Many of them responded to the imagery in his plate; some even offered to name the work. The response was so overwhelming, in fact, that Diediker began to think about the unique collaborative elements that Facebook offered him. The Wax Onion was born out of this serendipitous happenstance. "I didn't start the Facebook Wax Onion project thinking that it would be a movement. It was more of a 'What if?,' which is how I work in my studio or how I approach any project... 'What if I use an under-painting of acrylic, sand it down, and put oil paint on top? What if I fold and arrange a bunch of dollar bills to make them look like an image?' The project kind of evolved on its own."

In its inaugural year, the Wax Onion group grew to nearly a thousand participants, proving that Diediker's idea for the collaboration of art holds considerable appeal. "In my encaustic work, I try to forfeit complete control," says Diediker. "I take a complete chance abstract and then I post it to the Wax Onion for opinion and direction. The art isn't necessarily the finished piece hanging on the wall. I truly believe that the art is in the collaboration of the Wax Onion community."

The collaborative process requires Diediker to navigate many people's varying impressions of each of his encaustic plates, a task that can sometimes feel daunting but bears notable rewards. Diediker has said that he finds it fascinating when a participant makes a thoughtful observation that challenges the imagery he sees, prompting him to examine his work through a different point of view. "It's so exciting to weave the tapestry of comments together to create a finished piece," he says. The piece titled 'River monkey King in high heels flying the banner of his people followed by two Crocs' provides a prime example of how Diediker weaves together the 'tapestry' of each piece. "Each element of the title was influenced by specific elements of the comments posted," says Diediker. Ultimately, Diediker reworks the imagery in each piece based on the comments that resonate with him the most.

As a final component of inclusion, Wax Onion participants fall – if only minutely – under the umbrella of Diediker's notoriety, adding the 'cool factor' to the list of benefits of inclusion. The ripples of his presence surface when his personality occasionally peeks through, as it did in Plate 6 - Sewing Sunbear: "Play-Dough? ouch baby... very ouch."

In ancient cultures, honey was sometimes used to embalm the dead. In a similar fashion, using beeswax as an encaustic medium serves as a time capsule, "embalming" modern experiences to commemorate them, celebrating the present moment and preserving the ideas of the moment forever. "It's so interesting that when asked 'What do you see?' people make reference to things that are representative of our here and now," says Diediker. "And, in a way, these pieces are collective journals of humanity as it exists today." Diediker hopes that his encaustic pieces will endure as time capsules, representative of this unique collaboration. "I'm interested in the idea of these works hanging on a wall 500 years from now with all the comments and suggestions from the Wax Onion sealed on the back," says Diediker. "Even though we may be gone, the evidence of this collaboration will exist enfolded within the finished work, as a time capsule and as a symbol of the evolution of our communication as human beings."

"The art isn't necessarily the finished piece hanging on the wall..."

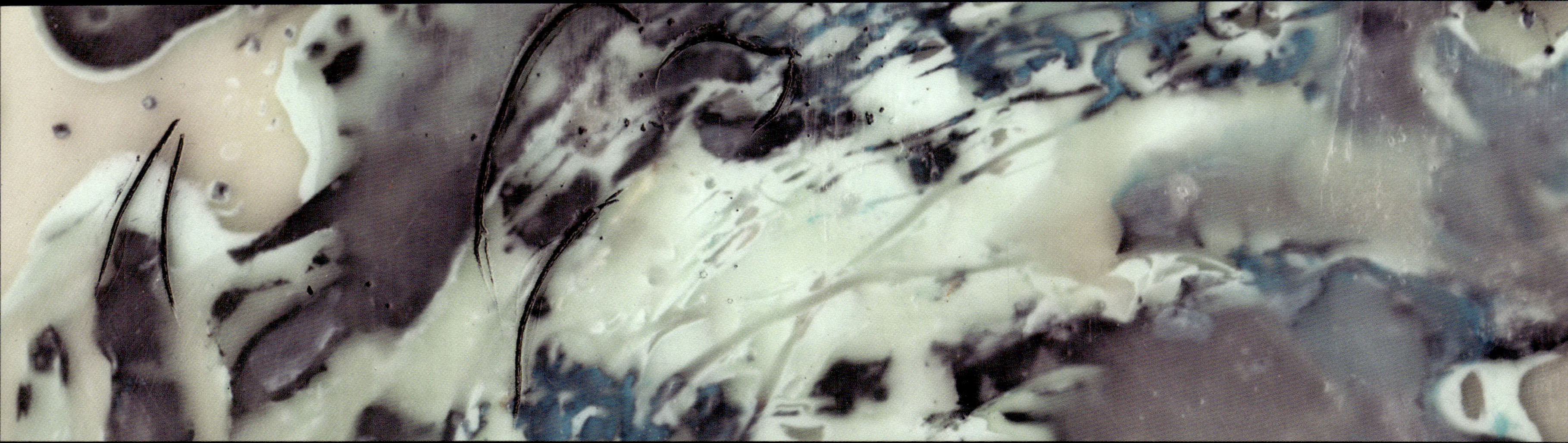

Surfer at Pipeline

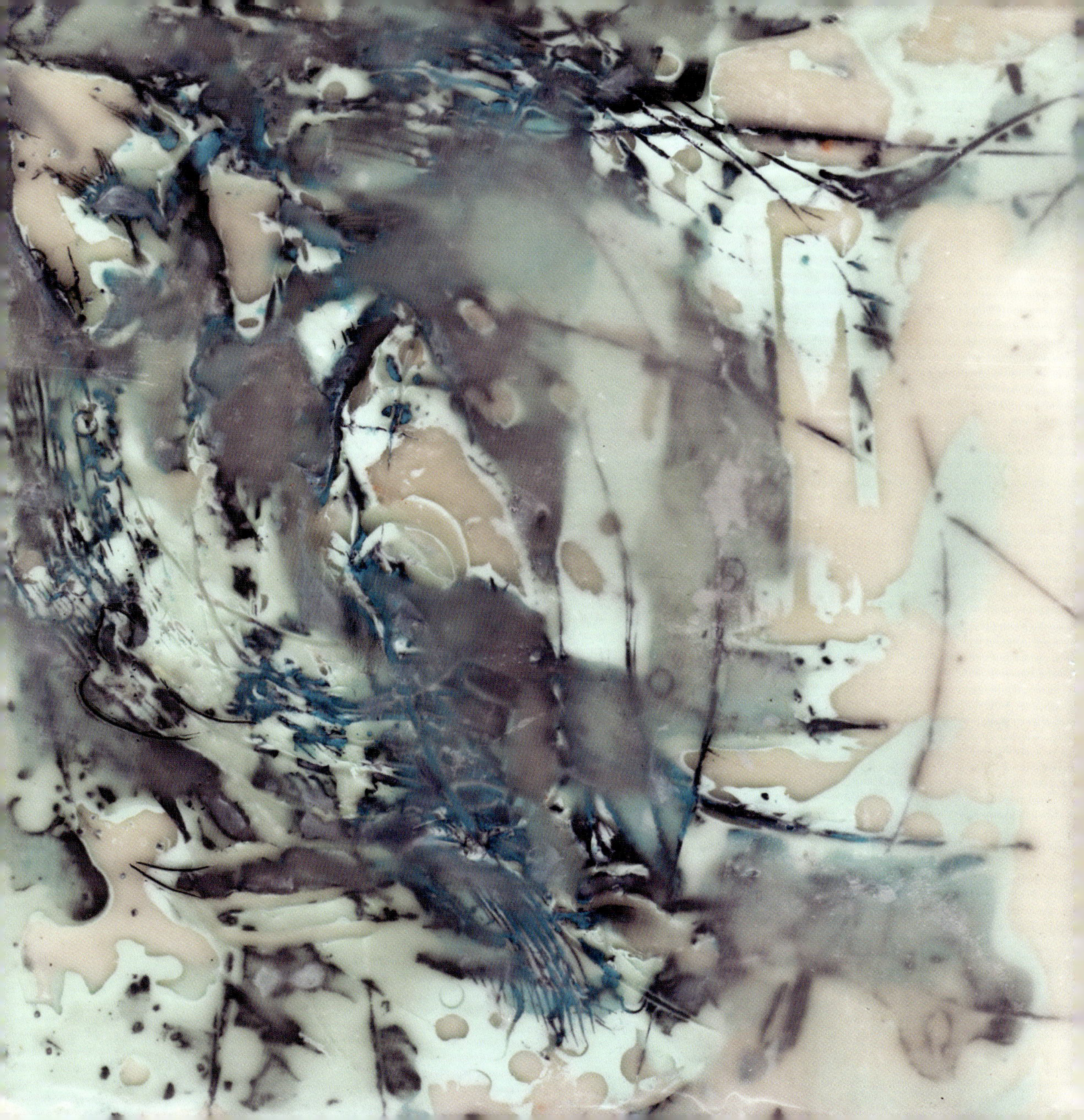

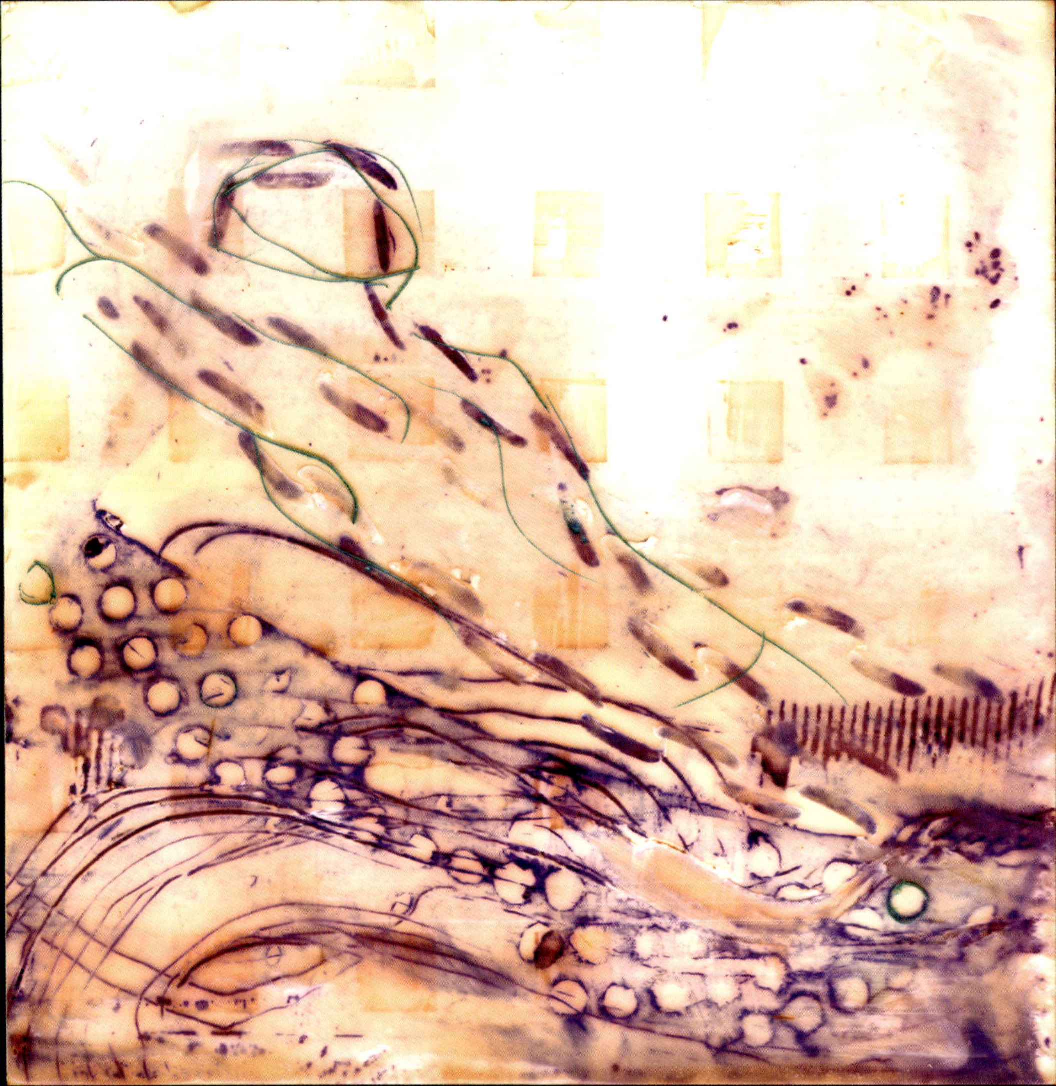

Michael Phelps 2009
Encaustic on clayboard
8 x 8 in.

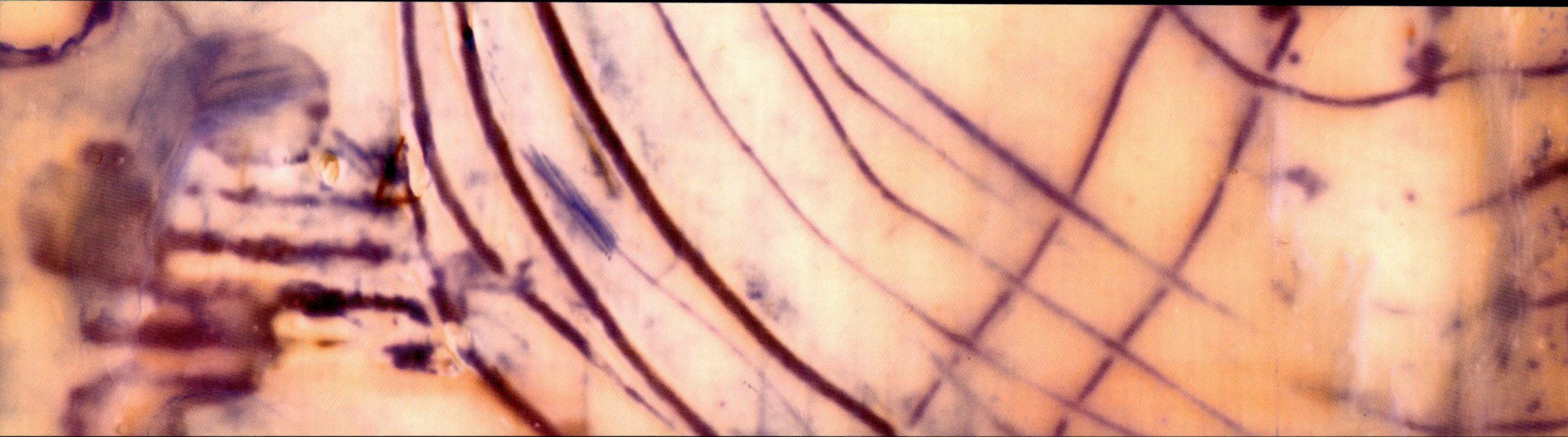

Michael Phelps

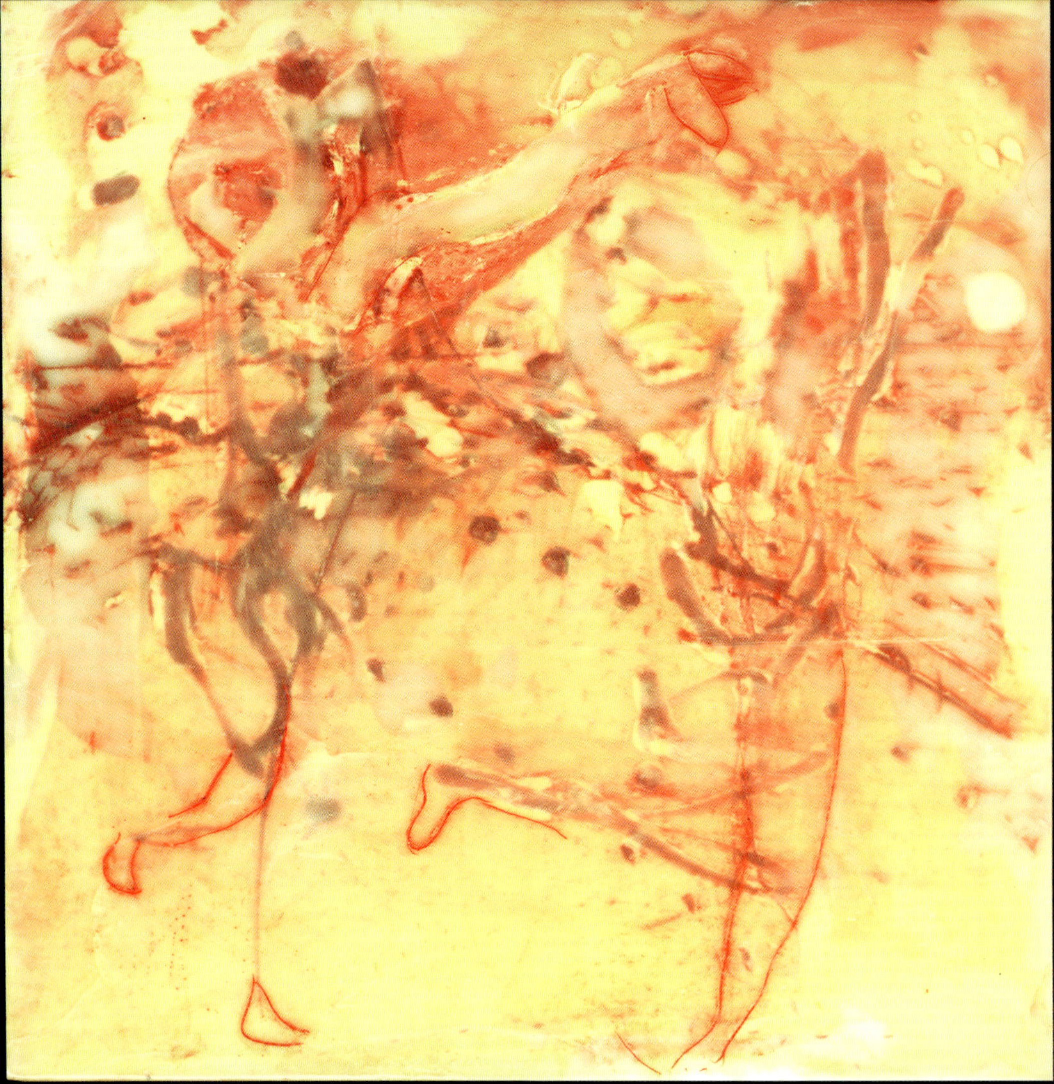

Lovers dancing away from the
World of War-Craft because
they found their lucky charms
2009

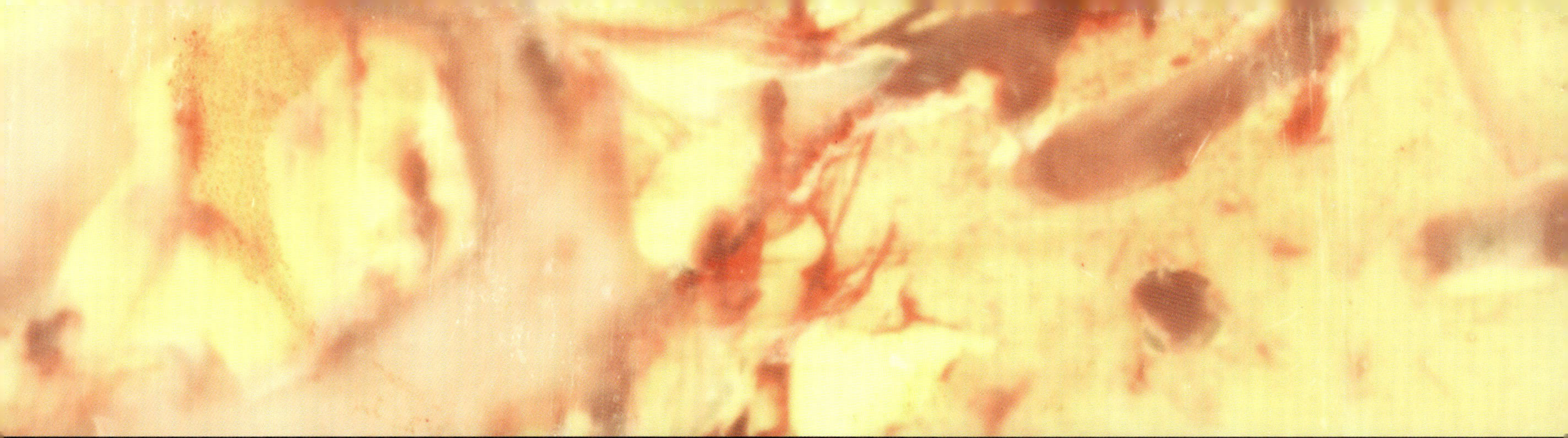

Lovers dancing away from the World of War-Craft, because they found their lucky charms

She stepped up on stage...Stared at the sea of blue faces...held her breath...and took it off

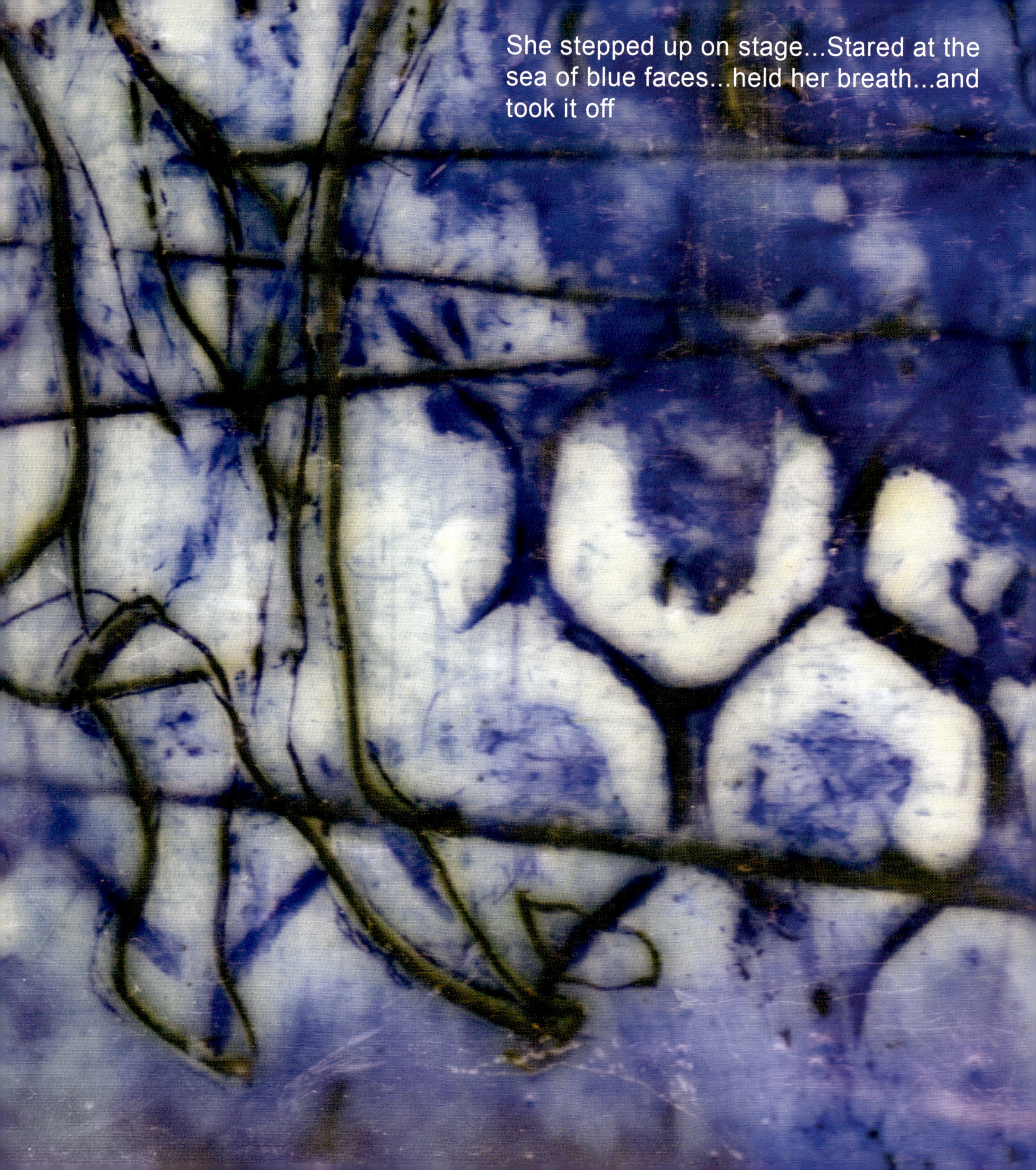

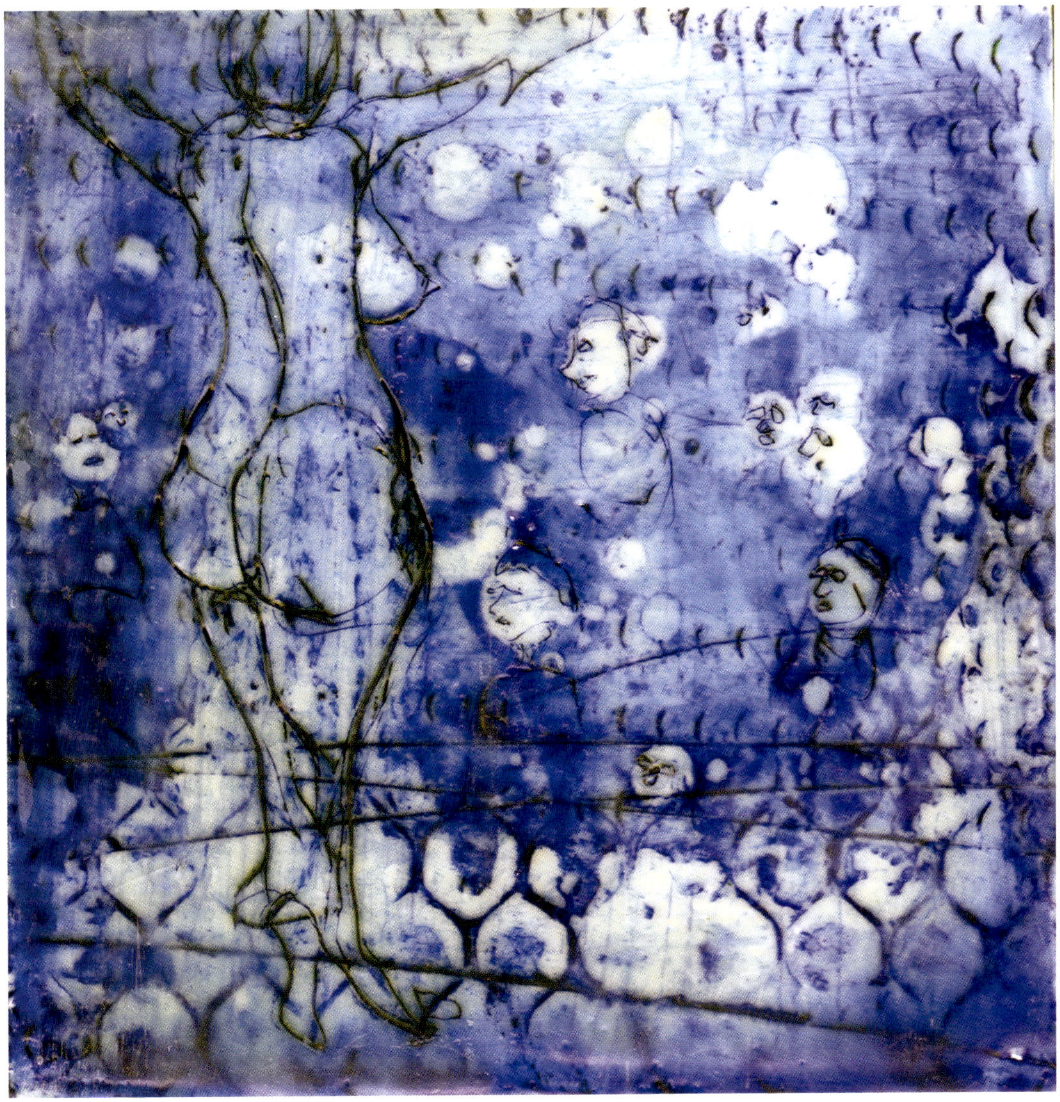

She stepped up on stage
stared at the sea of blue faces
held her breath
and took it off
2009
Encaustic on clayboard
8 x 8 in.

CHAPTER 2

The Cusp

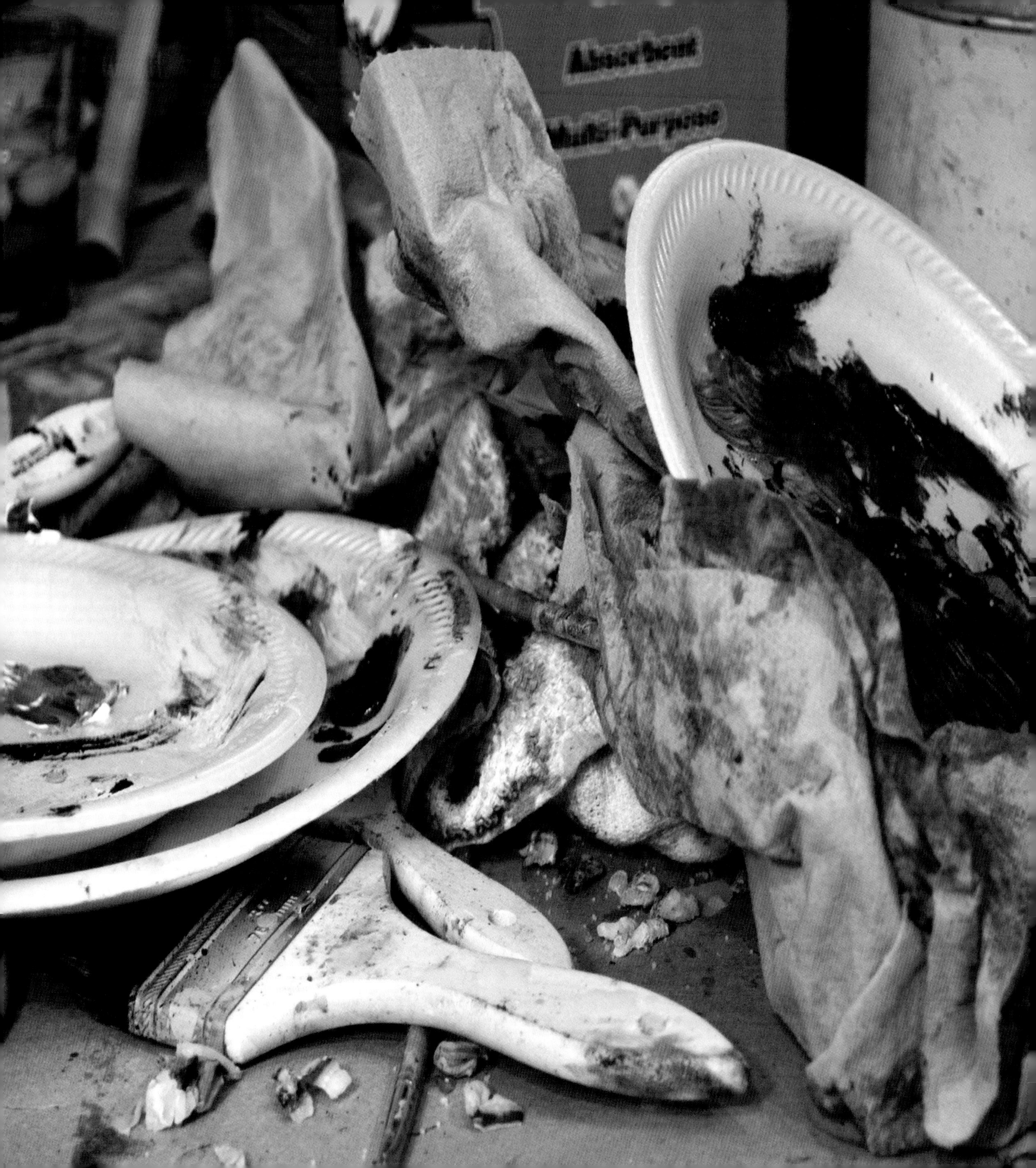

The Cusp

Some of the most controversial and influential movements in art sprung from periods of social change and upheaval. The Renaissance emerged as a bridge from the Middle Ages to the Modern Age - bringing with it an attention to perspective, realism, the effects of light and shadow, and studies of commonplace subjects and scenes. It brought with it, too, an interest in nature, naturalism, and anatomy. The movement used the printing press as its primary means of spreading new ideas throughout Europe, broadening social awareness and understanding where before it had been impossible.

Similarly, Impressionism was born from changes originally wrought by Napoleon as an alternative to the prevailing rules of academic art. Artists broke from devotion to the straight line in favor of short brushstrokes and vibrant colors intended to create an overall impression of a scene or subject. They worked en plein air to capture the evocative effects of changing light. They removed the veil of perfect composition to reveal movement and emotion.

After WWII and the McCarthy era crusades, which imposed an oppressive air of artistic censorship, New York became home to the Abstract Expressionists who responded in backlash response by breaking through all known accepted practices of the creation of art. The work stemming from this movement was steeped in the subliminal mind and the existential; it forever changed what it means to produce art. "To me, it seems as though the art pendulum over time has slowly swung from realism to abstraction, accelerating greatly in the last two centuries," says Diediker. He created the Wax Onion to "massage" the shift from the absolute image that prevailed in the Renaissance to the abstract image as it evolved in more recent art movements. "Perhaps we can push the pendulum back the other way by starting with a complete chance-driven abstraction and then extract imagery." The encaustic medium, beeswax, is an optimal vehicle for "playing" with image.

Three Chinese Warriors and a Praying Mantis releasing The Fenghuang 2009
Encaustic on clayboard
12 x 12 in.

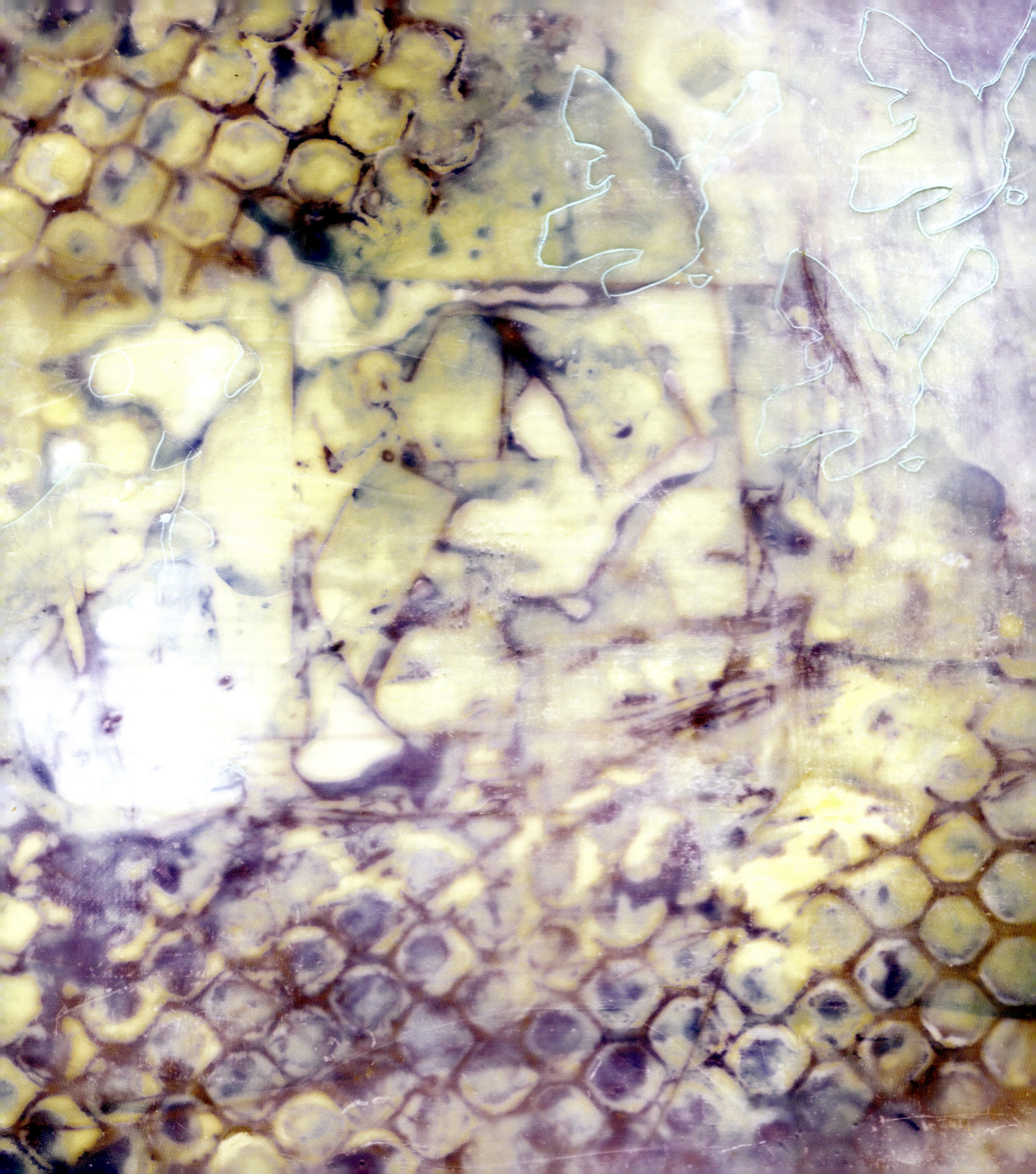

The Cusp

Perhaps in response to today's challenging economic and political times, there exists an opportunity to return from abstraction and reintroduce ourselves to finding natural imagery, a re-visioning of what we see and how we see it. In the advent of social media, global citizens are responding to the deconstruction of geographic communities and the resulting sense of loss and alienation by reasserting themselves and redefining their communities in the online setting. The human need to connect prevails, no matter how "unnatural" these settings may be. This is evident in how quickly social networking sites are growing in popularity. Perhaps the nihilism and disconnection of the recent past can be transformed into an opportunity for deriving real meaning and real imagery once again. From an abstract piece of melted wax and pigment, and from observations cutting across a seemingly disparate swath of ideologies and cultures around the world, the meaning of living today, in this moment, can be drawn forth and distilled to create a composite image of common life and common experience. This is connection.

For the sake of cohesive discourse, the modern return to the encaustic process might be called **natural revisionism**. Revisionism has historically connoted negative meaning, as in the case of the Holocaust revisionist movement or the Marxists. In this particular scenario, revisionism takes a positive cast, through which the artist and the audience mutually benefit by dint of their collaboration in the creation of art. The artist divines his inspiration from nature and draws forth an image, paying homage to nature's abundant beauty in every context: the medium, itself a natural product; the subject matter, as inspired by erosion and patterns in nature; and the creation of natural art. The artist "re-visions" the image. The participants also take part in the creation or re-visioning of the image.

Historically, artists have worked in solitude – in the studio or en plein air – adding layers upon layers of paint to a canvas, and culminating in a finished piece that is then revealed to the world. Natural revisionism turns this process on its head. Through this process, the audience provides insight on a work as it is in progress, thereby influencing and inspiring the artist to "revise" or "re-vision" the finished piece to reflect or encapsulate an informed and globally varied perspective.

In several ways, natural revisionism expressed through the encaustic medium encompasses many of the characteristics common to the movements that changed the art world as we know it. Facebook becomes analogous to the printing press, the vehicle that carried the Renaissance across Europe. Facebook becomes the vehicle that amplifies the idea of a gallery: instead of a limited number of viewers on the work of a limited number of artists, all determined by geography and softly publicized by word of mouth, an artist's work is now subject to appreciation by viewers around the world, any number of whom are welcome to respond to the art at any hour of the day, from any geographic vantage in the world.

The malleability of beeswax allows the artist to mimic the Impressionists through varied strokes and marks, by the effects of light, and with the use of vibrant color. Academic rendering sublimates itself to the impression created by the overall image and its effects on the viewer(s). Though the encaustic medium requires the use of tools, and therefore the use of a studio, it also relies heavily on sunlight to reveal its pools of color and its uniqueness of texture– the very qualities that comprise the beauty of the medium.

David Anfam, an expert on Abstract Expressionism, writes, "Abstract Expressionism is a landmark in the general history of art and of modern art in particular. Like the Cubist epoch it represents a revolutionary event which revises our view of things before and after...." In a similar way, Diediker uses the forum of social media to help him revise our view of things before and after. Of his own work, Picasso said, "A picture is not thought out and settled beforehand. While it is being done it changes as one's thoughts change. And when it is finished, it still goes on changing, according to the state of mind of whoever is looking at it. A picture lives a life like a living creature, undergoing the changes imposed on us by our life from day to day. This is natural enough, as the picture lives only through the man who is looking at it." The Wax Onion collaborative could not be more of a serendipitous analogy to Picasso's earlier vision.

As a result of the marriage of an artist's ingenuity and the strengths of social networking, unfinished artwork may now subject itself to global interpretation prior to completion. The influence of a global audience and the audience's varied and contemporaneous interpretations of art-in-process renders a final product that acts as a composite of the modern world and its briskly changing environment, a "time capsule" of modern associations and sensibilities, so to speak. The artist who participates in this process is charged to reexamine what he has created and "evolve" the final product. In a pointedly ironic way, art may now use technology – the antithesis of nature – to mimic nature's evolution and allow the process of making art to "organically" encompass any number of modern ideas and quirkily inspiring sensibilities.

This is notable on two important fronts: in the production of art itself and in the effects of transparency on the artistic process. The shroud of solitude disappears. The mystery of creation becomes transparent. Some may lament this loss of mystery in the production of all elements of art. Nevertheless, this new transparency is endemic to the rise of social media, in forums where sharing information and ideas is the very cornerstone of technological and social progress. Creation of art becomes a collaborative activity.

In essence, natural revisionism changes how art is produced, interpreted, and completed, nudging thousands of years of historical standards in art to adapt to the rapidly changing world and to the tremendous potential of technology as we know it today. Art will always be subject to interpretation; the process of natural revisionism simply changes when the interpretation takes place.

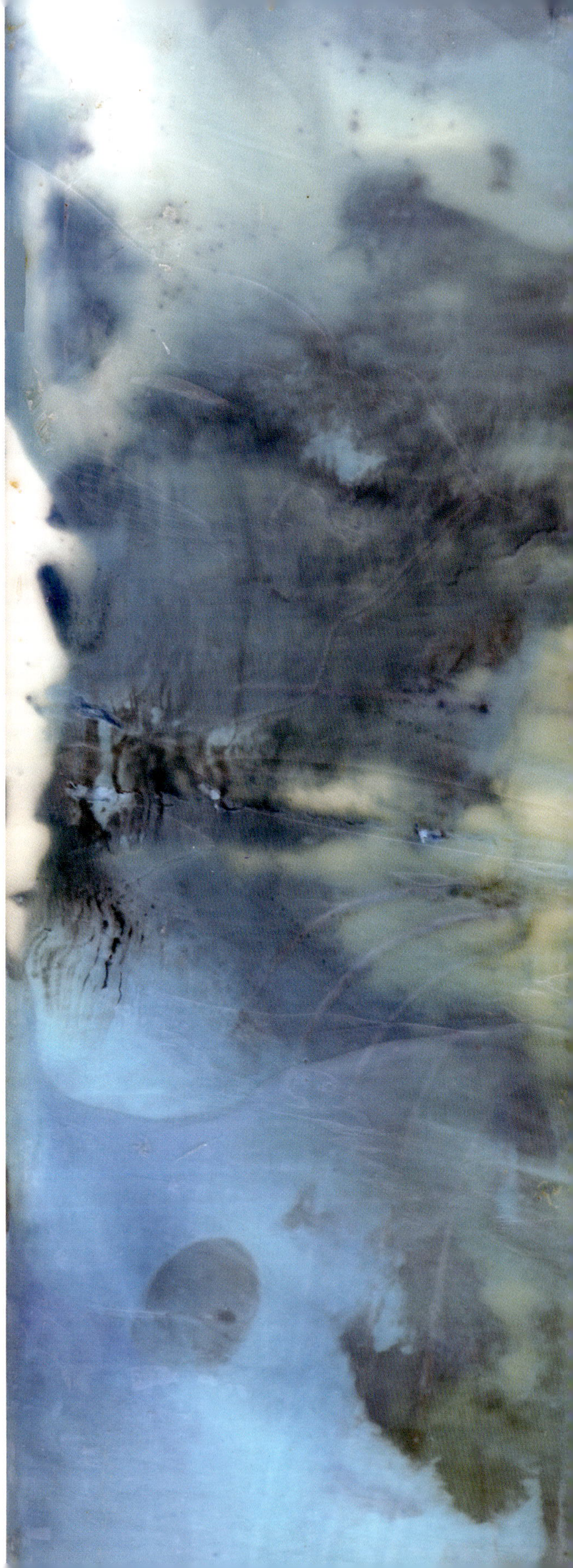

Sleeping Aqua King under talking Bear tree 2009
Encaustic on clayboard
8 x 8 in.

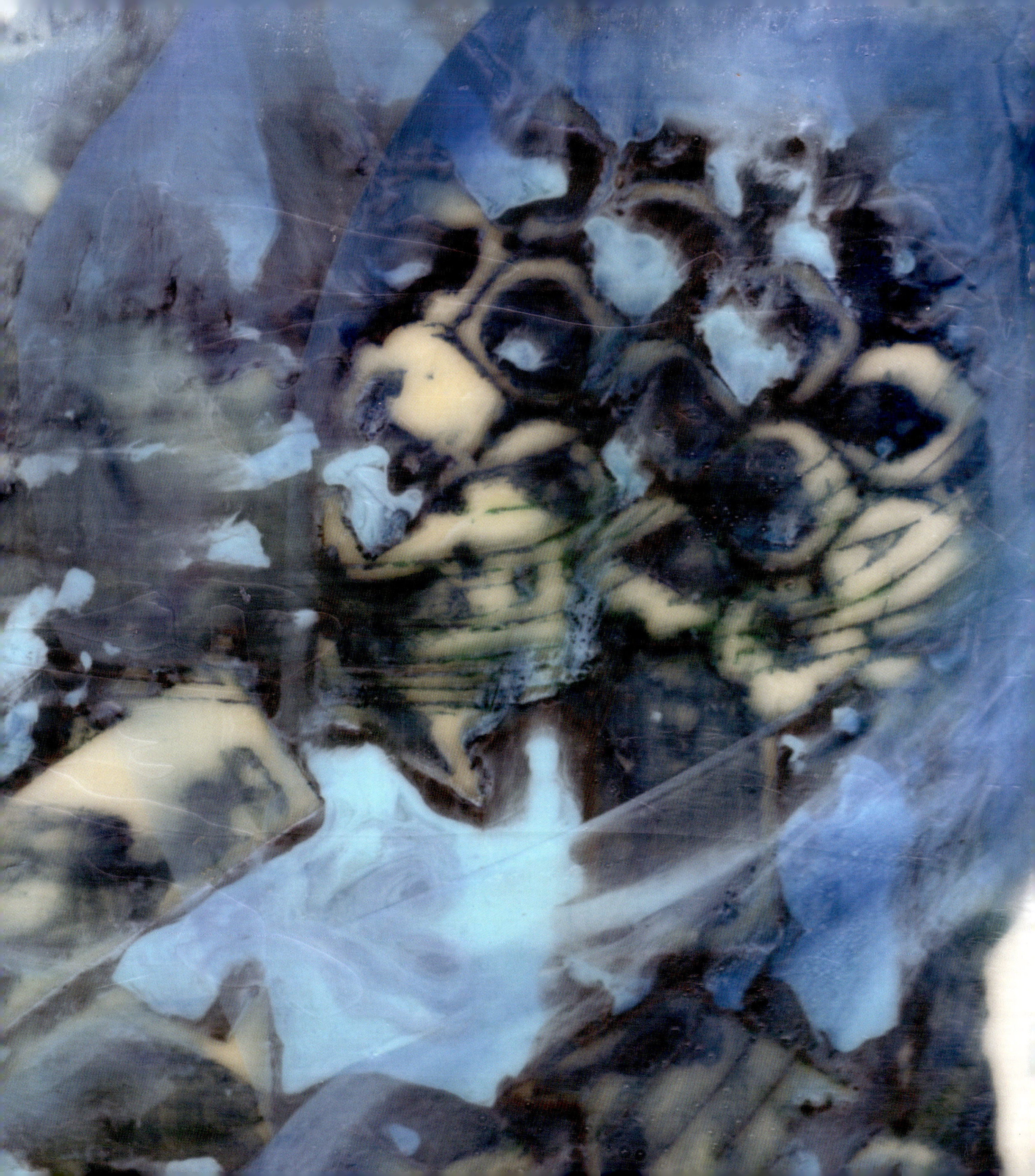

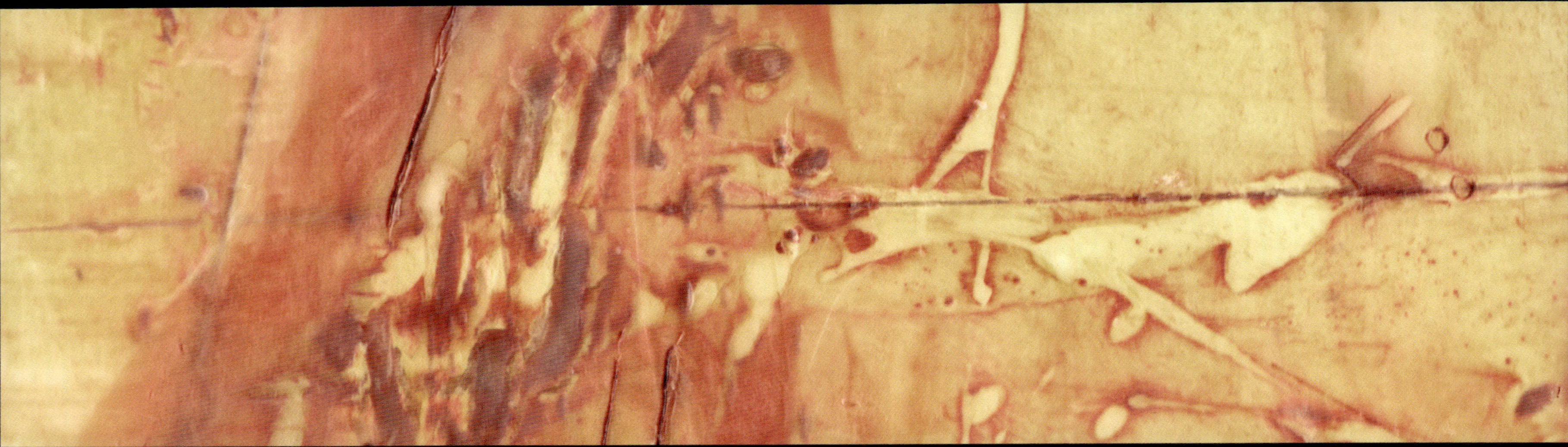

River monkey King in high heels flying the banner of his people followed by two Crocs

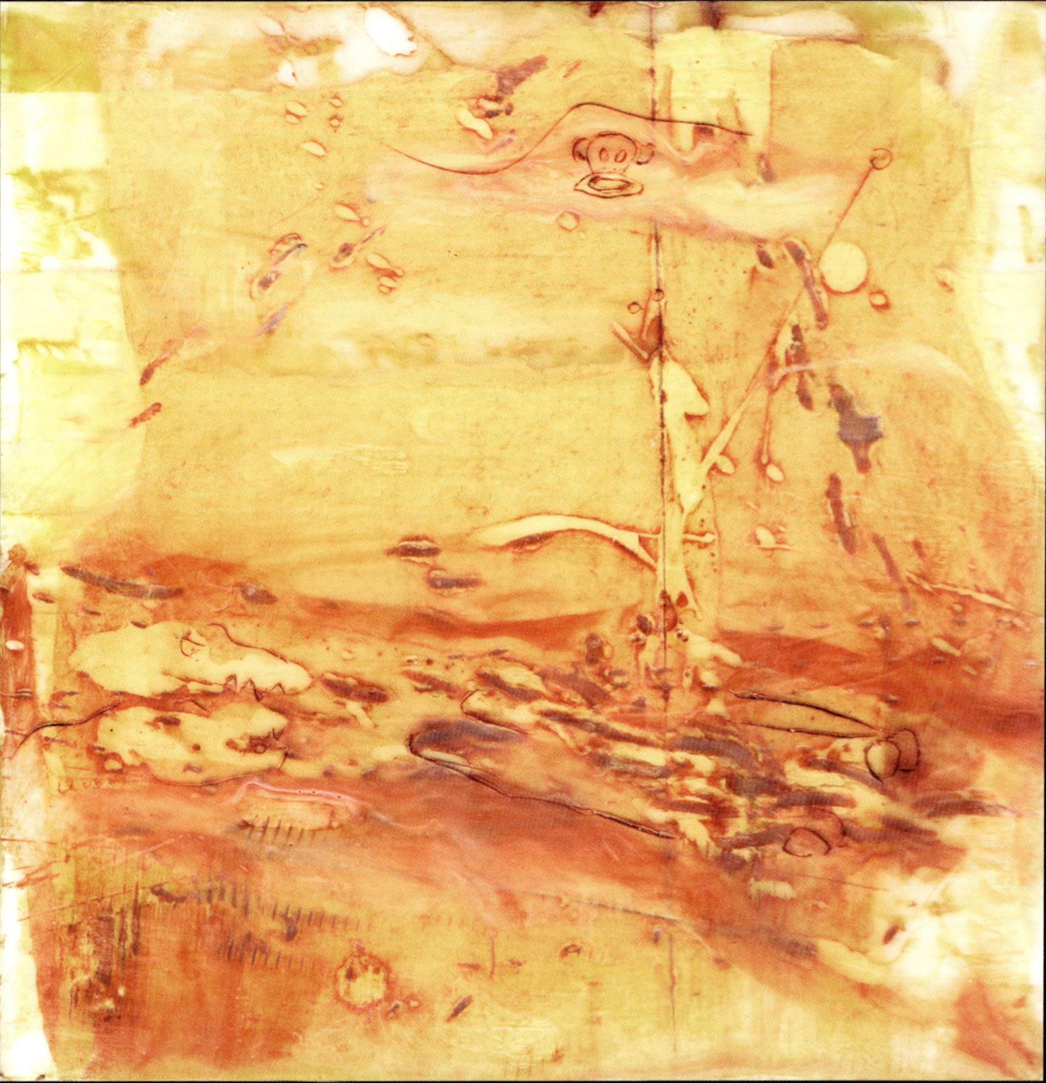

River monkey King in high heels flying the banner of his people followed by two Crocs 2009
Encaustic on clayboard
8 x 8 in.

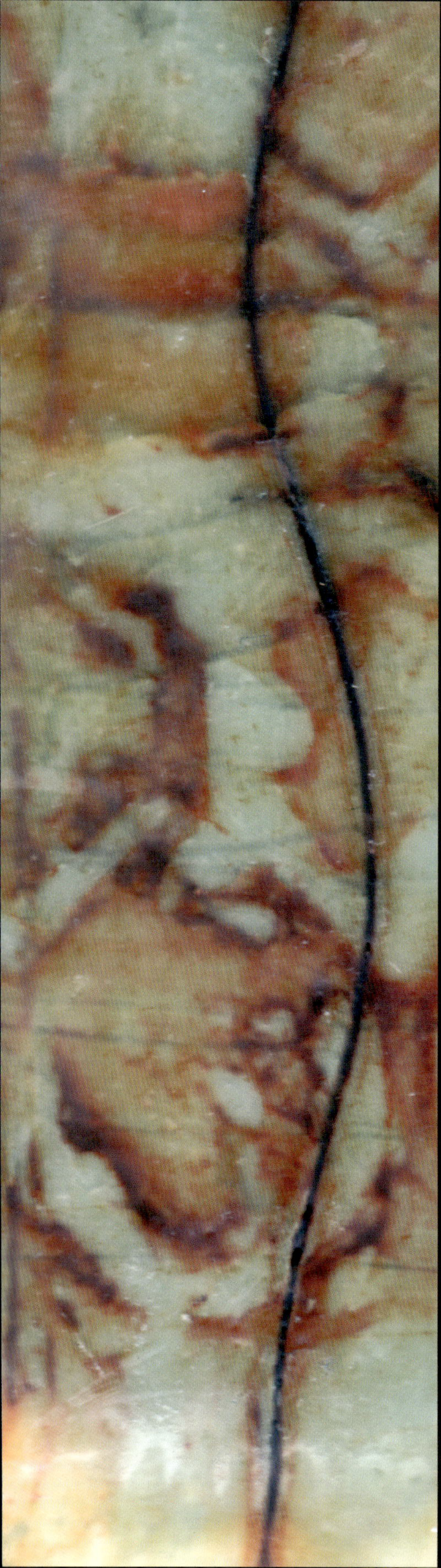

Skull Balloon

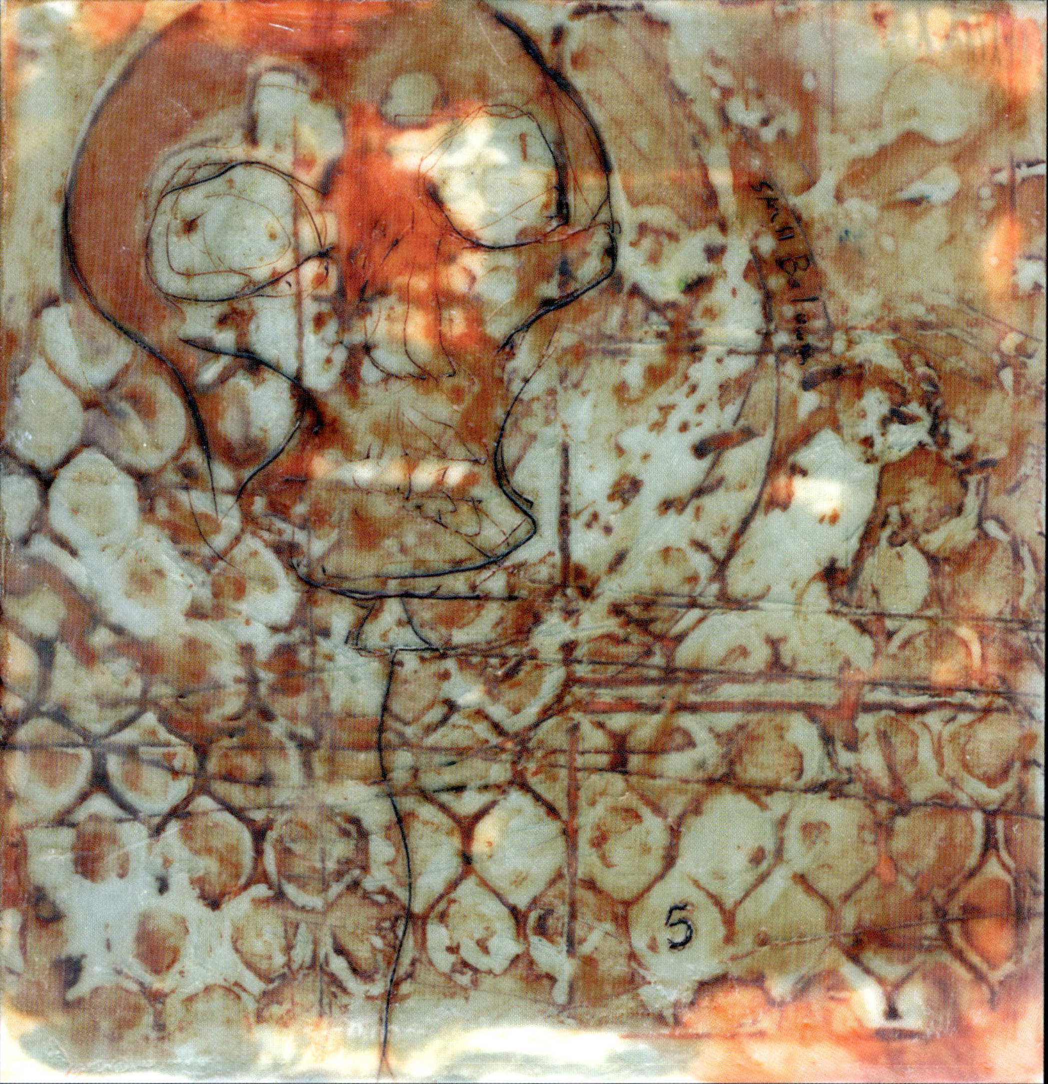

Skull Balloon 2009
Encaustic on clayboard
8 x 8 in.

Added November 16, 2009 · Comment · Like

Lisa Clarke Wow - this eerily reminds me of the collapse of the twin towers.
November 16, 2009 at 11:52am · Delete

Emily Dunster Birds flying around a secret city on a mountain top surrounded by misty clouds.
November 16, 2009 at 12:05pm · Delete

Ginny Millard I see an old man playing an organ in the lowe center. In the area just above his head is a fleeing man, a woman crawling up a flight of stars between the towers and two ghost-like figures in the clouds in fron of the building. Looks like uncontrolled chaos.
November 16, 2009 at 1:35pm · Delete

Anna James A zipper that is revealing a burning city.
November 16, 2009 at 1:41pm · Delete

Tony Schacher As versus controlled chaos? Any way... I see a woman ironing clothes in the kitchen, I think she may be day dreaming as she labors...
November 16, 2009 at 2:33pm · Delete

Wyatt Wilkerson this one is prbly my favorite. i see a woman walking in the distance and any eye looking over the world.
November 16, 2009 at 3:01pm · Delete

Micah I. J. Holt It's all pretty abstract, got some distinct urban / decay vibes going on. And I def see a skull in the top-left-middle, if that makes any sense lol.
November 16, 2009 at 3:33pm · Delete

Chris Walsh Tsunami hits oil rig
November 16, 2009 at 3:45pm · Delete

Maude Schellhous Ganesh dancing in a whirlwind.
November 16, 2009 at 4:41pm · Delete

Wendy Johnson Roberts A rip the fabric of time. The time zipper is busted.
November 16, 2009 at 5:15pm · Delete

Sarah Bostrom Foerster Waffles, A screaming skull in the upper left corner, a city falling into a sink hole.
November 16, 2009 at 6:52pm · Delete

Iva Ruth Kinkead No concrete images came to me! I just saw it and said, oooh, I like it. The mood is really good in this one. Maybe it's the golden glow in the upper left. There do seem to be structures in the center. Maybe an old city with flair.
November 16, 2009 at 8:11pm · Delete

Allison Leigh Smith I am with Tony. I see the woman. I feel like she's mending or sewing or comforting a child. And it seems she is haunted by memories in ruins.

Or entirely separate: a fist tightly grasping a newspaper reporting on a big story of a city.
November 16, 2009 at 8:32pm · Delete

Cynthia Wood Stott Demise of the Twin Towers
November 16, 2009 at 9:51pm · Delete

Michaelangelo Adam Krum nake woman swimming in cough syrup.
November 26, 2009 at 9:31pm · Delete

Rose Datoc Dall ghosts after the teddy-bear massacre...
November 30, 2009 at 11:08pm · Delete

Quinn Peterson a late night party in the video game realm
February 1 at 11:43pm · Delete

Kent Miller The pages of an architectural coffee-table book being torn down the middle.
February 1 at 11:44pm · Delete

Andy Lawler a pair of pale green pants with nobody inside them climbing a broken ladder notes with interest a high-bouncing rubber trapezoid, as a racecar driver reenacts the anguish of Gethsemane below.
November 16, 2009 at 11:54pm · Delete

Ark Idol I see a pair of Gecko's, perhaps mateing in a stream with pebbles and rocks. Their bodies cross each other in somewhat of an X.
November 17, 2009 at 10:06am · Delete

Dan Oldham I see bits and pieces of a broken zipper.
November 17, 2009 at 10:15am · Delete

Kirsten Thayne Elkins 2012
November 17, 2009 at 1:13pm · Delete

Sean Diediker these comments are brilliant im using many of them right now!!
November 17, 2009 at 1:59pm · Delete

Ben Stier peering through a window onto a war torn city.
November 17, 2009 at 4:45pm · Delete

Chelsey Hillman Browning Someone playing the piano, skull in the sky,a woman crying
November 17, 2009 at 7:15pm · Delete

Vanessa Harvard I see a woman in a freeezing iceland. She's running from something. Shes holding her dress up. I think she is pregnant... and she might have wings. I can't make up my mind.
November 17, 2009 at 7:52pm · Delete

Alyson Oldham Williams a long-nosed gnome is tossed out of a cave by the seat of his pants while little red riding hood (upper right) gasps.
November 18, 2009 at 12:45am · Delete

Rebecca Richards Sean..is it me or is Jim Morriosons face at the top and over a lillte?
November 18, 2009 at 12:17pm · Delete

Sean Diediker I was able to use so many comments on this one! it's for sure 9/11 related! bravo. the finished piece will be on display in Park City in 2 weeks. Thanks
November 18, 2009 at 1:14pm · Delete

Renae Mariena Phelps sorry so late, but it looks like a zipper thats being ripped open.
November 20, 2009 at 10:22am · Delete

Wade Stubblefield I see death here. At the top, a skull fragment and then what looks like bits and pieces of other bones broken, some spineage there on the mid-right. Some indistinguisable guts or insides. No real blood more more like stains perhaps of blood.

Oddly enough I am not a goth or grim person. This one just seemed dead. It could have something to do with me just studying about necrophiliacs and if they were real and what their problem is.
November 22, 2009 at 1:36pm · Delete

Marc Trombella spirits let loose
November 24, 2009 at 9:49pm · Delete

James M. Feezor regal zombie.
November 25, 2009 at 10:59pm · Delete

Write a comment...

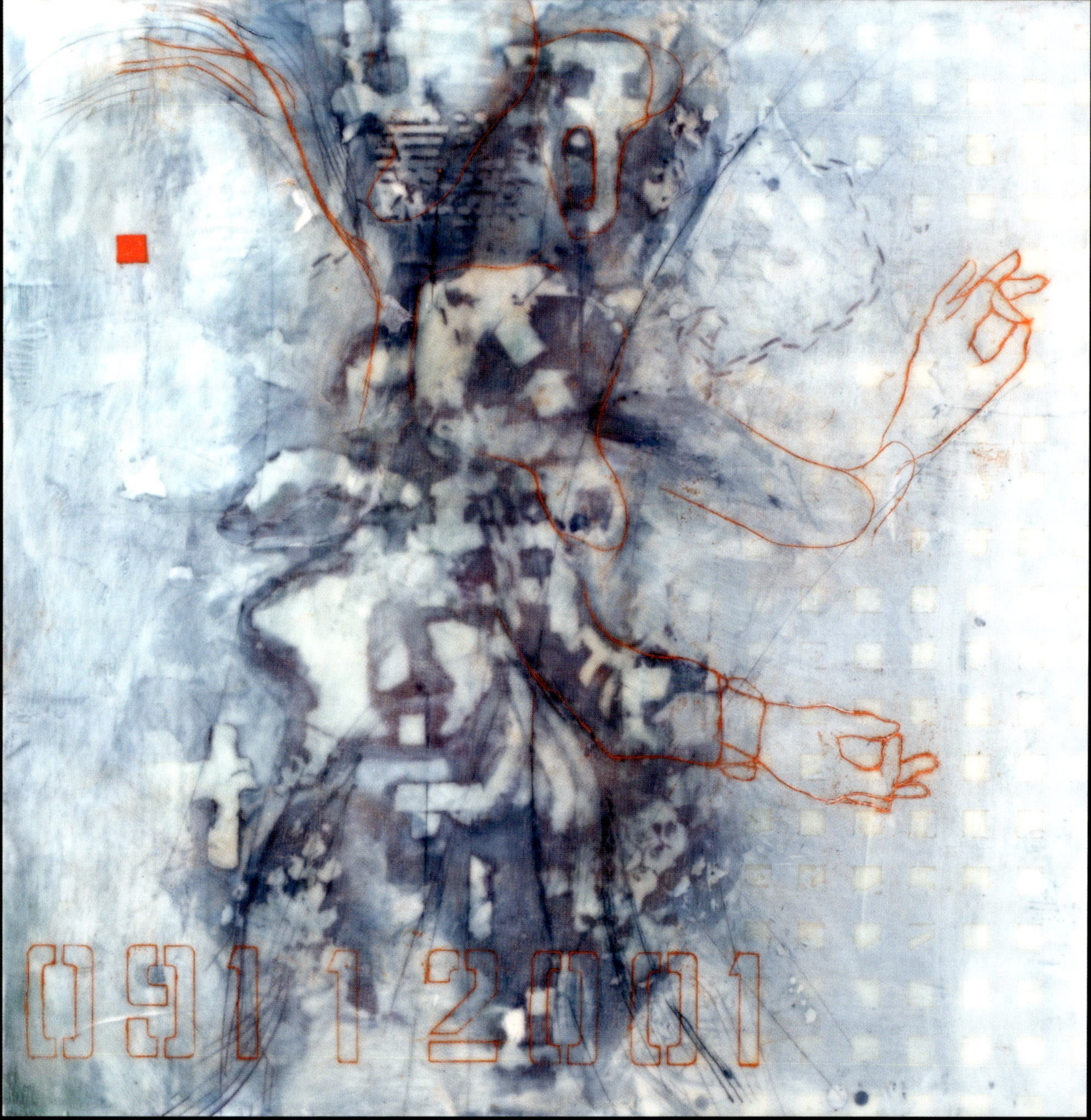

09112001
2009
Encaustic on clayboard
30 x 30 in.

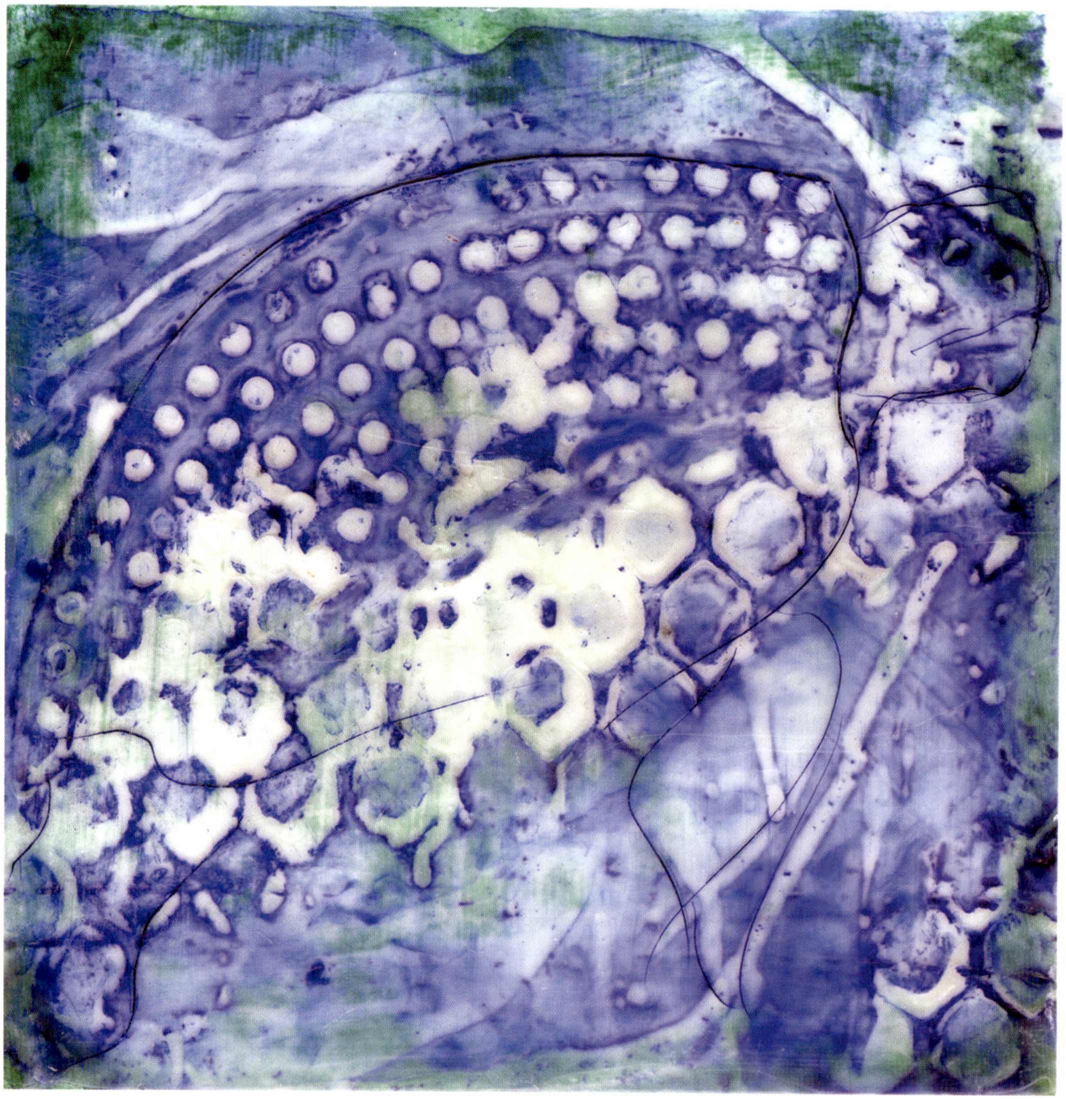

Sea Turtle 2009
Encaustic on clayboard
8 x 8 in.

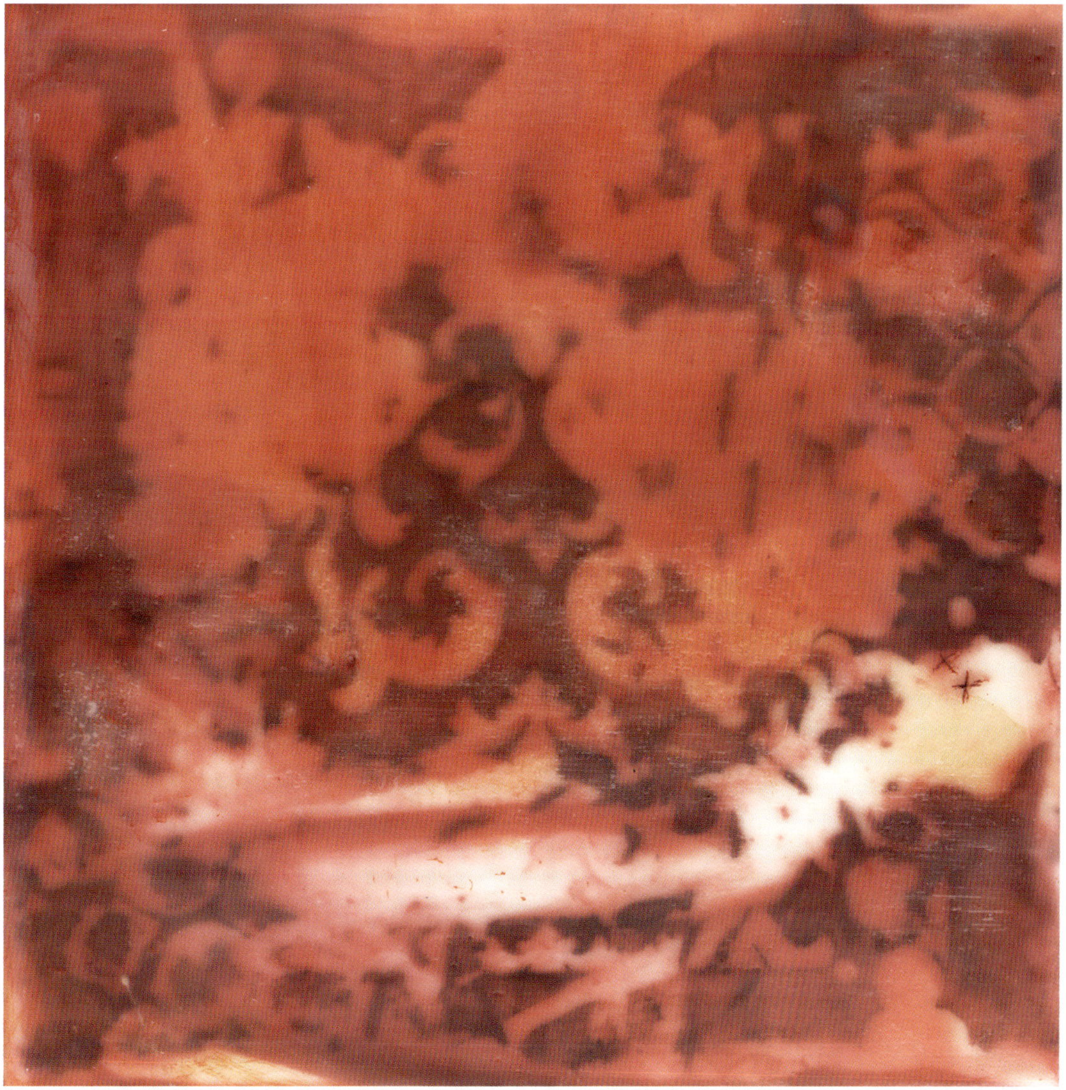

Assassination of Gonzo by Grimace
2009
Encaustic on clayboard
8 x 8 in.

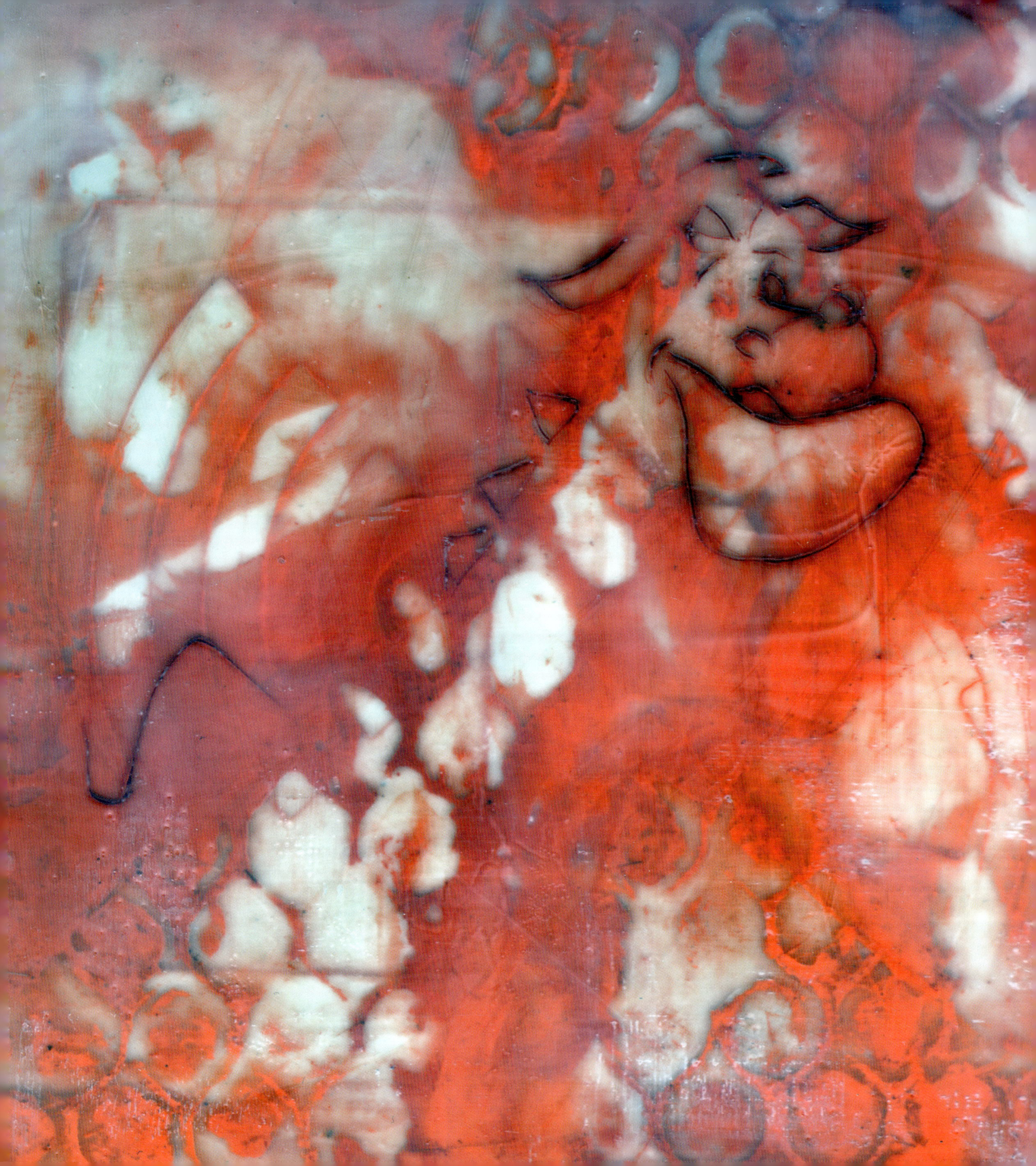

Pete's Dragon

Pete's Dragon 2009
Encaustic on clayboard
8 x 8 in.

(Next Page)
Intergalactic traveler from the Star Wars cantina (detail) 2010
Encaustic on clayboard
8 x 8 in.

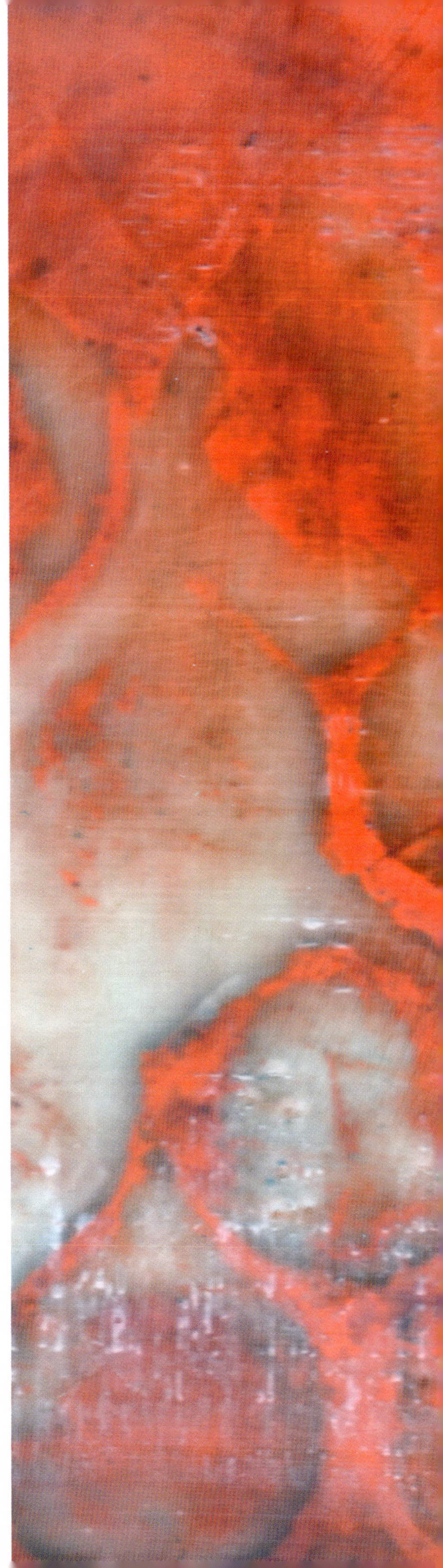

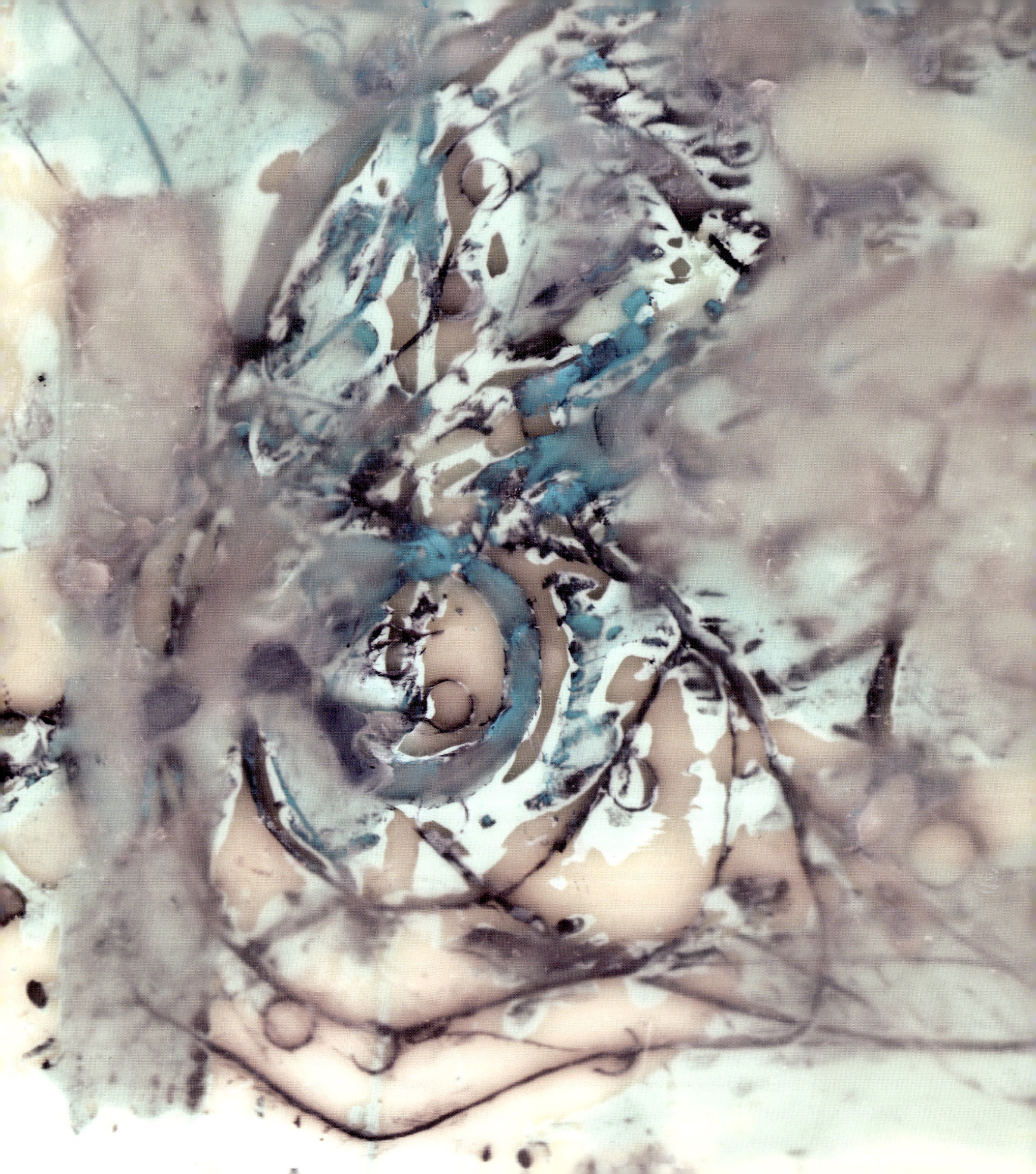

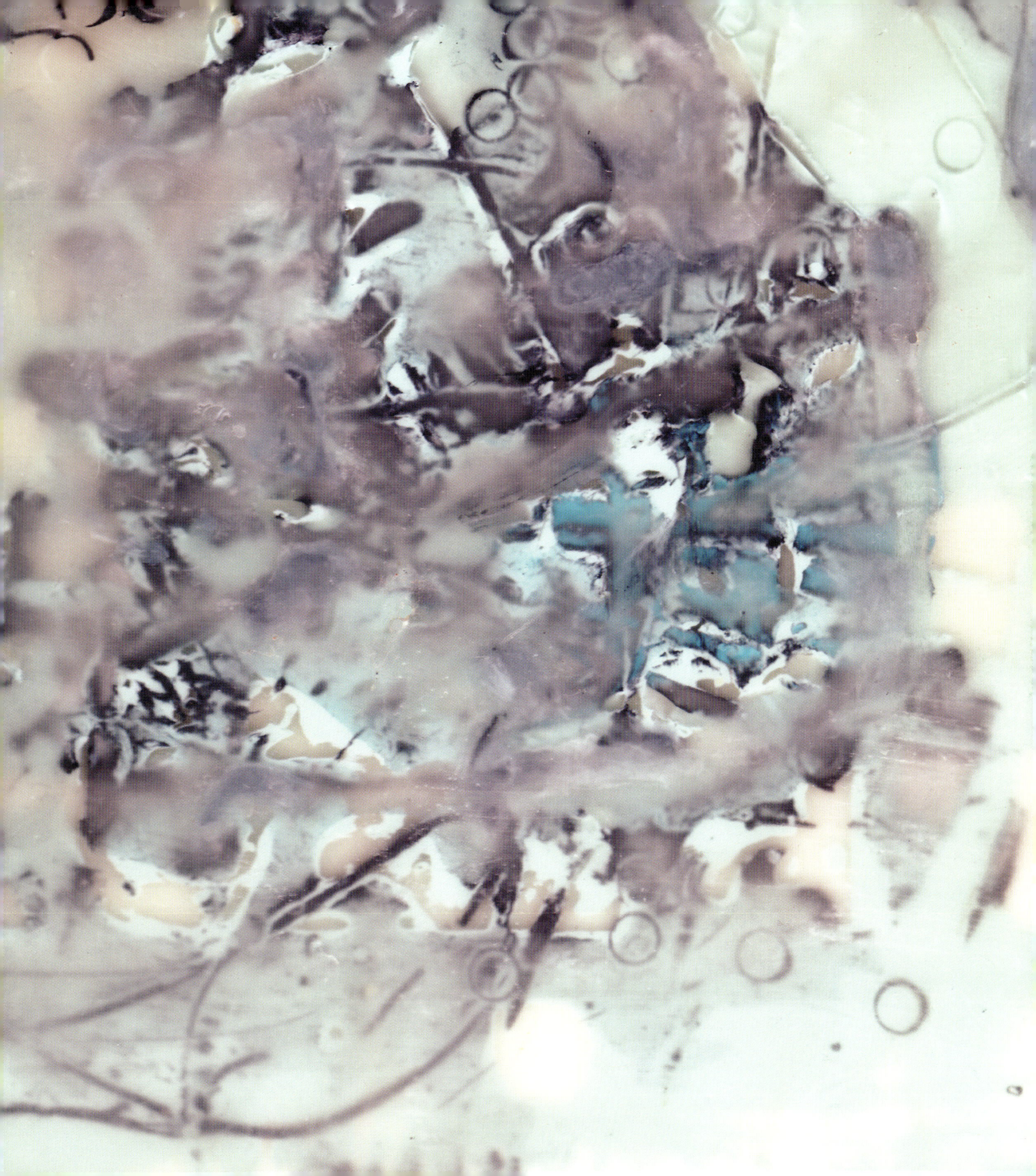

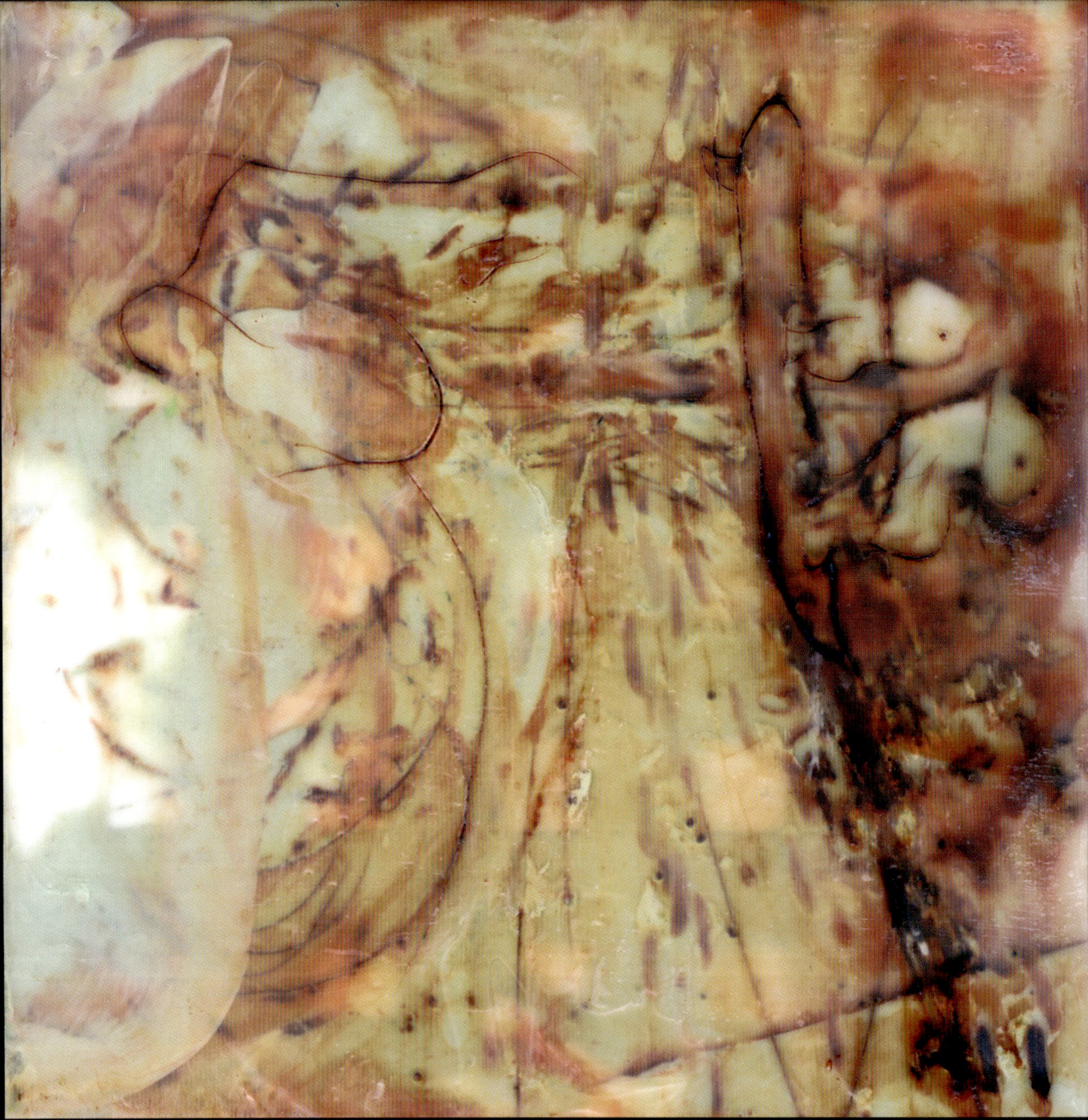

Picasso People surfing down the neck of a horse named Guernica
2009
Encaustic on clayboard
8 x 8 in.

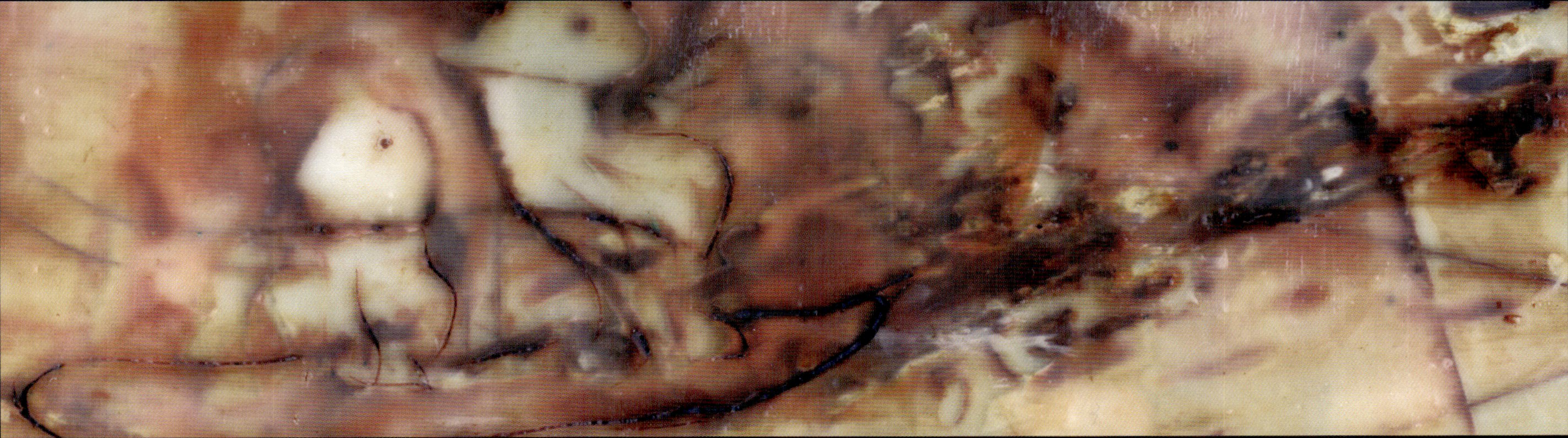

Picasso People surfing down the neck of a horse named Guernica

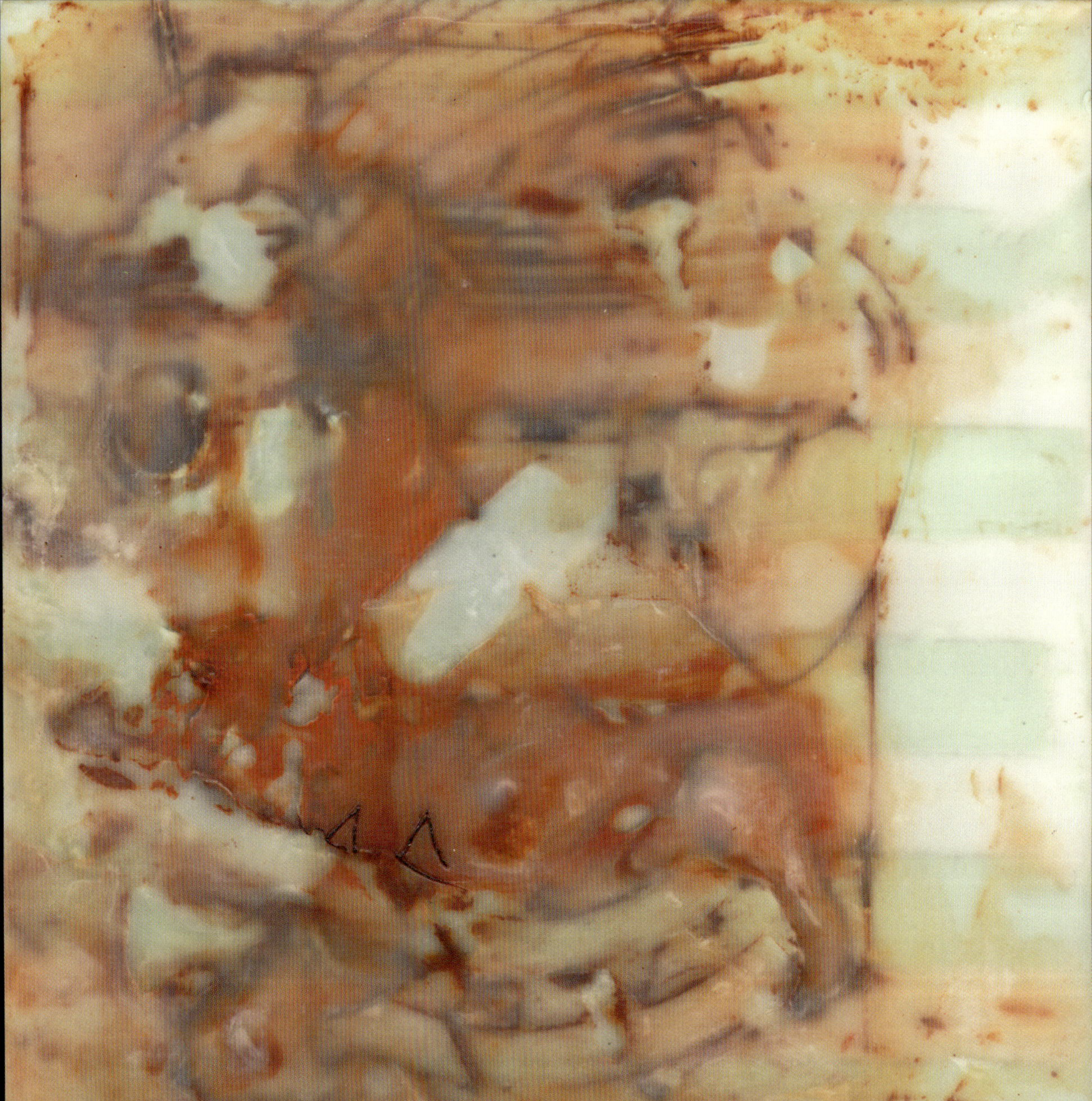

Inca Priest wishing he had become a baseball player while being eaten by a Great White
2010
Encaustic on clayboard
8 x 8 in.

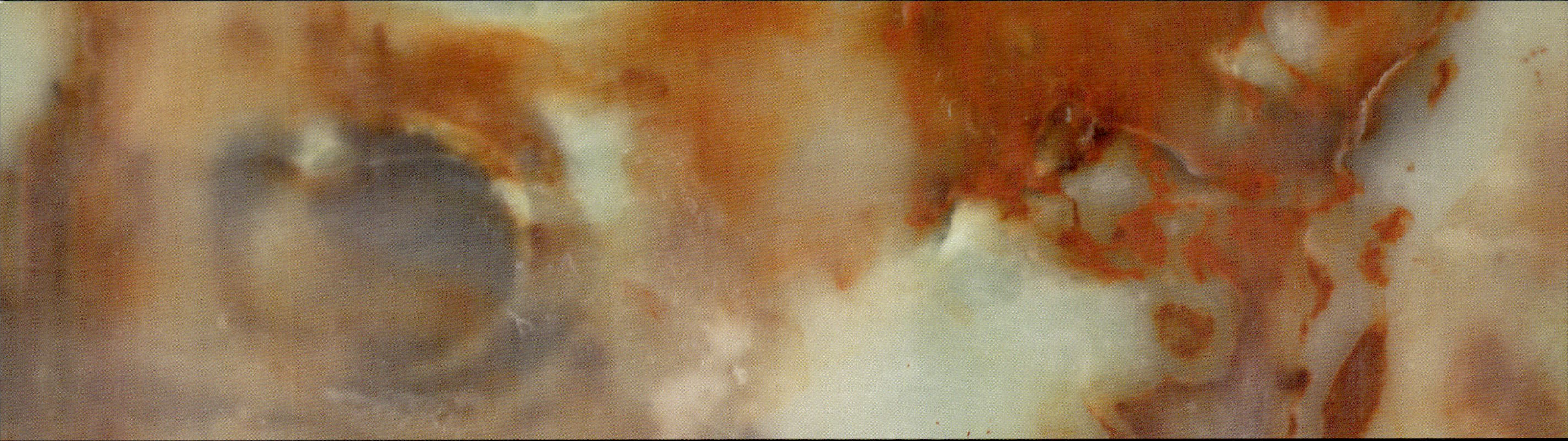

Inca Priest wishing he had become a baseball player while being eaten by a Great White

CHAPTER 3

Birds, Bees, & Mormons

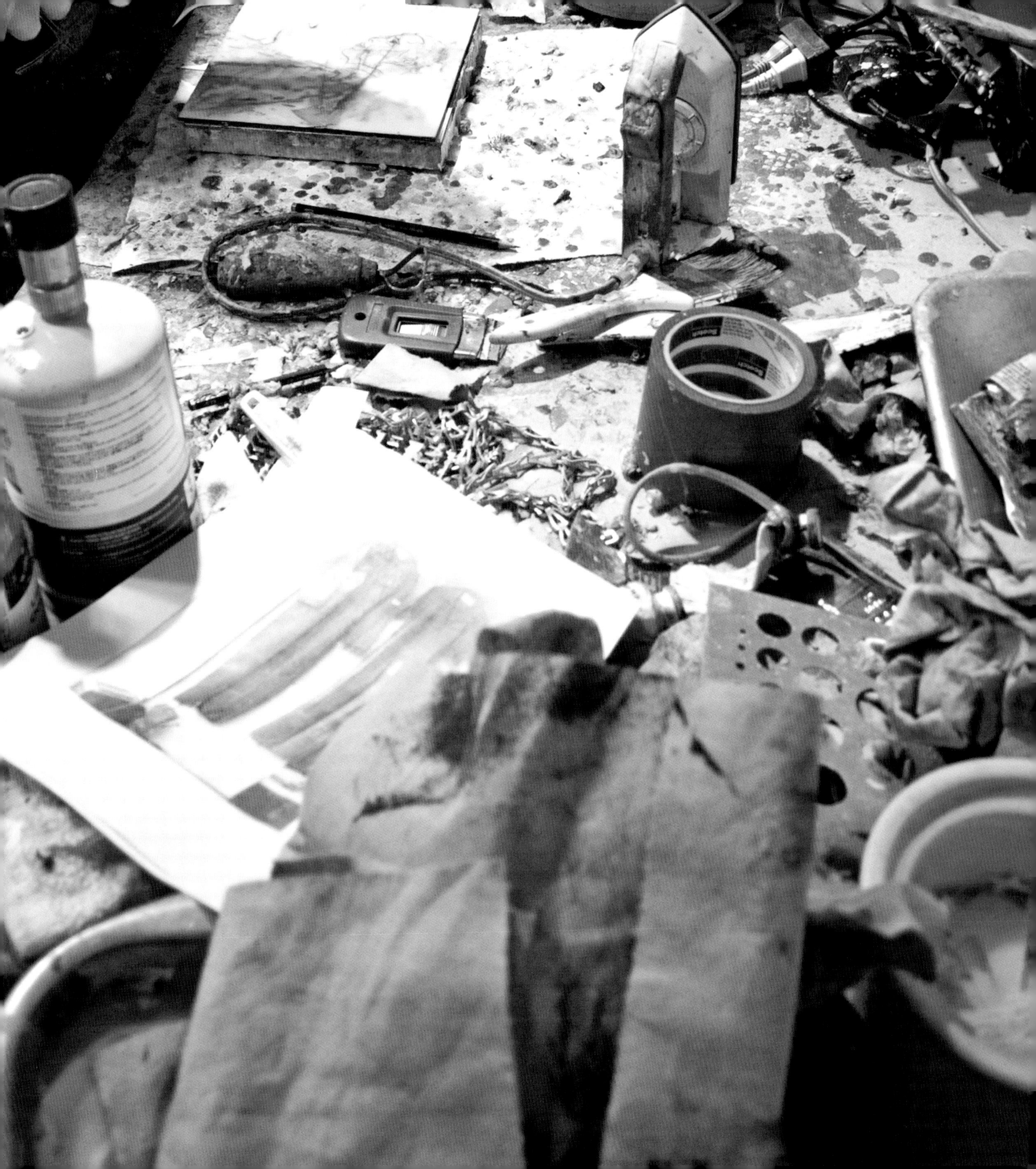

Birds Bees & Mormons

Those artists often deemed to be masters relied on the effects of sunlight and shadow on form. Diediker, whose paintings also rely heavily on the interplay of light on surfaces, turns to encaustic as a temporary respite from paint, a deepening of his artistic command, and the ultimate affirmation of the value of light on a medium. His studio is spacious, with many windows that offer him the benefit of maximum daytime exposure to sunlight. This condition allows the sun to reveal the nuances of color, depth, and texture in each encaustic work. As light pools and shifts on the surface of each plate, the glory of color reveals itself in ever-transforming brilliance and tone. Much like the way sunlight reveals crystals shining on the snow's surface, sunlight reveals pools of color in the encaustic medium.

The encaustic medium mimics evolution in nature by allowing the artist to "evolve" the natural image, but at a much faster speed. Diediker notes that, traditionally, man has not taken cues from nature, imposing human will on art and its presentation. Through the encaustic medium, Diediker symbolically takes inspiration from nature, evolving and building heated wax to mimic nature's beauty and the beauty inherent to the changes made to surfaces during the progression of millennia. "I have a great affection for the-abundant and inspiring transitions in nature," says Diediker. **"The encaustic medium allows me to mimic the long-term build-up and erosions found in nature on a much more accelerated basis, and the very medium itself – beeswax – is a testament to the earth's evolutionary genius."**

Though figures vary, several pounds of honey are needed to yield a single pound of beeswax. A small, finished encaustic clay board plate (8 square inches) uses approximately half a pound of beeswax to create. The larger plates, which are 48 square inches, may require a few pounds of beeswax. Sue Hubbell, an apiarist and writer, has said, "One bee would have to fly the equivalent of three orbits around the earth in her foraging flights (using one ounce of honey as fuel for each orbit) in order to produce a single pound of honey." It's amazing to think of bees traveling the circumference of the world thousands of times to make the many pounds of honey that enable Diediker to explore his craft in the encaustic medium. Even more amazing is their biological imperative to work in conjunction with nature to do what they are evolved and inherently compelled to do: create beeswax and protect their colonies. As a natural and abundant byproduct of daily bee life, beeswax is the ultimate sustainable ingredient, born out of millennia of evolutionary perfection and available at no

"You have to suppose, with or without much knowledge, that we don't attach ourselves to a place merely to get away from one another. While human culture seems to be acquiring the role of a substitute for nature, I suspect we also learn from whatever reaches are left inside us to match the earth's, and whatever of its sensual messages we innately receive. Otherwise, why should we roll in the first snow, or rejoice all over again at being visited by the fragile, white blossoms of the shadblow in early spring? Have we not experienced them before?"

-John Hay

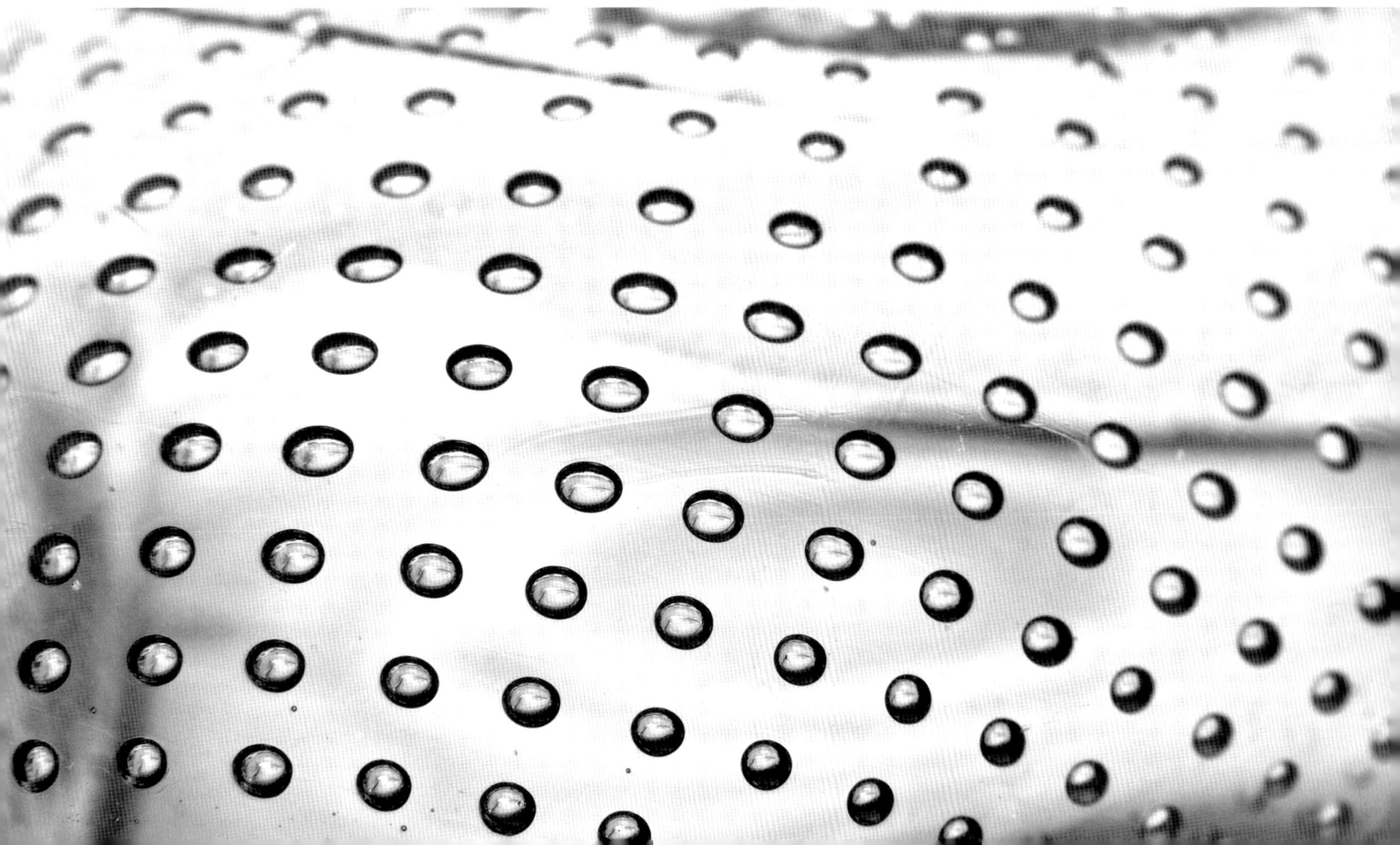

apparent 'cost' to the little workers who happily create it.

Moreover, the things that bees require to make honey, and therefore to render beeswax and sustain their colonies, are the very things that artists have historically turned to for inspiration: flowers and trees. Without the pollen and resins from these natural elements, bees would not be able to survive. As a result of the varied characteristics of these simple natural elements and because of the unique ways in which the bees process them, the color of beeswax deepens from clear to yellow or brown. The encaustic process, then, acts as a mirror to the natural formative condition inherent to beeswax by "growing" its opacity and deepening its color through each layer.

Beeswax and honey work symbiotically. Honey is the sustenance consumed for energy to make the hive and, in its consumption, creates the very byproducts required for construction. Once the beeswax is molded into a hive - in a hexagonal pattern that is considered to be a model of exceptionally sound engineering, allowing a maximum yield of honey with the least constructive effort - the wax serves to protect the young, thereby enabling honeybees to perpetuate the species and continue honey-making and pollination.

As a product of nature, beeswax has evolved to benefit human societies in many arenas, many of which require additional and often chemical processing, as is the case with cosmetics or pharmaceuticals. The encaustic process celebrates beeswax in its purest form with minimal additional processing, which is perhaps why encaustic art has remained present for so long. Ancient Romans used wax-coated tablets as a means to communicate, carving messages into the tablets, which could then be heated, smoothed, and reused indefinitely once the message was read. In this same vein, an encaustic piece can be heated to be reworked or re-visioned to communicate a new message or image. The only processing required is the application of heat, natural pigments, and simple tools.

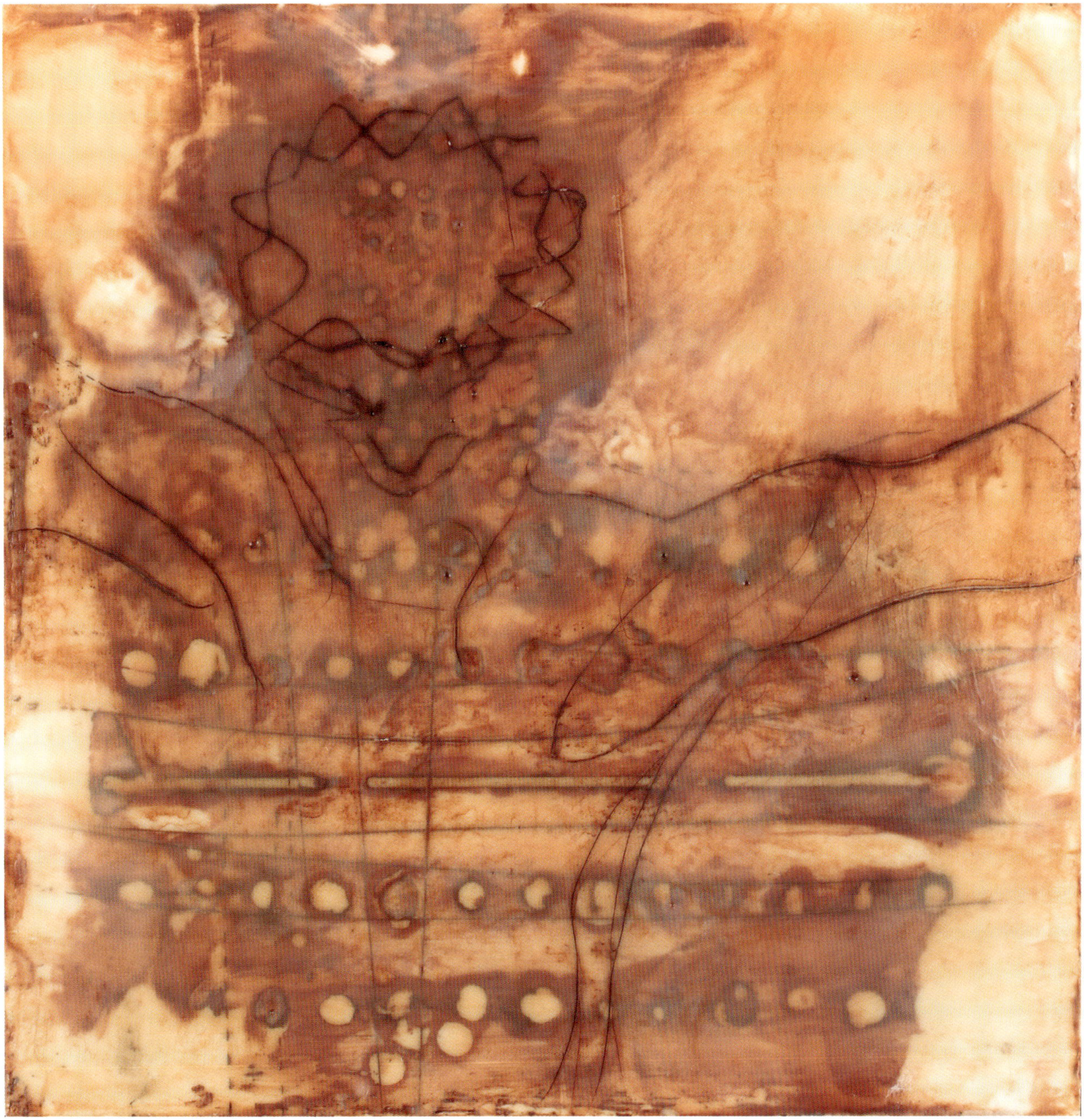

Christ 2009
Encaustic on clayboard
16 x 16 in.

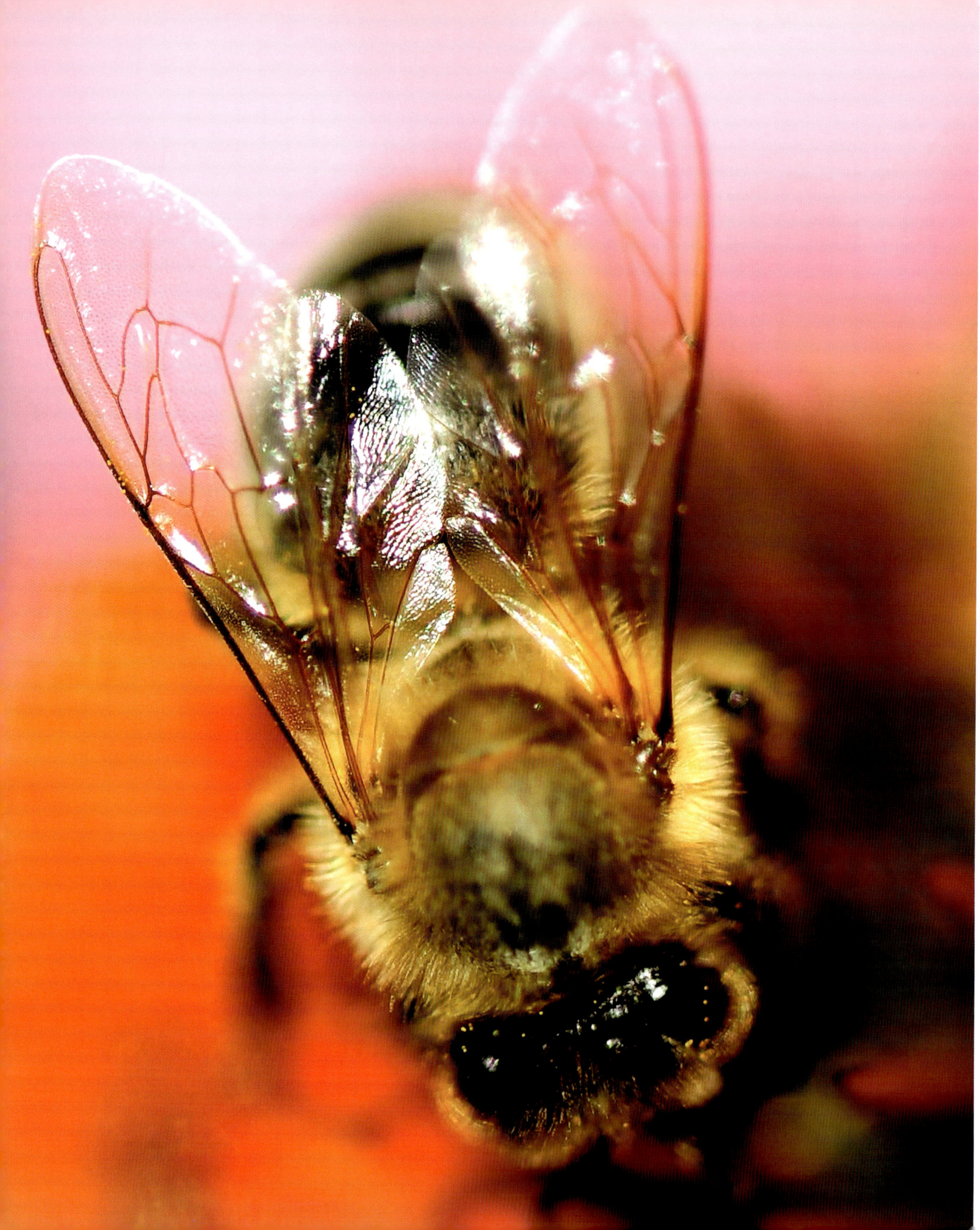

Birds Bees & Mormons

An artist using encaustic turns his space into part-studio and part-laboratory, where common household items are used to coax and conjure imagery from layers of beeswax and pigment. A common slow cooker, a skillet, an iron, and a paintbrush... These basic household items take on new use to draw beauty from the beeswax as it cool from a heated state. Stencils and pigment further draw an image forth. The wax is layered and manipulated until an image appears. Water and wind erode stone and rock, weathering away patterns and colors over thousands of years. In this same way, the artist "weathers" out an image from the encaustic plate, mimicking the beauty of erosive patterns present in nature.

Humans recognized the potential of creating imagery through the manipulation of heated wax very long ago, and made wax art well before the advent of chemical agents available to artists today. Diediker's turn towards encaustic painting takes a cue from thousands of years of artistic wisdom, lauding the ecological and evolutionary genius of the simple honeybee. Working with beeswax, respecting its malleability and finessing it to reveal the depths of its beauty, is as much an act of respect and communion with nature as is meditatively studying the patterns of ponderosa pine needles while hiking through a forest or rubbing one's fingers appreciatively over the soft, furry beard inside an iris.

Of the humble quahog clam, Robert Finch once wrote: "When dug up, quahogs have a rich, weathered, blue-and-gray cast to them, as though they had lain beneath the mud for ages, forming slowly like minerals in the earth. Their smooth, rounded, gracefully asymmetrical shape fits satisfyingly in the palm, and their shells are covered with patterns of growth rings that reflect their environment: rippled sand flats, expanding waves, a concentrically spreading world. They take their color and form from where they live and possess that perfection of completeness, of circumference, like the compassed tufts of beach grass whose blade tips draw rings around themselves in the dune sand." This passage nicely illustrates the very human tendency to draw beauty from even the least likely sources present in nature. The beauty that nature makes on its own, as a result of its uninterrupted and unintruded naturalness, the patterns of erosion, wind, rain, and fire... this is the beauty that Diediker tries to channel in his encaustic work.

the humble quahog clam

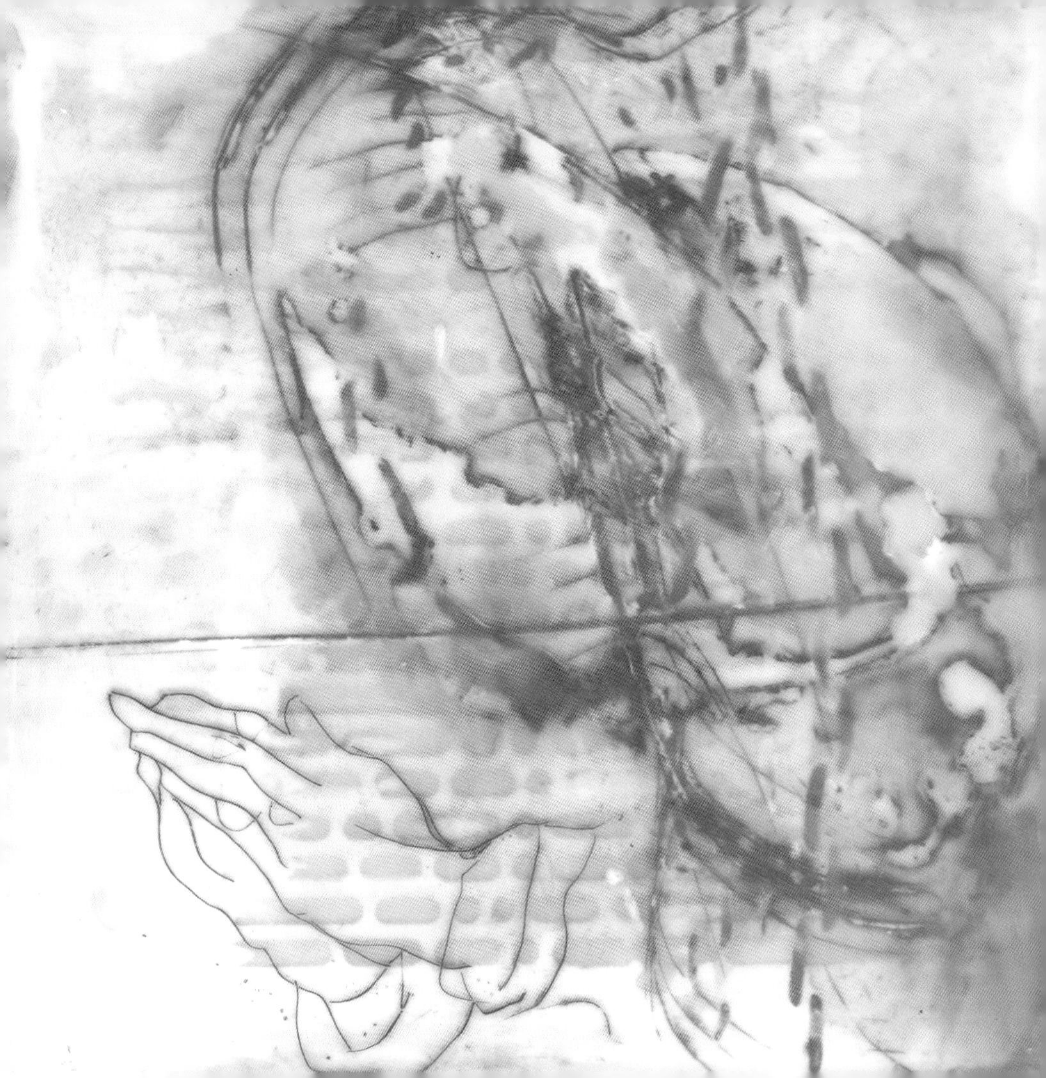

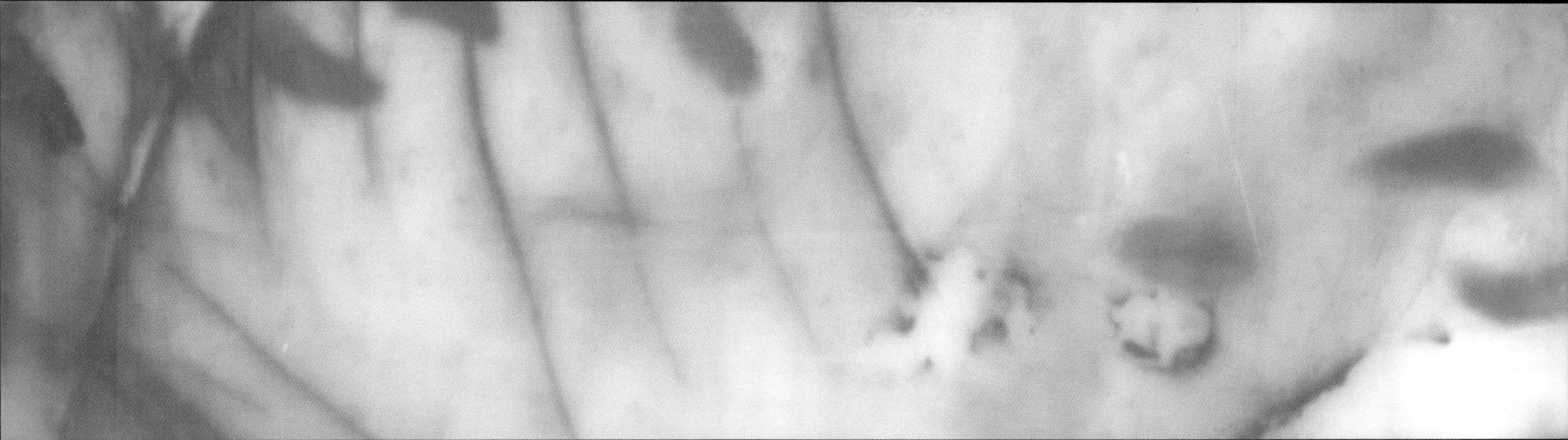

PRAYER

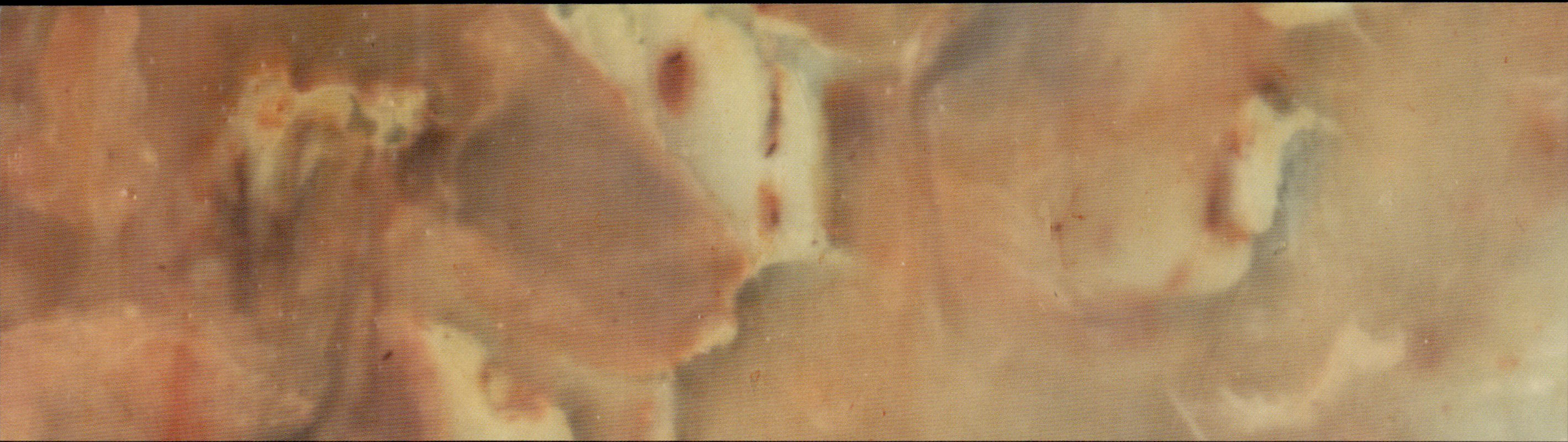

Reading under a tree next to a cat telling inside jokes

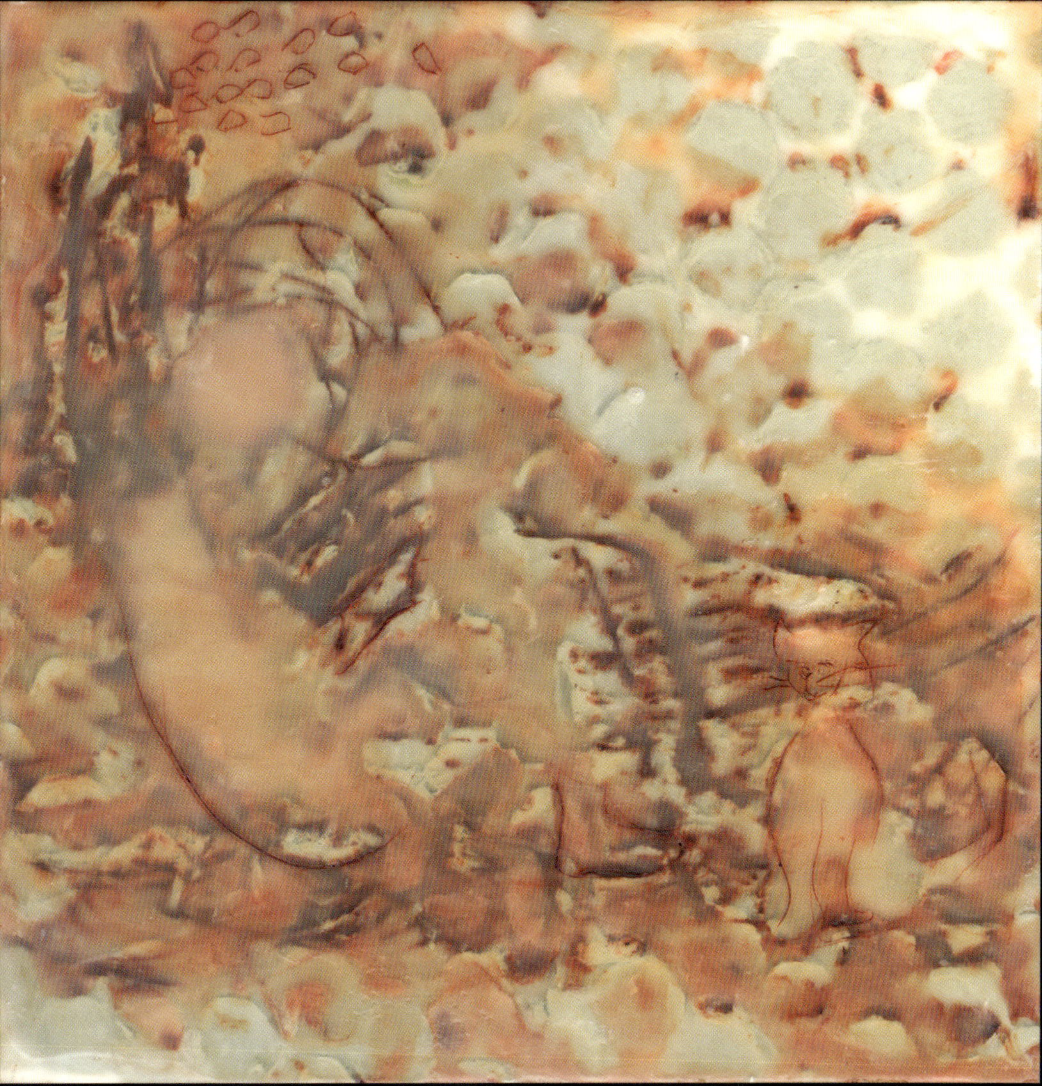

Reading under a tree next to a cat telling inside jokes 2009
Encaustic on clayboard
8 x 8 in.

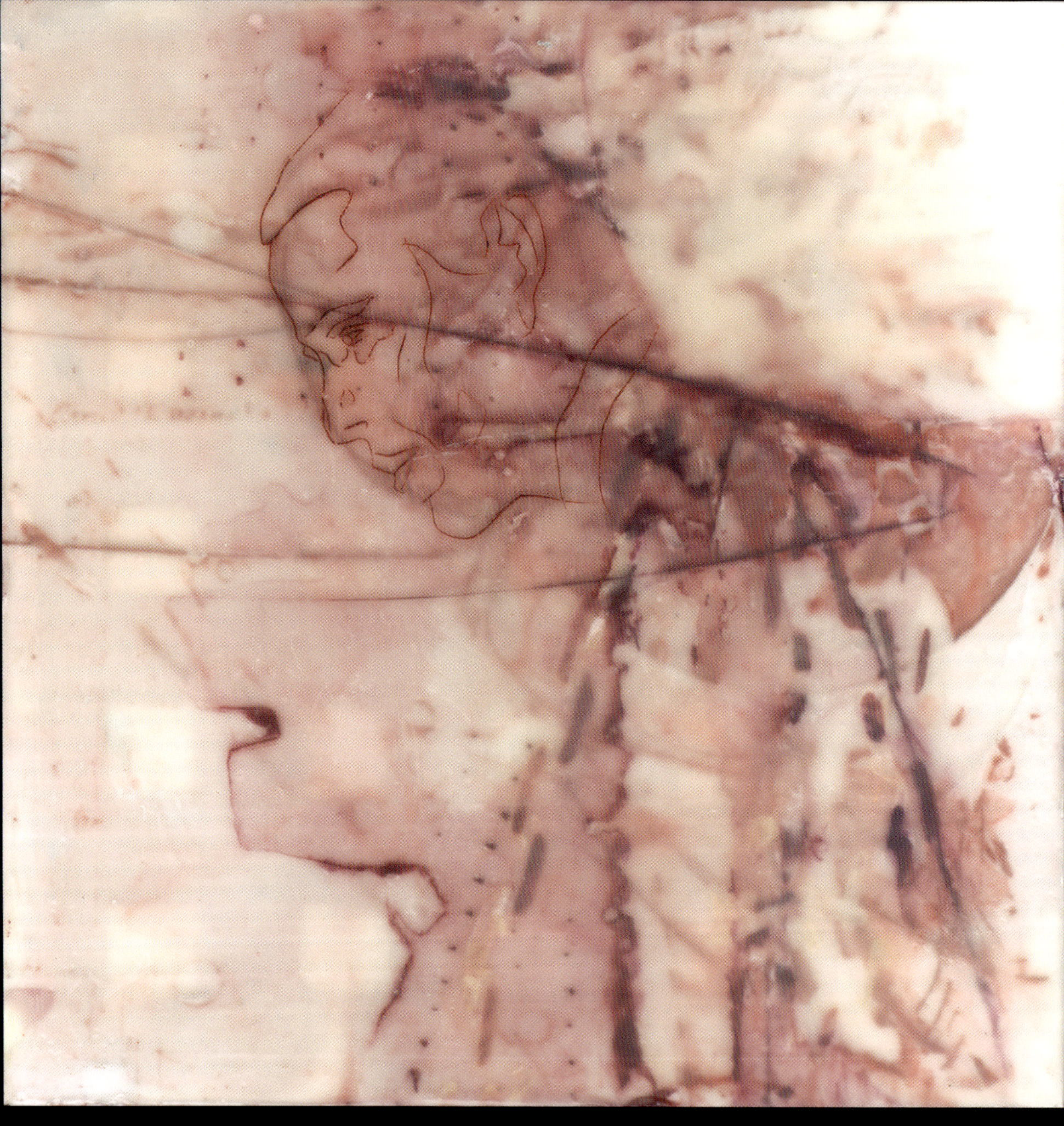

Obama in Hoodie 2009
Encaustic on clayboard
8 x 8 in.

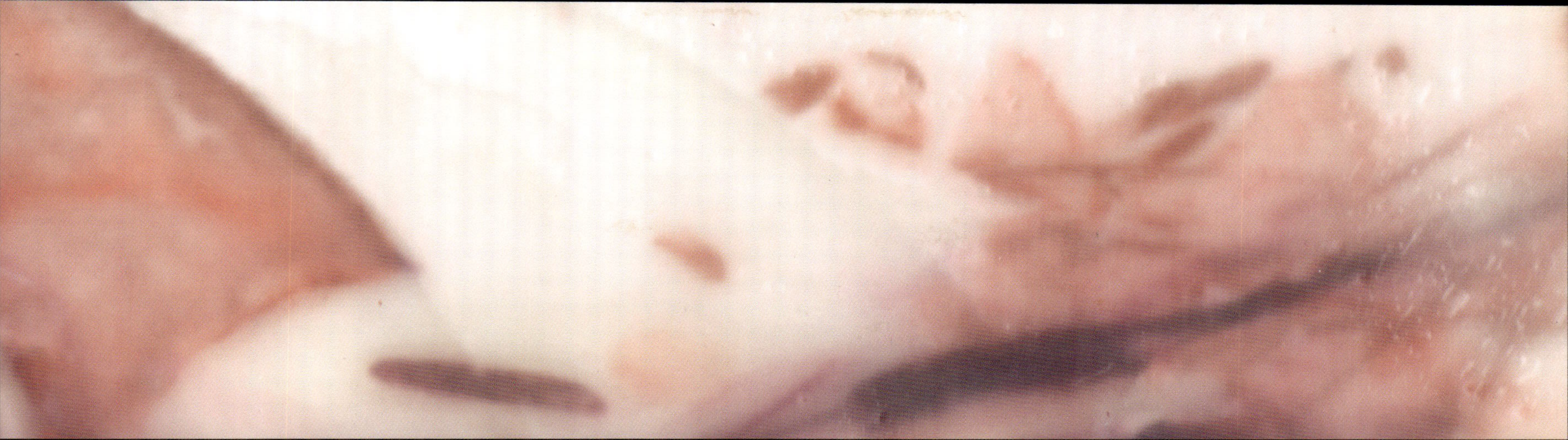

Obama in Hoodie

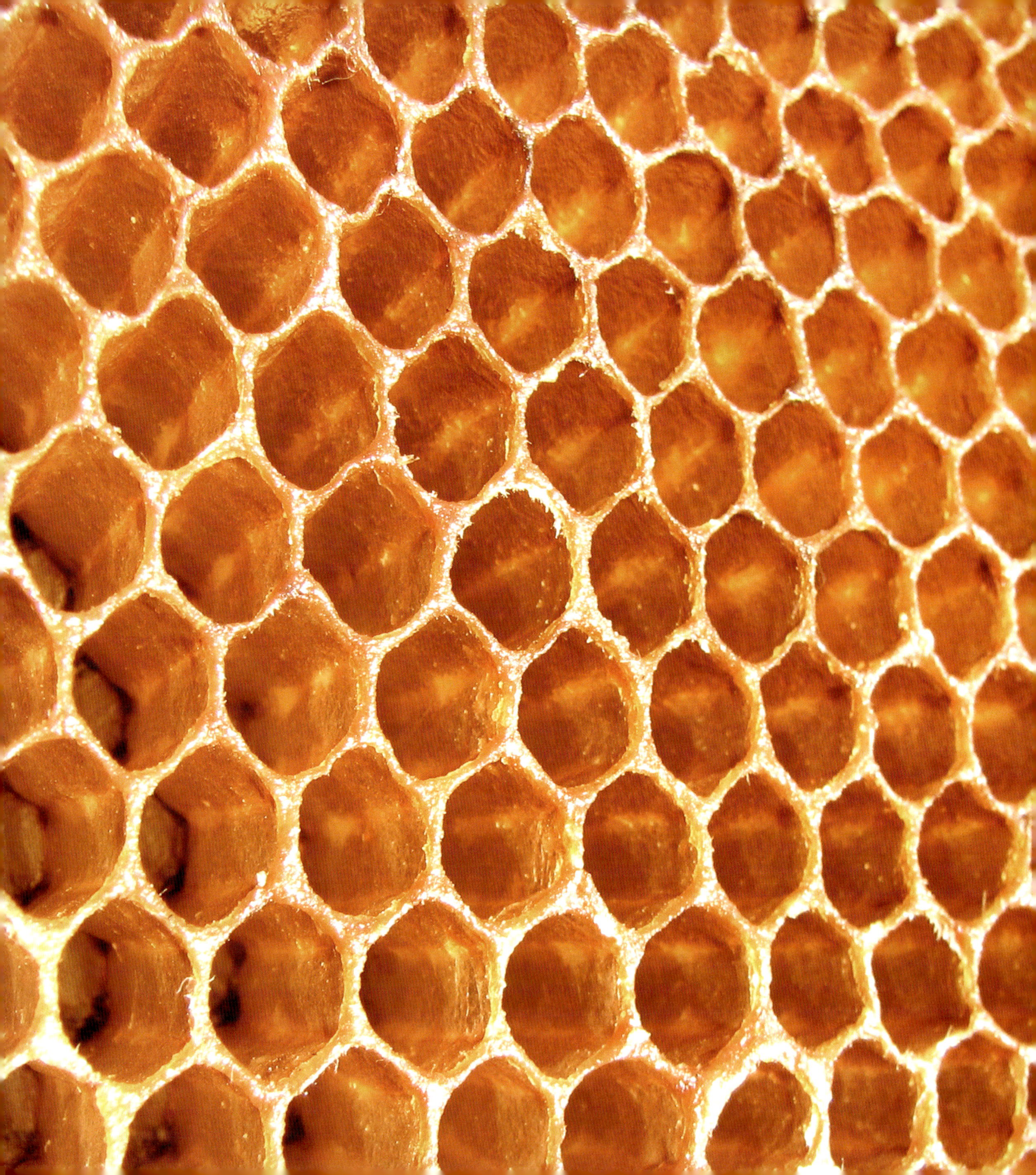

Birds Bees & Mormons

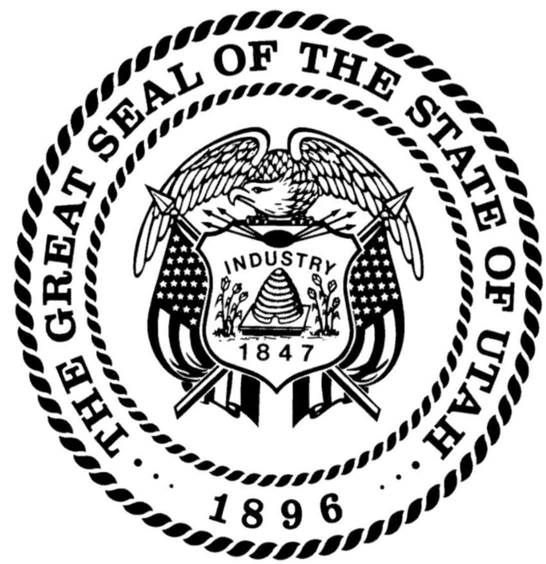

The honeybee figures prominently in history as an emblem of industry, but particularly in the state of Utah, whose culture has built itself around the symbol of the honeybee. It seems appropriate, then, for an artist who studied at Brigham Young University and settled in Spanish Fork, Utah, to take inspiration from the deeply-rooted and multi-faceted bee influences pervasive within his environment.

Utah's bee culture began with Brigham Young, who served as President of the Church of Jesus Christ of the Latter-day Saints (the Mormon Church) for thirty years and was seminal in settling what later became the state of Utah. In his writing on the settlement of the Great Basin, Michael Durham states that Young pushed to name the land the State of Deseret. "Deseret is a term from the Book of Mormon, Ether 2:3. 'And they did also carry with them deseret, which, by interpretation, is a honeybee.' As a symbol of industriousness, the beehive appears in the State Seal of Utah. Brigham Young's house in Salt Lake City is called the Beehive house." Though Congress ultimately renamed the short-lived State of Deseret to the Utah Territory, the word 'deseret' remains present throughout the state today, giving an additional layer of significance to the place of the honeybee and the beehive in the use of beeswax as a medium within the state.

In the years in which Mormons first settled the Great Basin, the early winters were difficult and common daily tasks, such as procuring food, required a dogged open-mindedness. "The first winter was hard, particularly for a people who believed they had arrived in the Promised Land. The poor harvest that year was made even more meager when livestock got loose in the field and raised havoc with the planted crops," writes Durham. The settlers' livestock, another potential food source, was later stolen, diminishing supplies further.

Birds Bees & Mormons

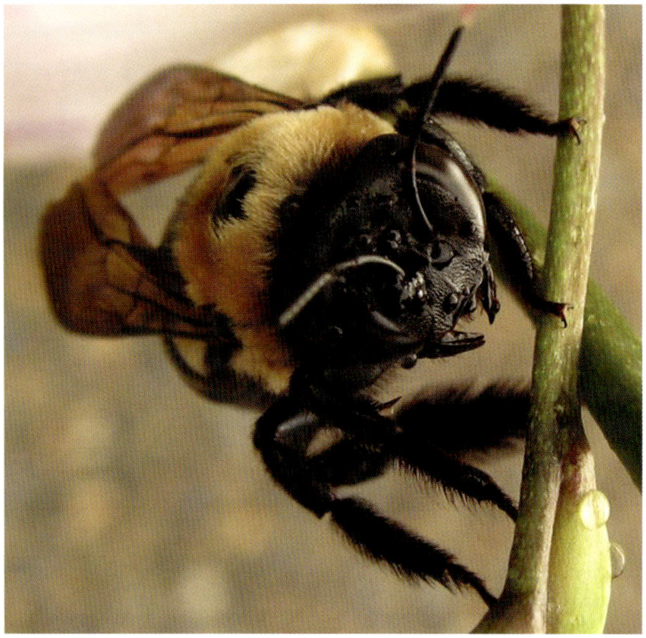

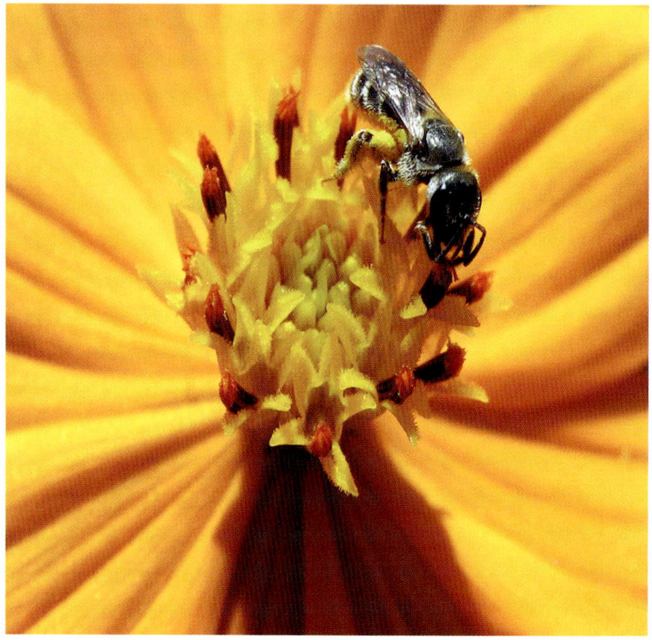

In response, the settlers sought out alternative proteins and turned to the earth – to roots, bulbs, and indigenous plants – for sustenance. According to Durham, one such creative protein turned out to be crickets. "Once the crickets were in hand, they ground the bodies into a coarse meal, which, when mixed with honey, made a tasty cake. [John] Taylor, who, after Brigham Young's death in 1877, would succeed him as president of the Mormon Church, took some of the meal home to his family... They found the mixture delicious, although Taylor never told them about the unusual ingredients."

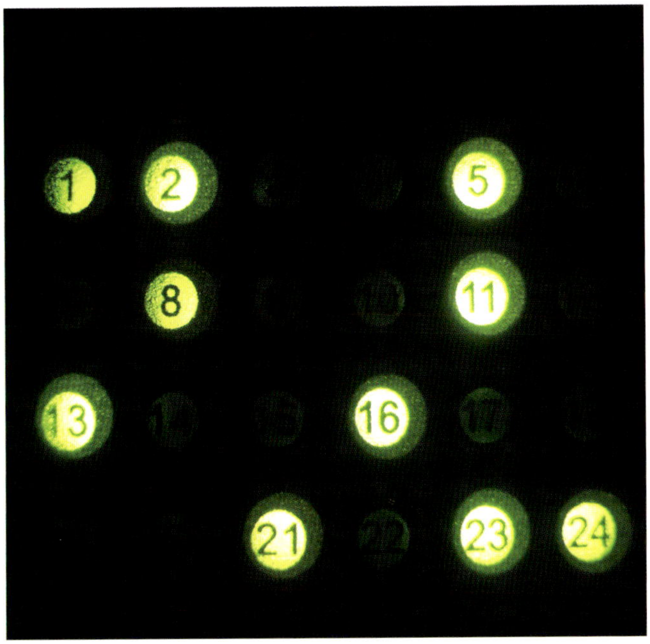

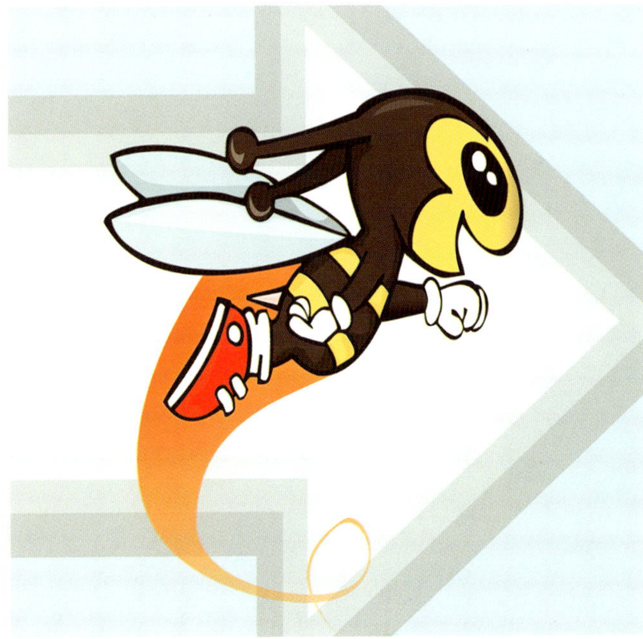

Current inhabitants of Utah

have moved onto more savory fare, but the symbol of the honeybee has remained with them. Bee iconography continues to proliferate in Utah. Honeybees, known for their complex social behavior, specialized roles, and organized societ-ies, remain the state insect of Utah. The honey comb remains on the state flag of Utah, as does the word Industry, which refers to life inside the hive. State troopers are plainly recognized by the symbol of the beehive on their state vehicles.

In a more localized context, the culture of the honeybee has several parallels with the culture of most Utah residents, the majority of whom are

Mormon. The dynamics within beehives are directly comparable to the dynamics within Utah homes. "Mormons often include cooperativeness among the virtues symbolized by the beehive," notes Durham. Bees are fiercely loyal to their hives and, once a hive has been established, all members work diligently to support the community, raise their young, and produce enough honey to nourish the hive through the long winter months. Similarly, Utahns commonly store extra food in their homes for the protection of families and communities and for emergency preparedness.

In a thriving hive, the output of honey is prolific, the structure of the comb sound, and the workers busily contented to perform their assigned roles and responsibilities. Sue Hubbell, an outspoken apiarist, writes that when a problem arises in the hive, such as when a disease is introduced or the hive has been attacked by robber insects, the bees seem to lose their morale and are no longer able to defend their hive. In extreme cases, the bees die.

Hubbell notes that within the hive, bees live and work in a "tightly insulating cluster to hold the warmth" generated by "metabolizing fiercely" to convert calories into heat. Though the outdoor temperatures may be freezing, the inside of each hive is held balmy and warm to ensure the survival of the brood. In Utah's climate, renowned for its abundant snow and long winters, bees as well as humans hold tight to the principles of staying in 'tight clusters.'

Honeybees have endured through millennia by dint of their evolutionary success. They are a prime example of the beauty of the natural order that Diediker's encaustic work celebrates.

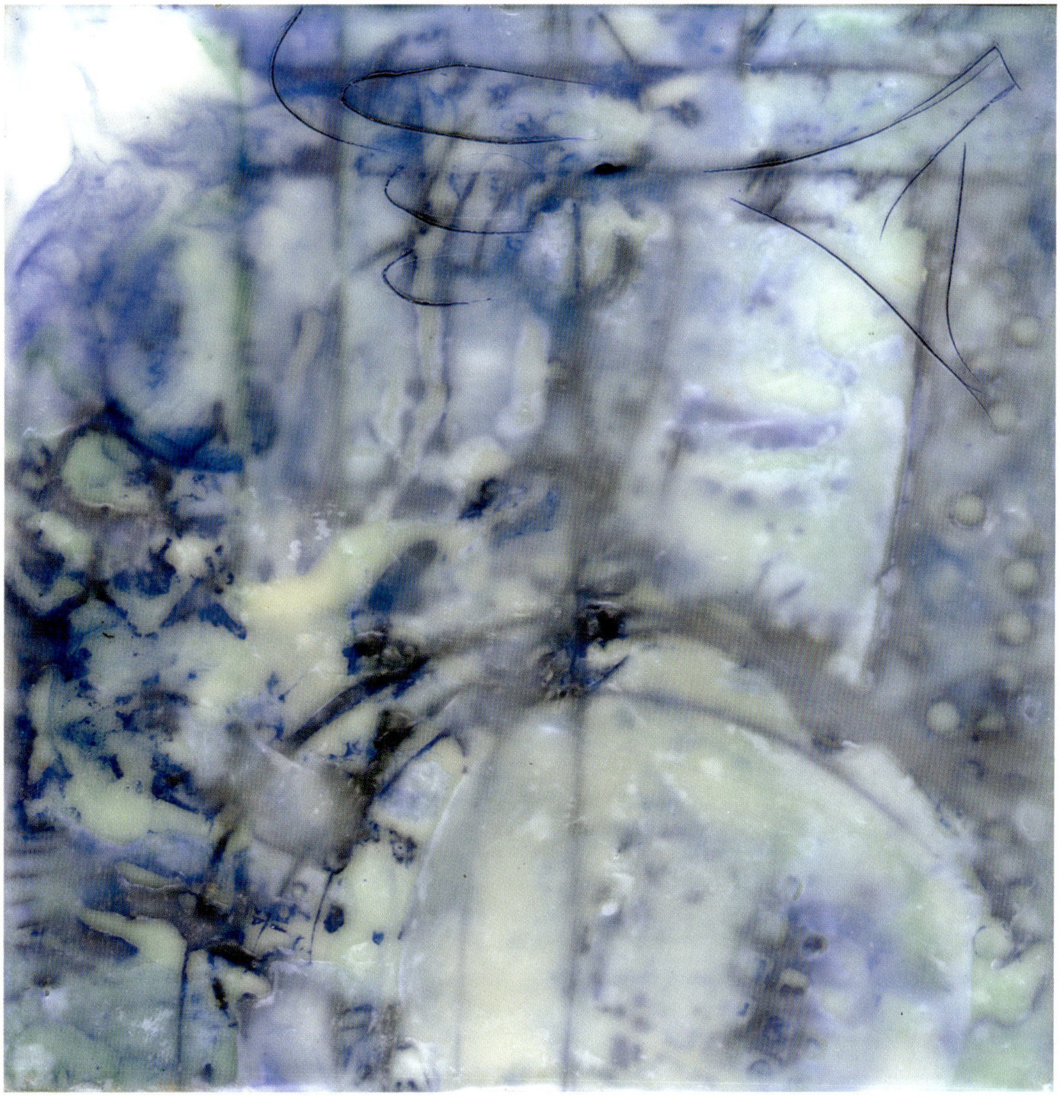

Blue Tin-Man with Tornado
2010
Encaustic on clayboard
8 x 8 in.

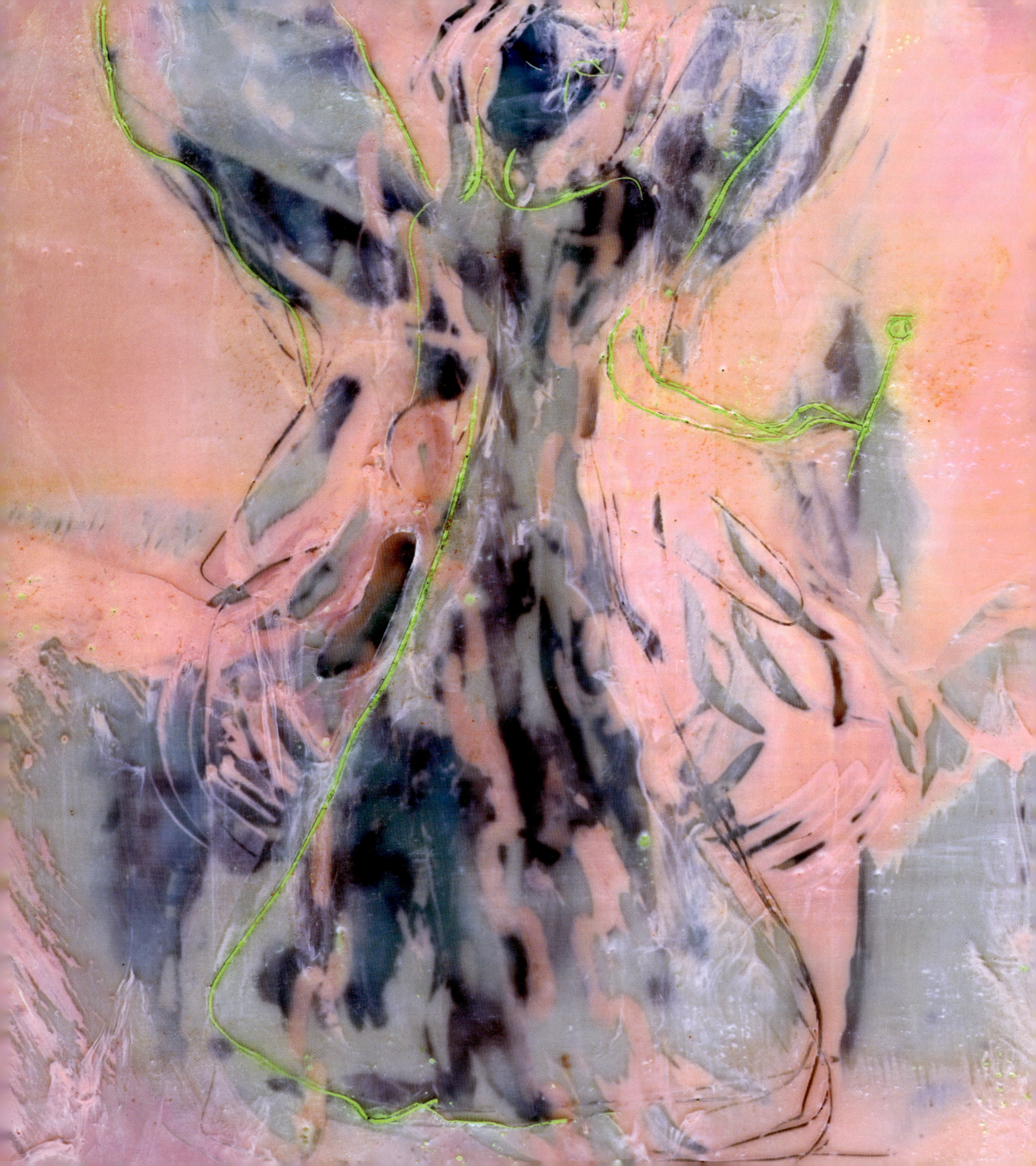

Blue Fairy

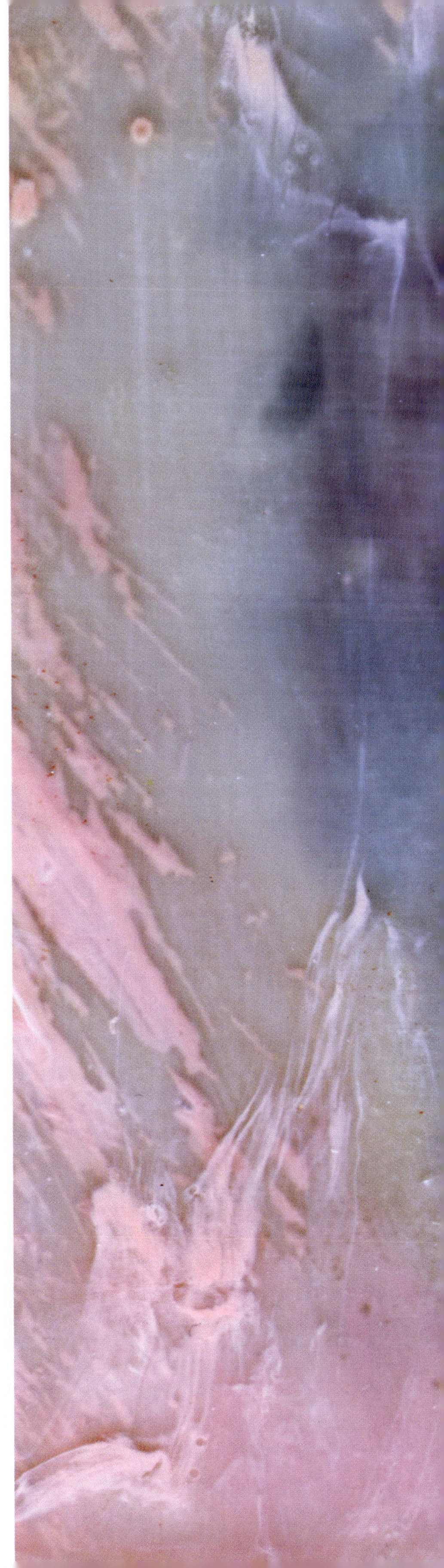

Blue Fairy 2009
Encaustic on clayboard
8 x 8 in.

CHAPTER 4

The Natural Man

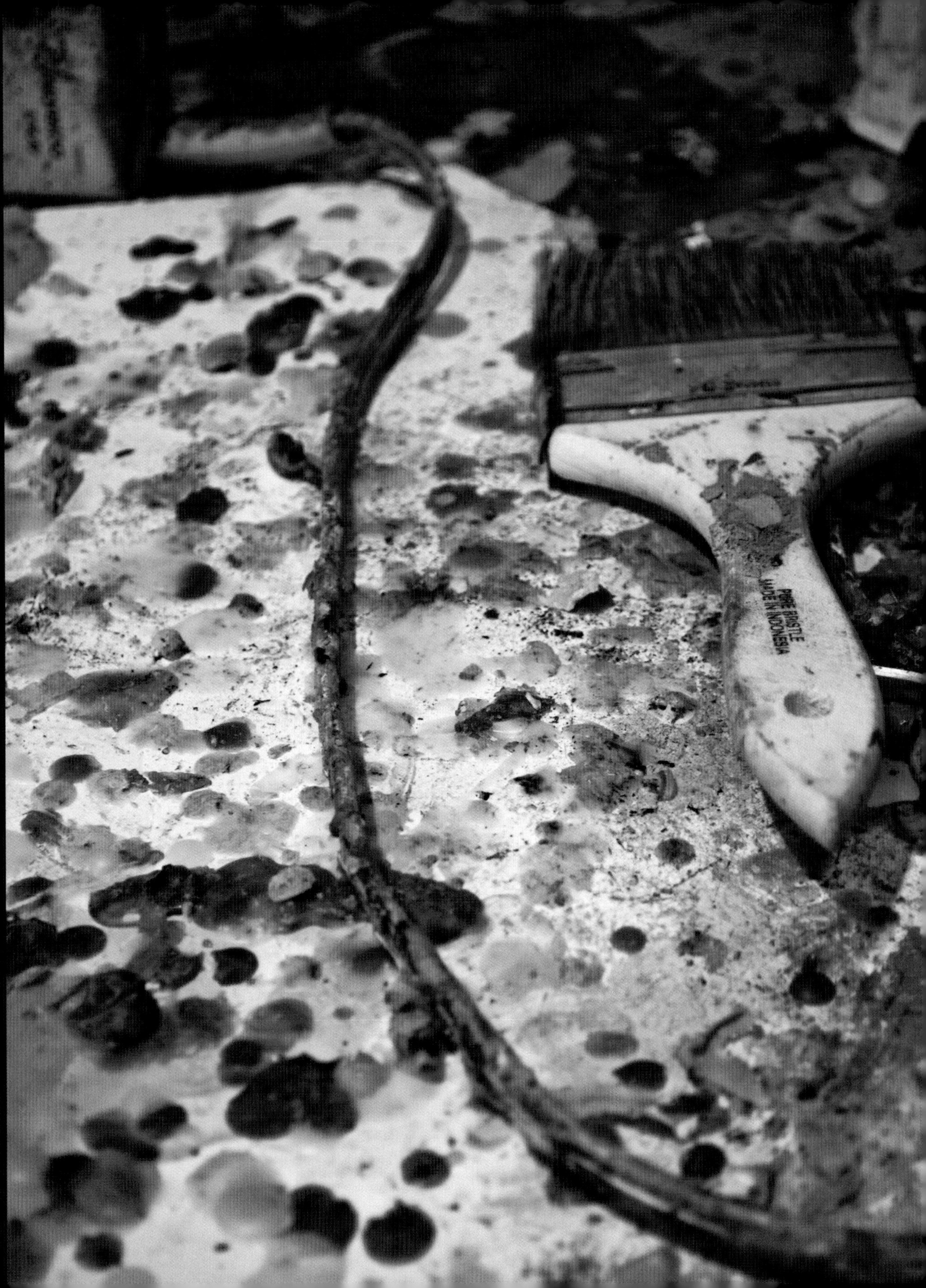
PURE BRISTLE
MADE IN INDONESIA

The Natural Man

By now, examples of humanity's encroachment on nature are ubiquitous. In North America alone, the history of settlement and imposition of human will on the landscape is long and its effects profound. This story is one that repeats itself among cultures and ecosystems throughout the developing world. As a collective, humans have fallen to an ideology of dominion over nature, often to nature's detriment.

However, there are some contemporary cultures which still depend on natural ways of living, co-existing with nature the way their predecessors have. Indigenous Australian (Aboriginal) culture, for example, is marked by a sacred reverence for the land. Their relationship to the environment rests at the heart of their cultural and spiritual existence. The Aborigines are noted for their artwork, which draws from the natural environment thematically and spiritually; is made with items that commonly exist in nature, such as rocks, leaves, sand, and wood; and is traditionally painted with naturally occurring colorants, such as ochre pigments, ground bone, or blood. The Aboriginal landscape artist, W. Rabuntja, has said, "Doesn't matter what sort of painting we do in this country, it still belongs to the people, all the people. This is worship, work, culture. It's all Dreaming. There are two ways of painting. Both ways are important, because that's culture."

Diediker's work with the medium of beeswax bears striking parallels to the tenets of indigenous art, particularly in terms of the influence of environment, respect for nature, and use of a natural medium to represent what nature itself has created. His work is an example of a practice that considers, respects, and ultimately pays homage to the beauty inherent to the natural world, including patterns of wind, water, and erosion. In his day-to-day work with beeswax, he mimics the day-to-day (and year-to-year) work of natural forces to render images created in their image and honor, an act of deference and respect to the natural world. This work stands in juxtaposition to the classical paintings of artists such as Vermeer, whose life work was characterized by total control over the medium and a strict dedication to careful artistic rendering of an absolute image, made even more painstakingly accurate through his use of the camera obscura. Diediker's encaustic work presents an antidote for those confined by such unwavering control of the medium. One type of art doesn't invalidate the other; the encaustic medium merely represents a different approach, a different way of making art.

Hole 18 2009
Encaustic on clayboard
8 x 8 in.

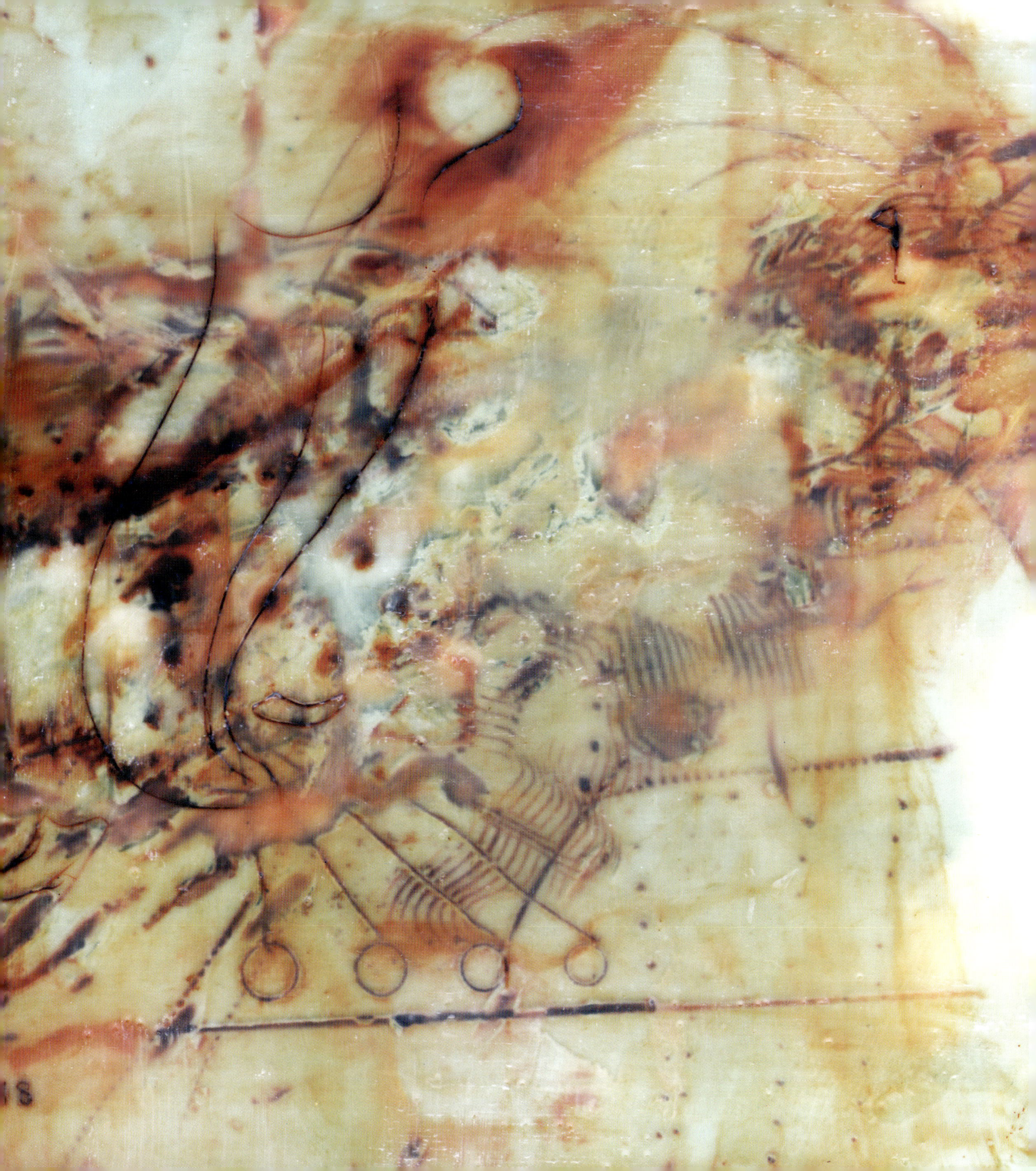

The Natural Man

An ecologist named Nancy Langston has suggested: "The answer perhaps is to figure out some way of ... forming close connections to a place but also being willing to adapt to the character of the place." That is, re-structure human behaviors in ways which take into consideration the strengths and challenges inherent to a specific place, and, as residents of that place, act in ways which promote its environmental success for the long-term. Fortunately, many people are beginning to think about their responsibility to the environment, both personally and as societies, and are amending their actions accordingly. A critical step in this process is realizing that we are part of the ecosystems in which we live.

As part of his Utah ecosystem, Diediker's use of beeswax reflects an understanding of Langston's ecological philosophy. He appreciates the medium's strengths and respects its limitations, submitting himself to all aspects of its nature. In doing so, he acts in a way that promotes environmental success for the long term, because his medium is a sustainable natural by-product of the daily work of honeybees. The light-transforming malleability of beeswax renders muted and delicate surfaces unlike those of Diediker's traditional paintings. Yet it also limits Diediker's ability to begin an encaustic plate with an image he has preconceived.

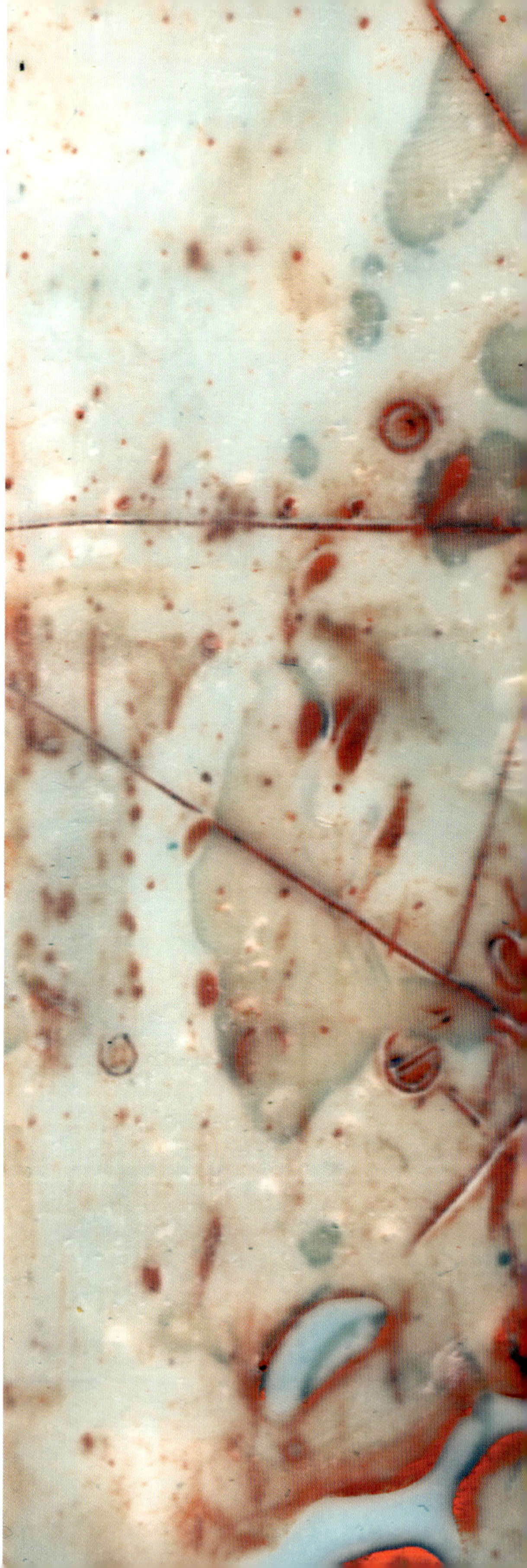

Boy with really good hearing emerging from the Surf 2010
Encaustic on clayboard
8 x 8 in.

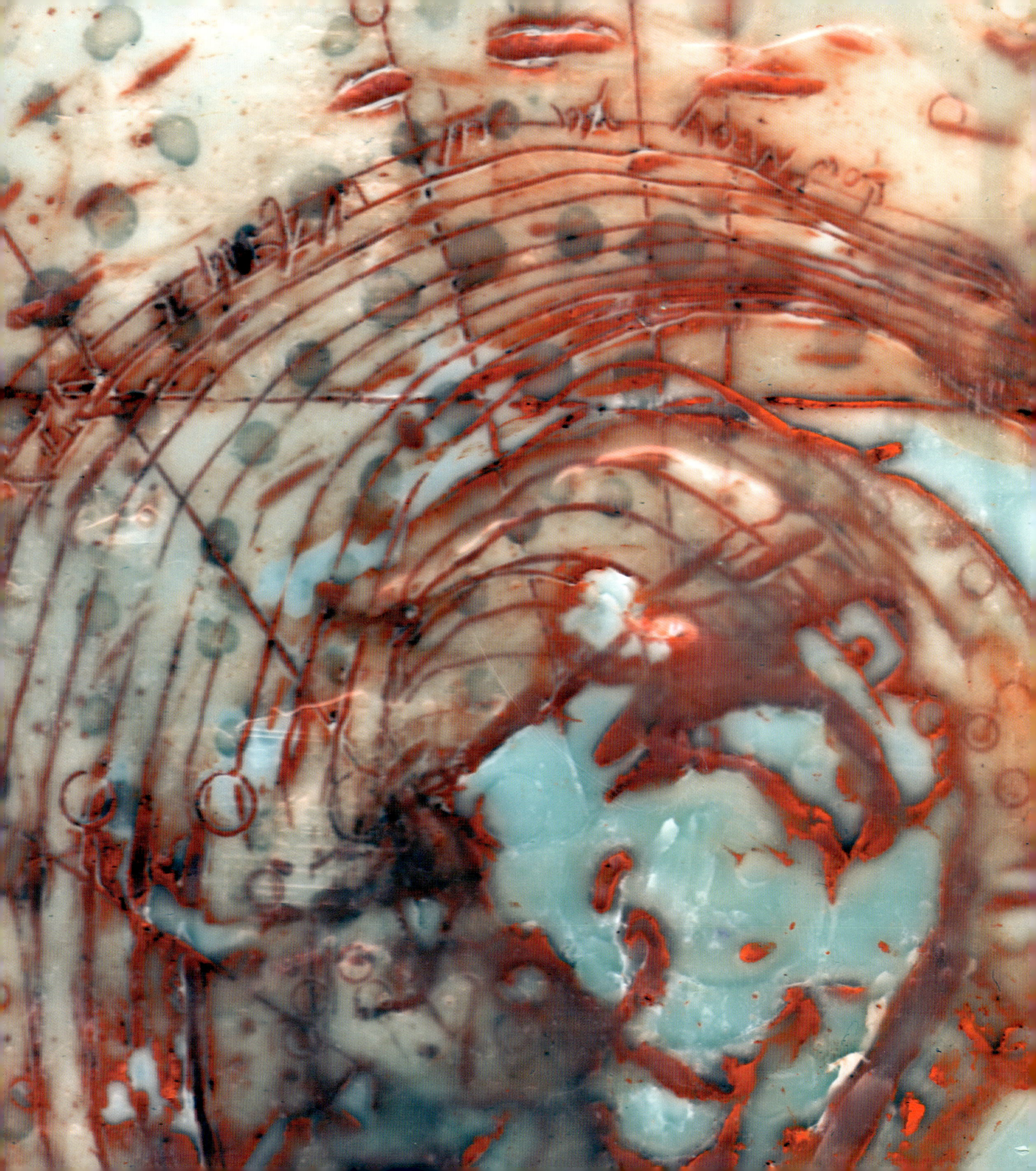

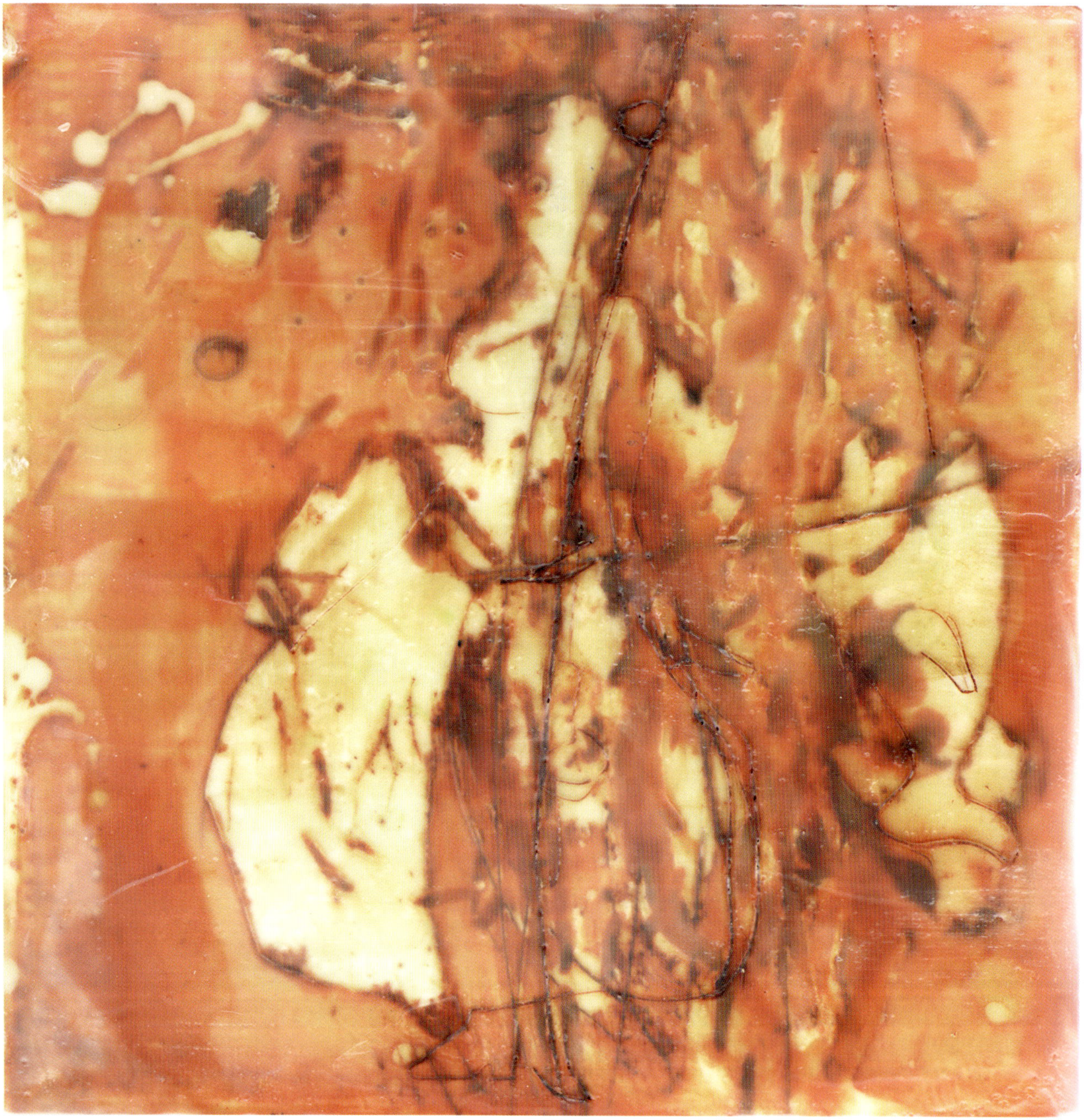

Fisherwoman in big dress with happy Snook 2009
Encaustic on clayboard
8 x 8 in.

The Natural Man

In 1749, Peter Kalm, a visitor to the developing New England region, said: "We can hardly be more hostile toward our woods in Sweden and Finland than they are here: their eyes are fixed upon the present gain, and they are blind to the future." This story played out time and again as settlers forged new frontiers throughout the continent. In 1964, North American forests, deserts, and wild untrammeled spaces won a small victory when the United States adopted the Wilderness Act. This act defined and protected wilderness areas so that ecosystems could operate without interference or restraint by humanity. In 1973, dwindling species received protection under the Endangered Species Act. There have since been many bills passed (and modified) to legislate and control man's interactions with nature. All of these decisions were made in response to a problem that stemmed from man's imposition on the natural environment.

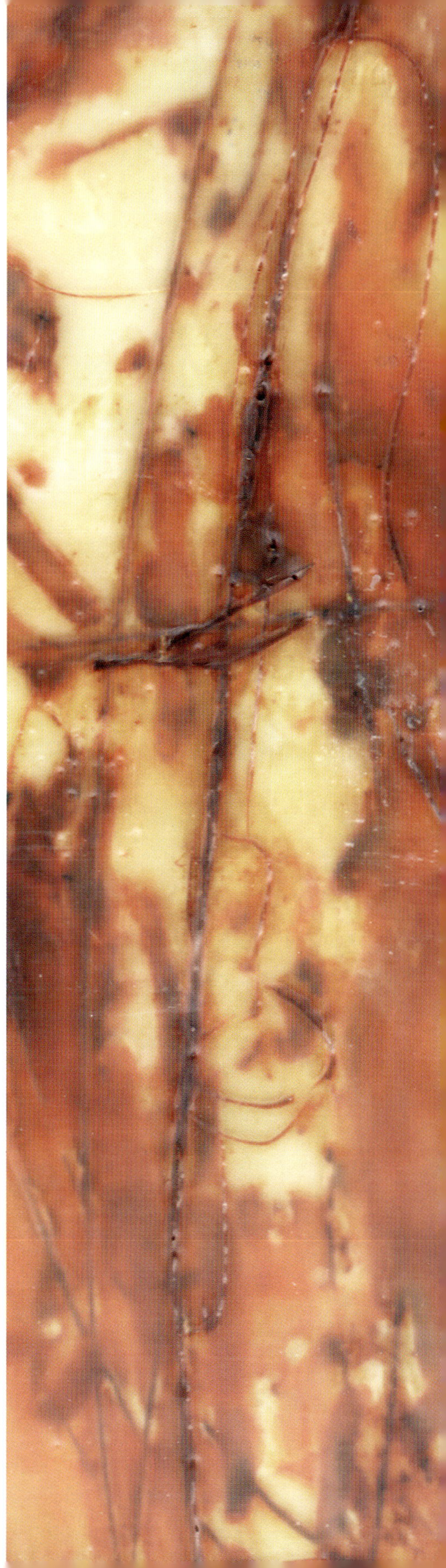

Fisherwoman in big dress with happy Snook

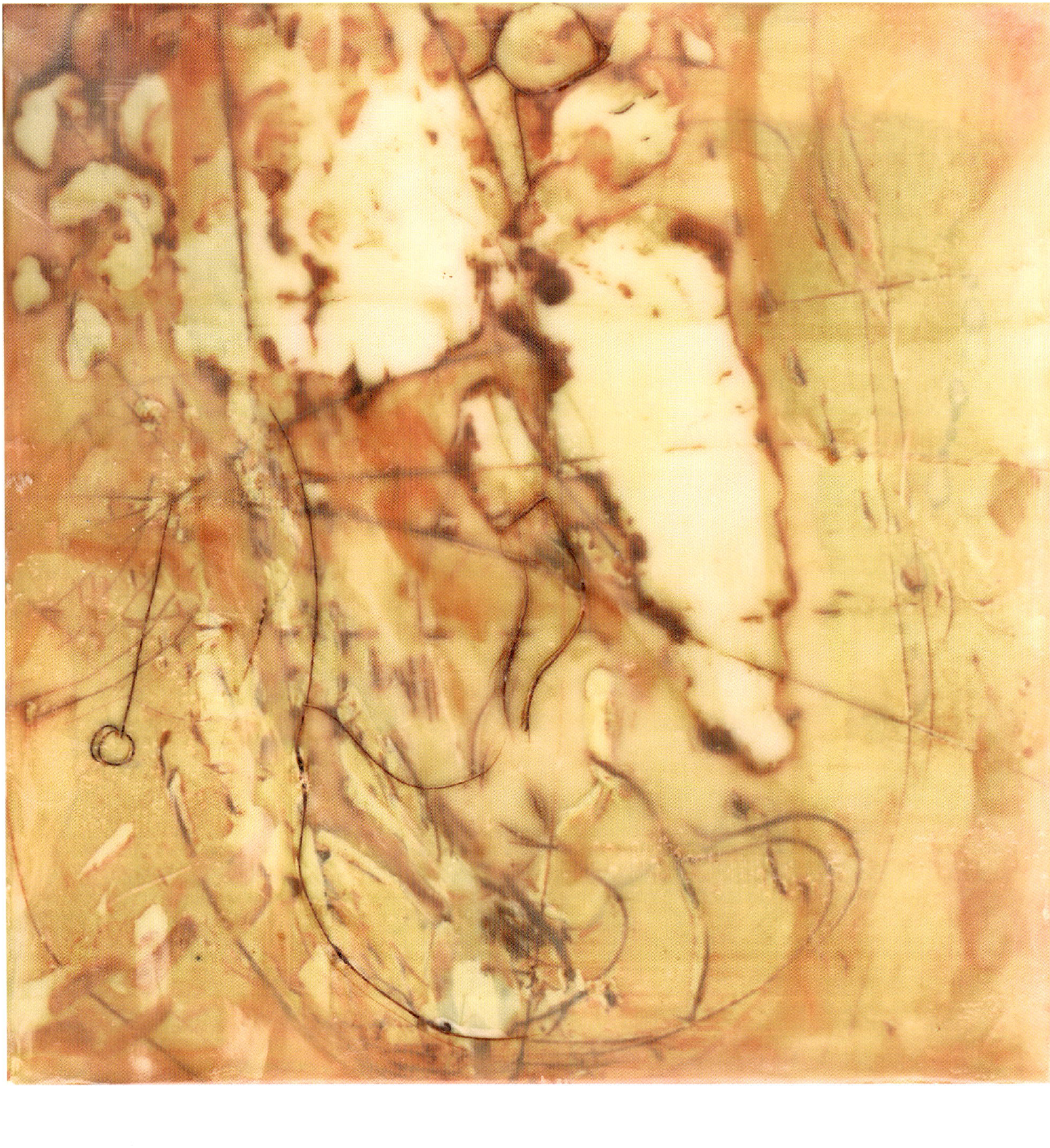

Caterpillar Mom with Baby on back twirling a yoyo 2009
Encaustic on clayboard
8 x 8 in.

The Natural Man

Perhaps now is an ideal time to consider more constructive, less ecologically devastating ways of being citizens of the natural world. It is difficult to dispute that much insight can be garnered from nature, which, when left to itself, has evolved in a certain harmony and order. Prior to human intervention, nature contended successfully with itself. Bees are a prime example of this. They work in conjunction with – not in opposition to – other natural elements. As a result, bees have sustained their societies and thrived over millions of years, much like the Indigenous Australians, who have become one of the oldest human cultures. These cultures – bee and human alike – have flourished as citizens of the natural world by performing their roles within their larger ecosystems in ways that respect and uphold environmental integrity and healthy biodiversity.

William deBuys has said it is clear "that a society cannot long preserve its culture without also conserving the resources that give it life. People everywhere ... have proved the truth of that. The hardest task is to accept the truth of what experience has proved." In his encaustic work, Diediker shows acceptance of the truth of what experience has proved, and he inspires others to do the same.

Caterpillar Mom with Baby on back twirling a yoyo

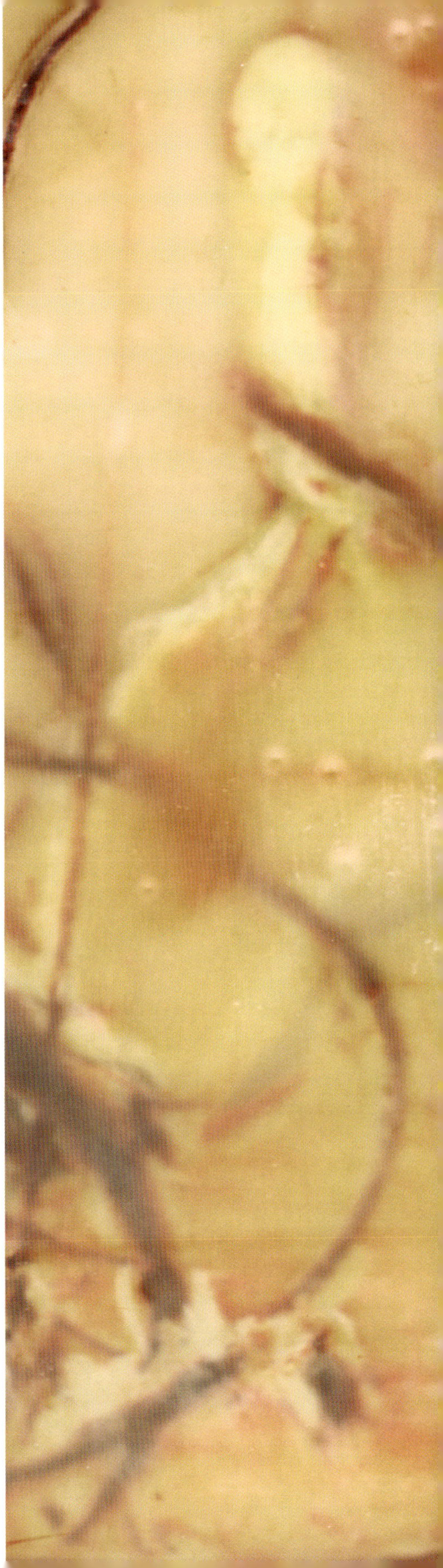

"A society cannot long preserve its culture without also conserving the resources that give it life. People everywhere

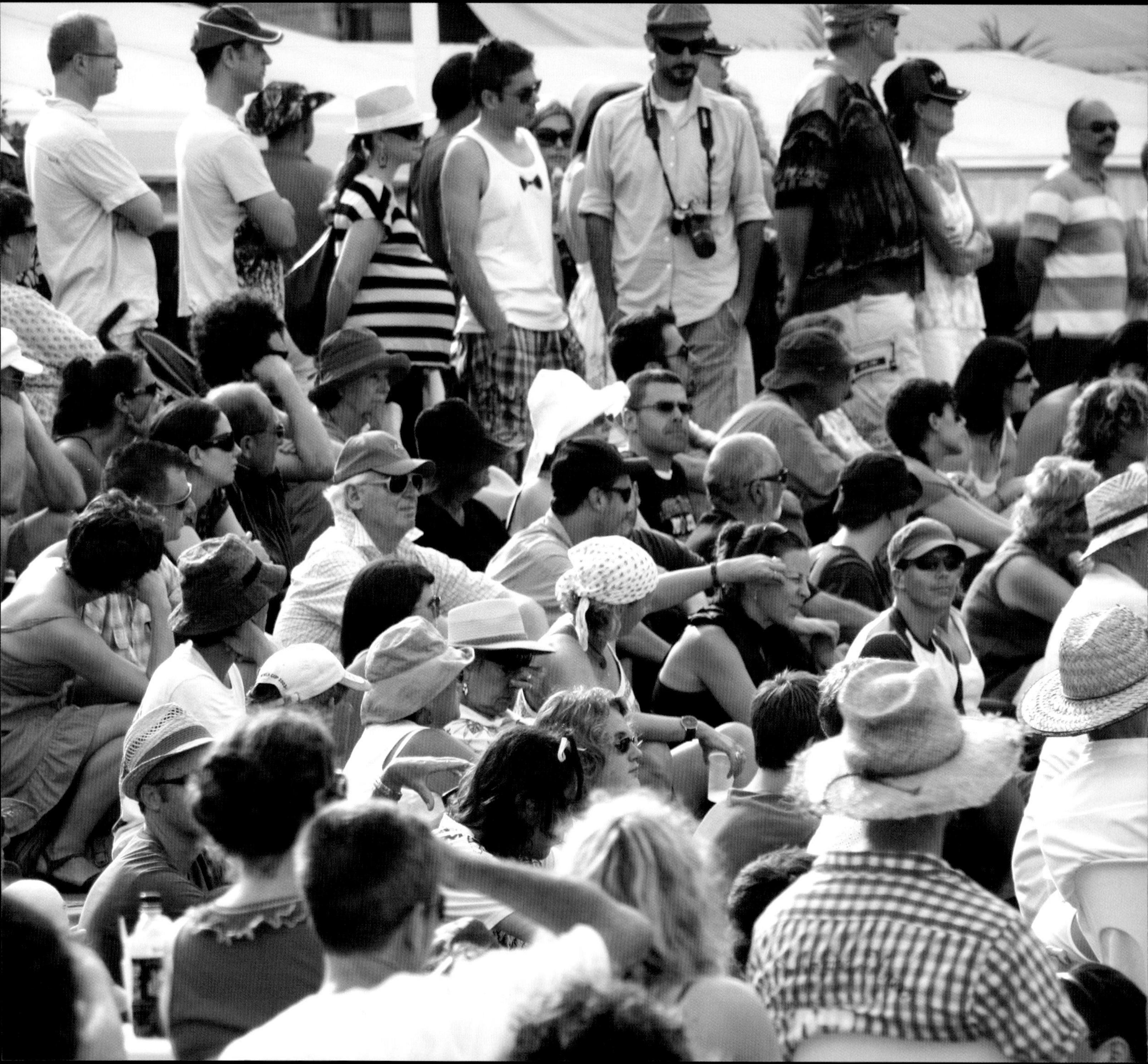

have proved the truth of that. The hardest task is to accept the truth of what experience has proved." -William deBuys

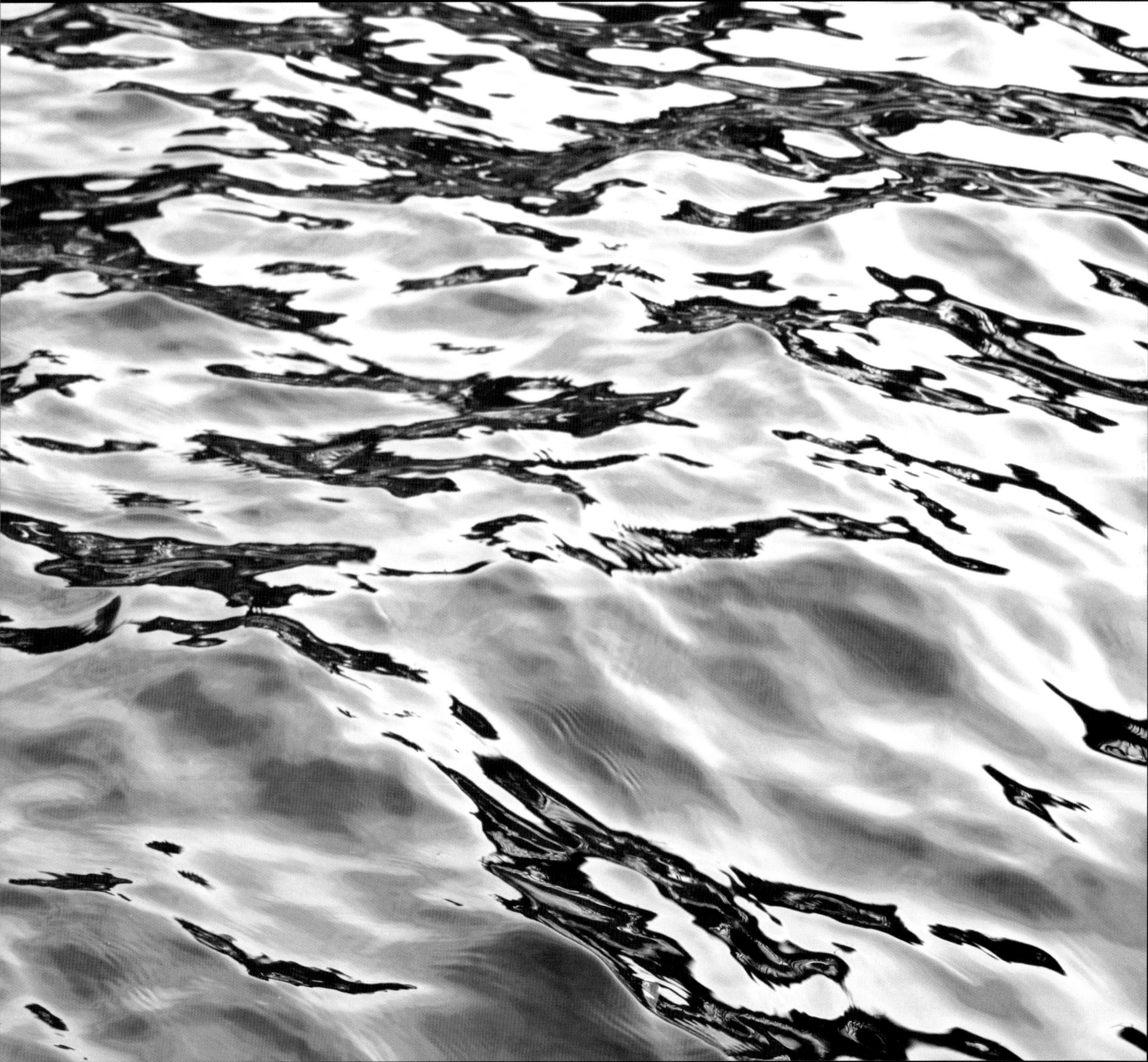

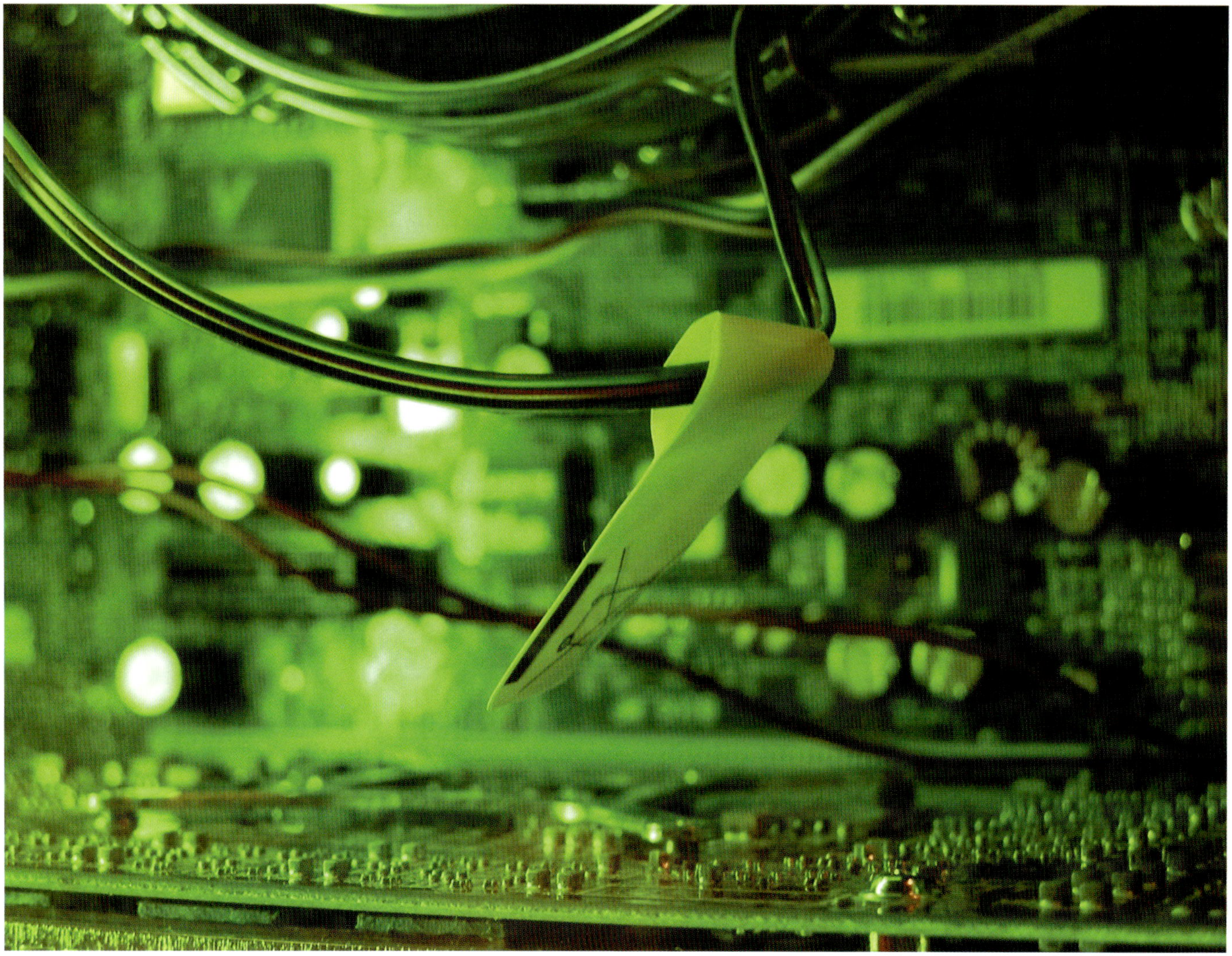

The choice is Not Between Two Landscapes,

One with and one Without Human influence;

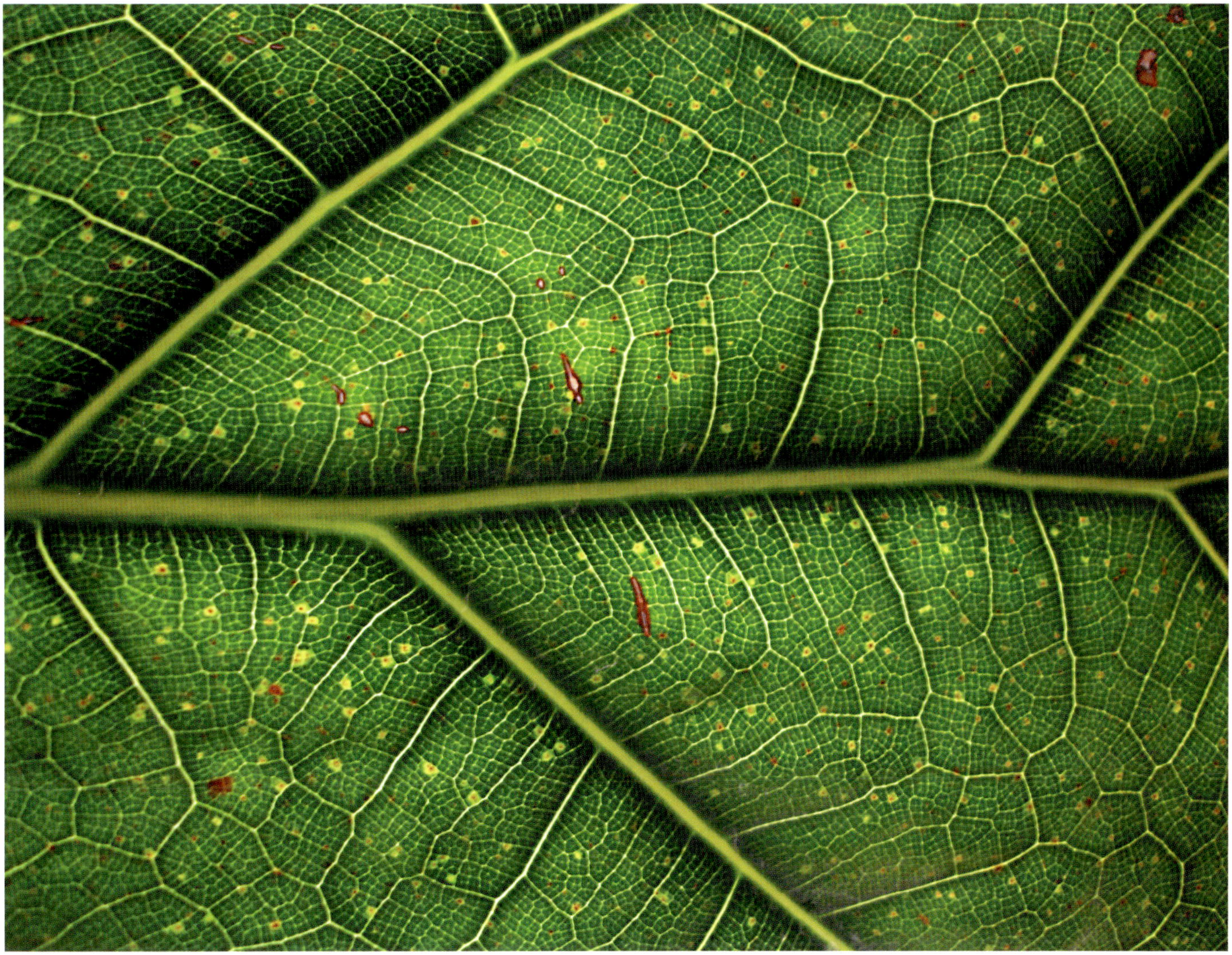

It is between two human ways of living,
two ways of belonging to an ecosystem

- William Cronon

Snoopy and Woodstock laying in Central Park discussing Clouds

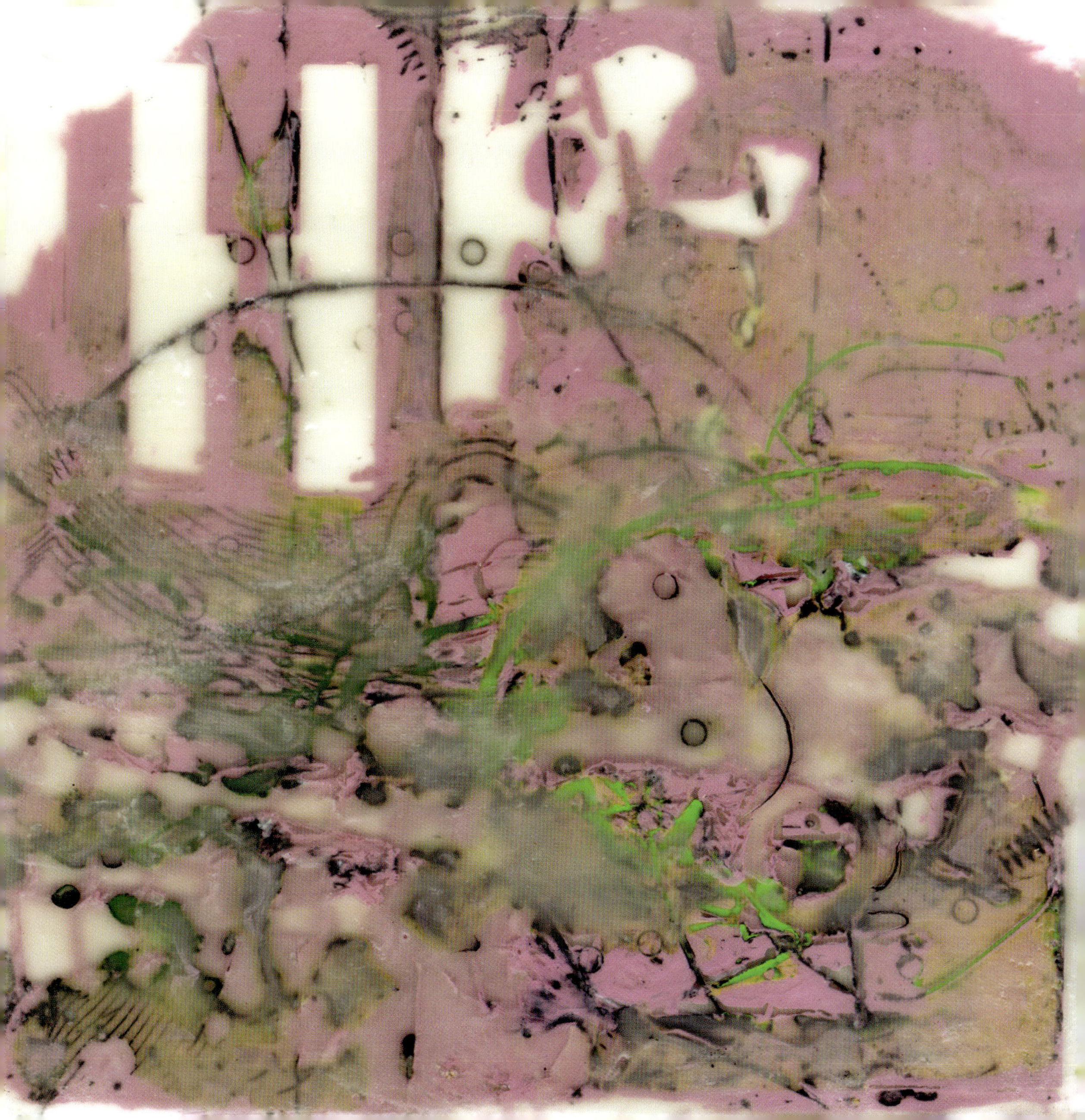

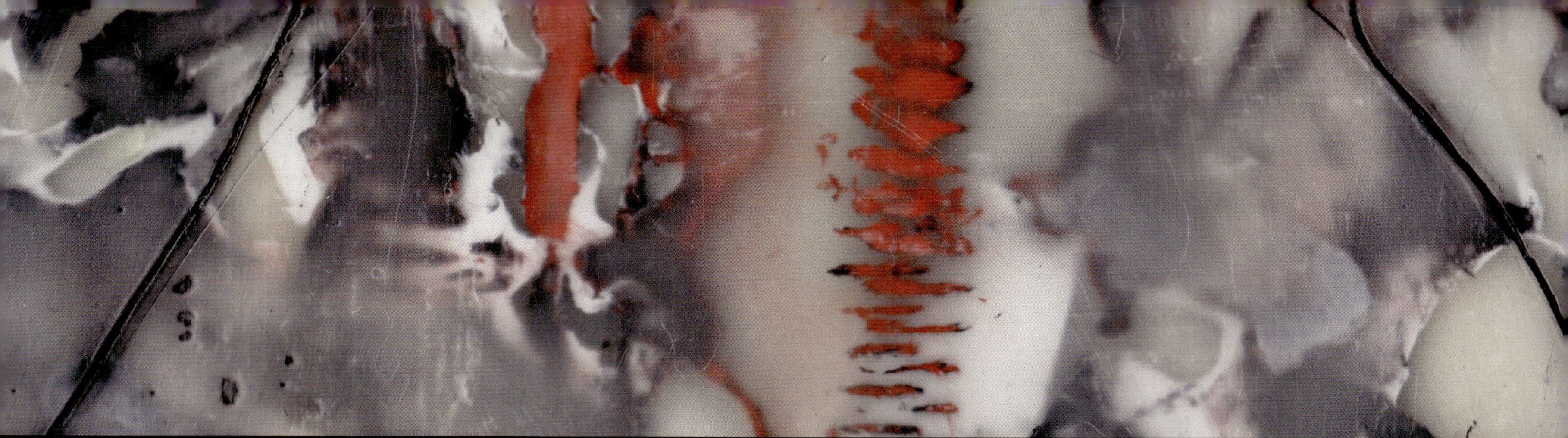

Austin Powers Mechanical Shark with a "Frickin" laser beam

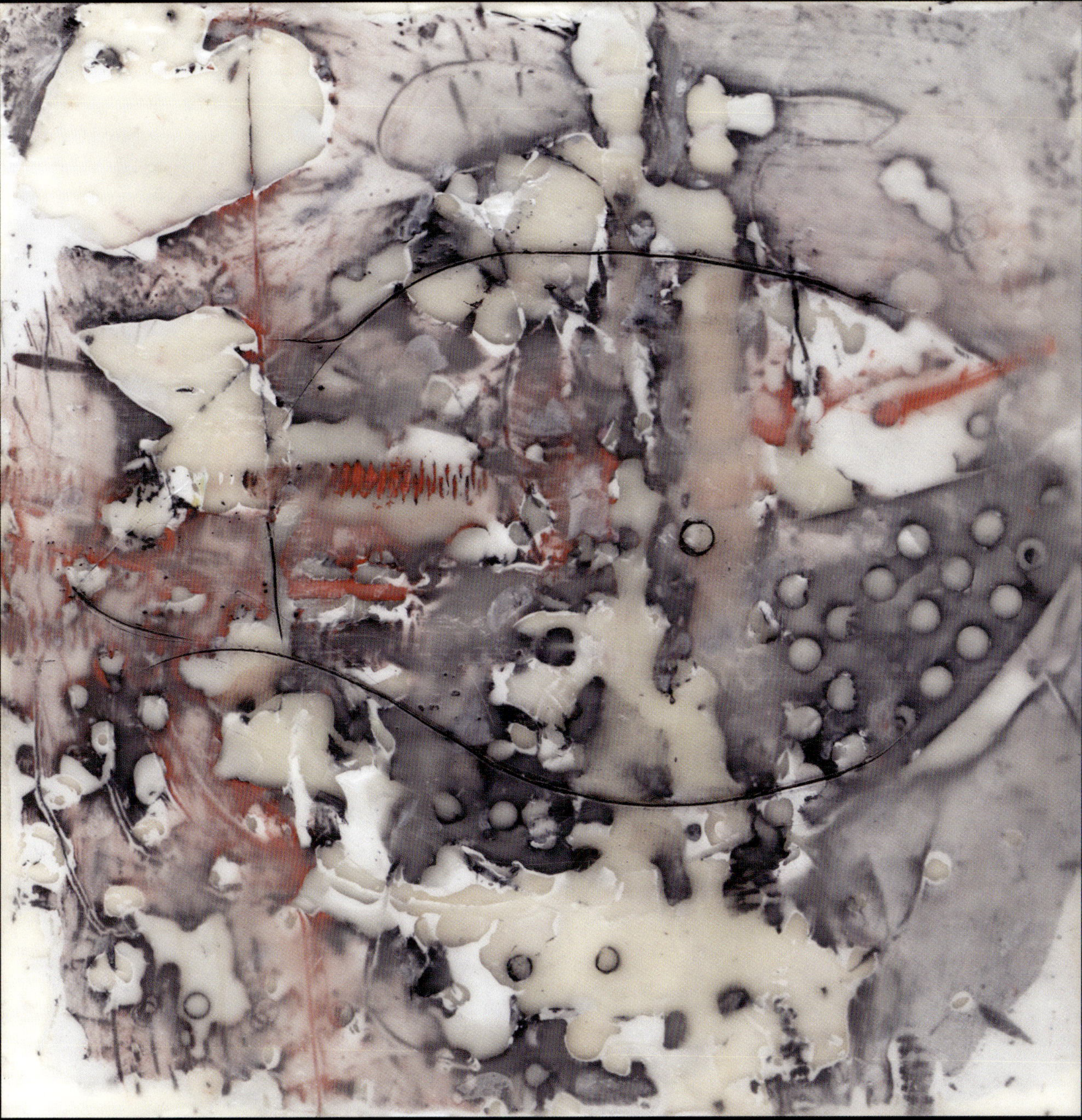

Austin Powers Mechanical Shark
with a "Frickin" laser beam
2010
Encaustic on clayboard
8 x 8 in.

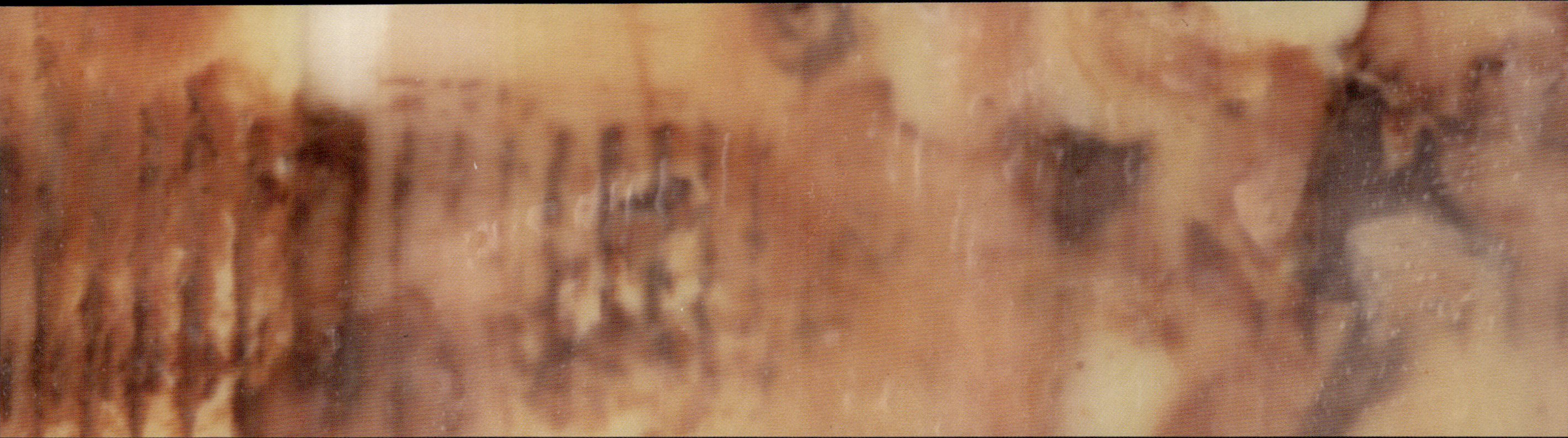

Picasso Warrior Battling Rumors

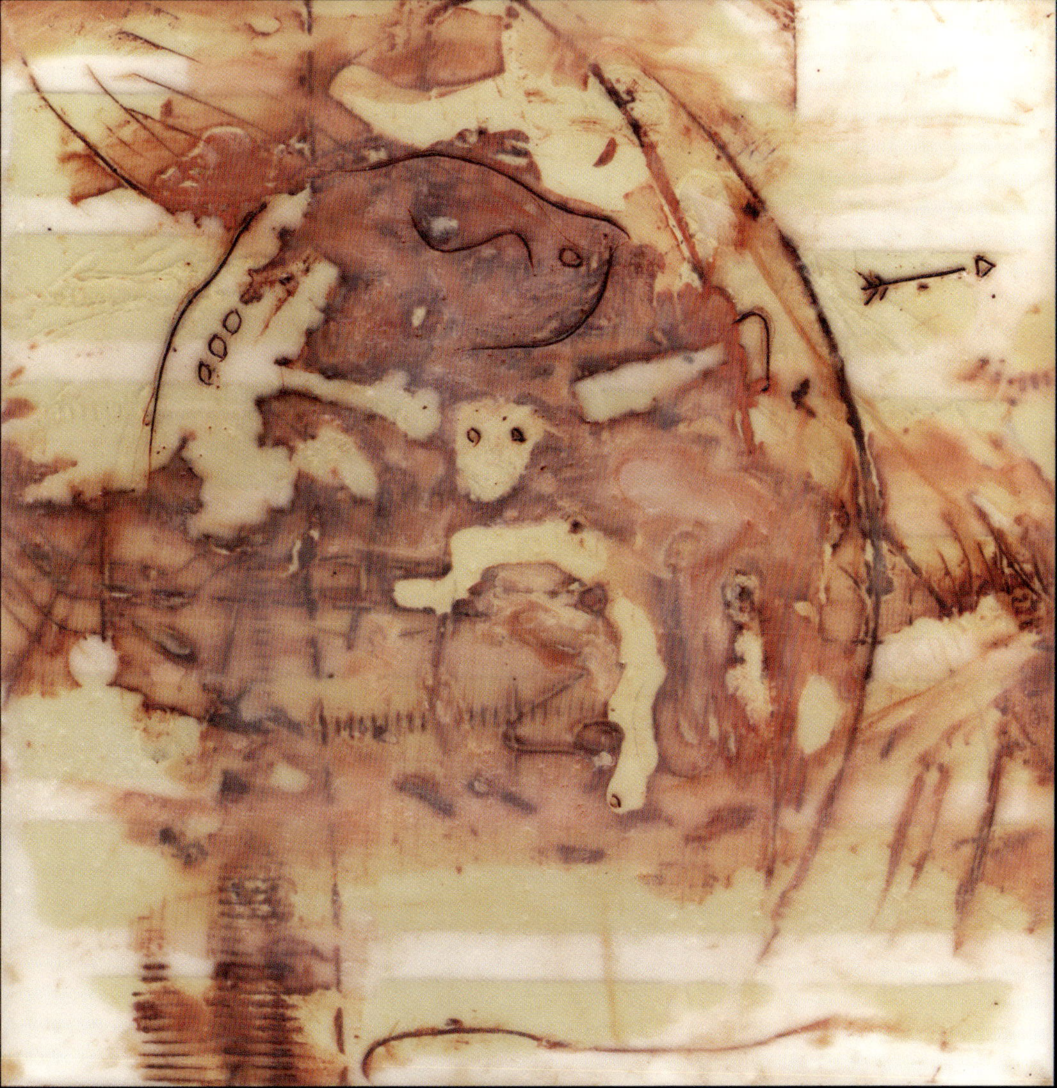

Picasso Warrior Battling Rumors
2010
Encaustic on clayboard
8 x 8 in.

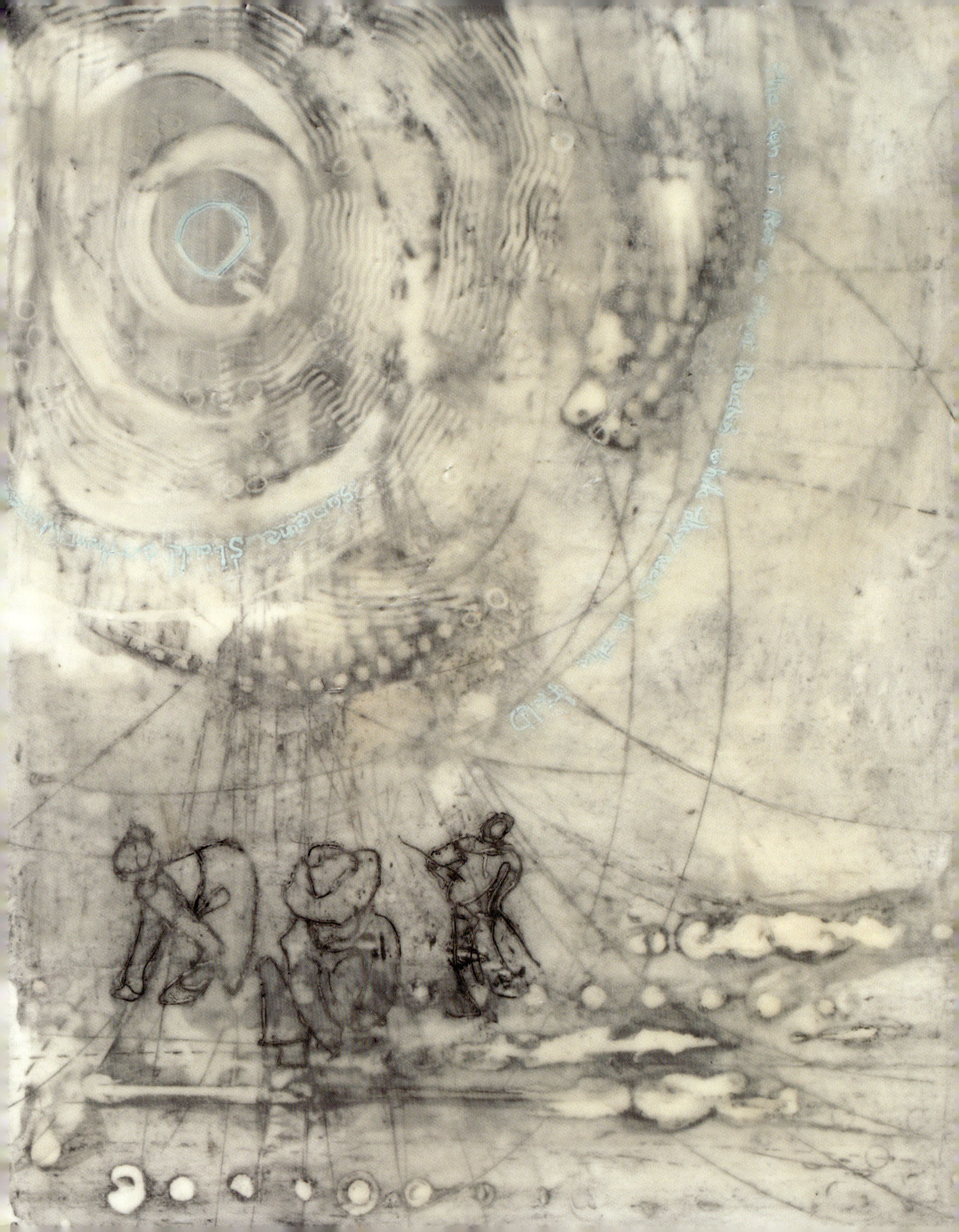

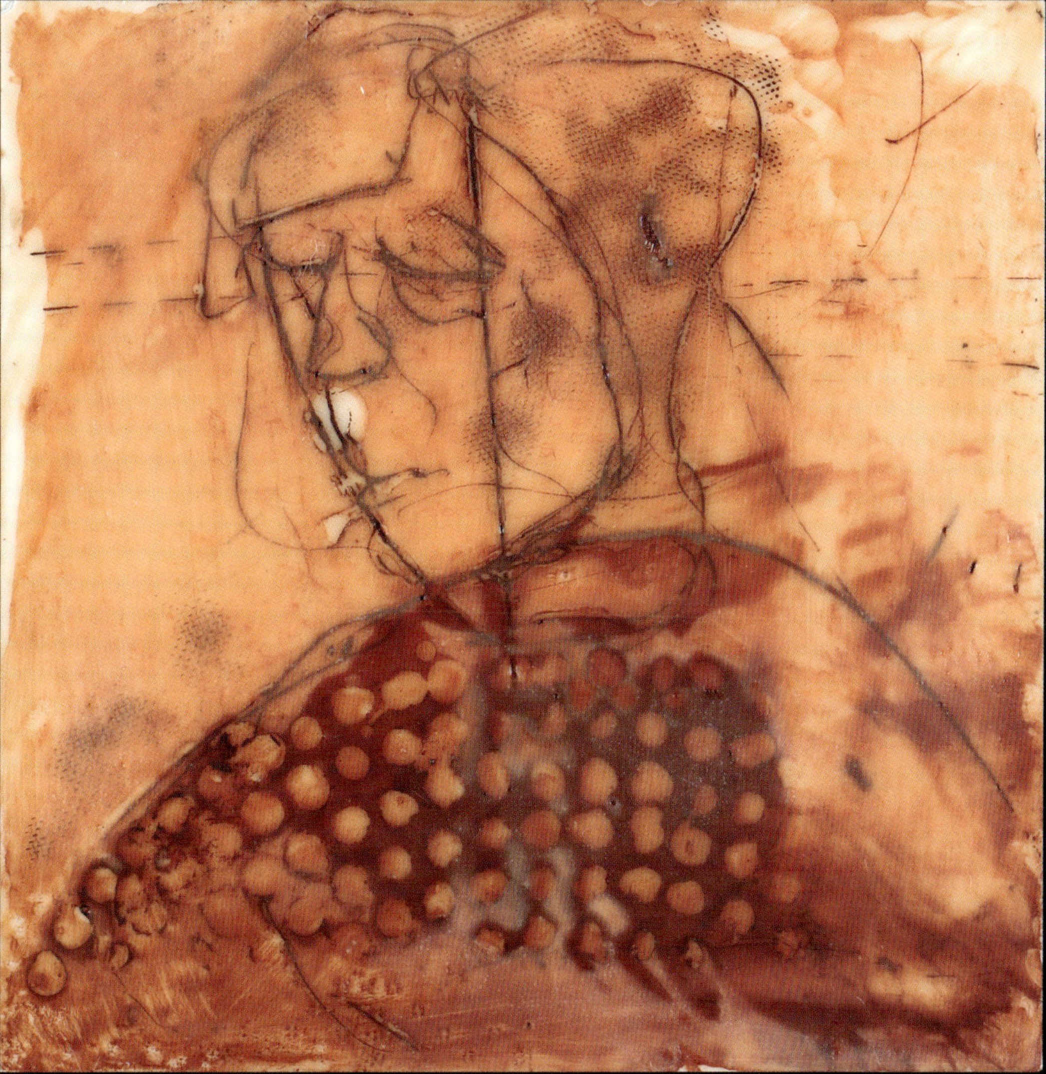

The sun was hot on their backs while they worked in the fields
2009
Encaustic on clayboard
20 x 16 in.

Her new Jacket 2009
Encaustic on clayboard
8 x 8 in.

Nemo being fed to Bird in Nest

Nemo being fed to Bird in Nest
2010
Encaustic on clayboard
8 x 8 in.

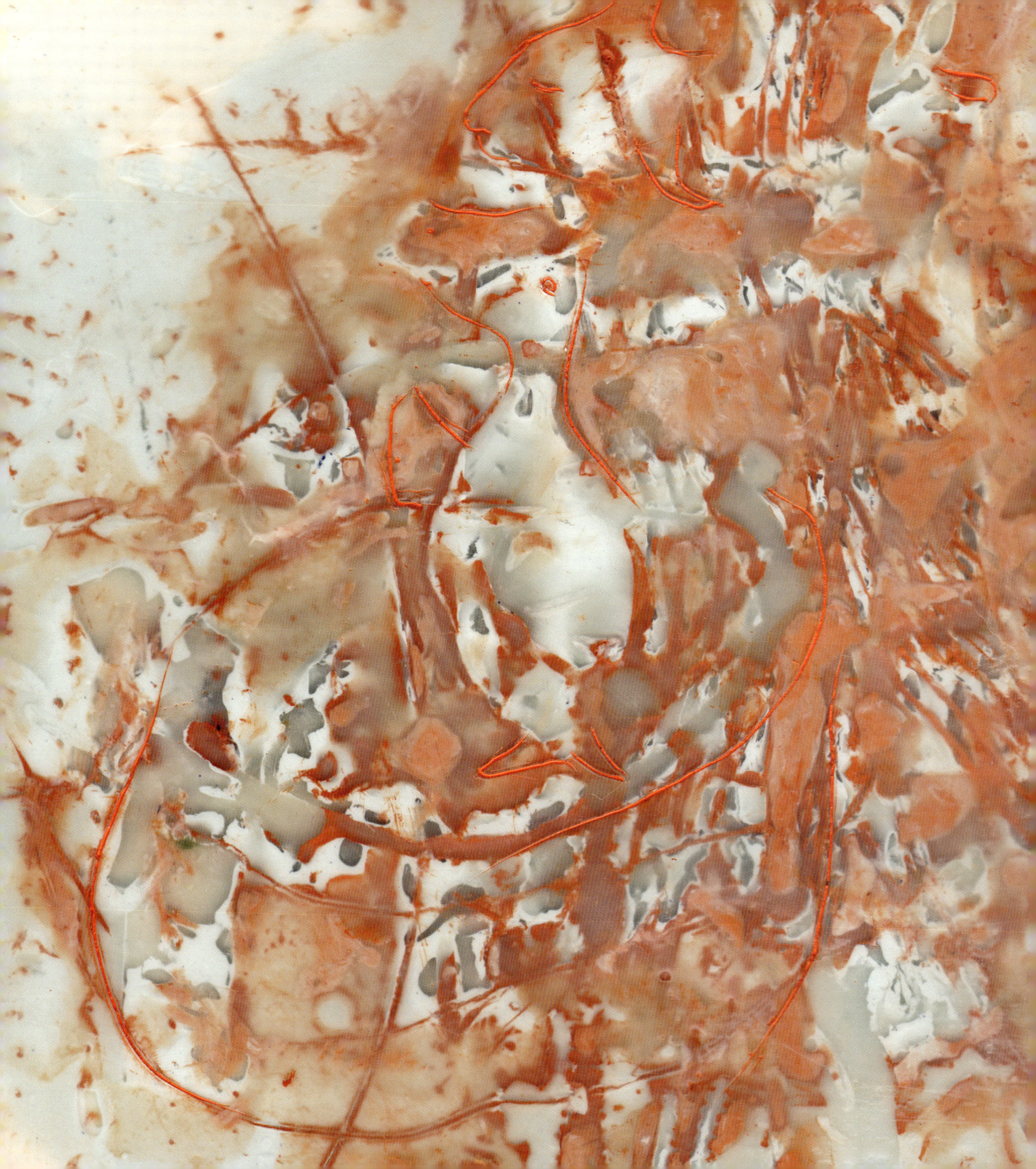

CHAPTER 5

The Small Things

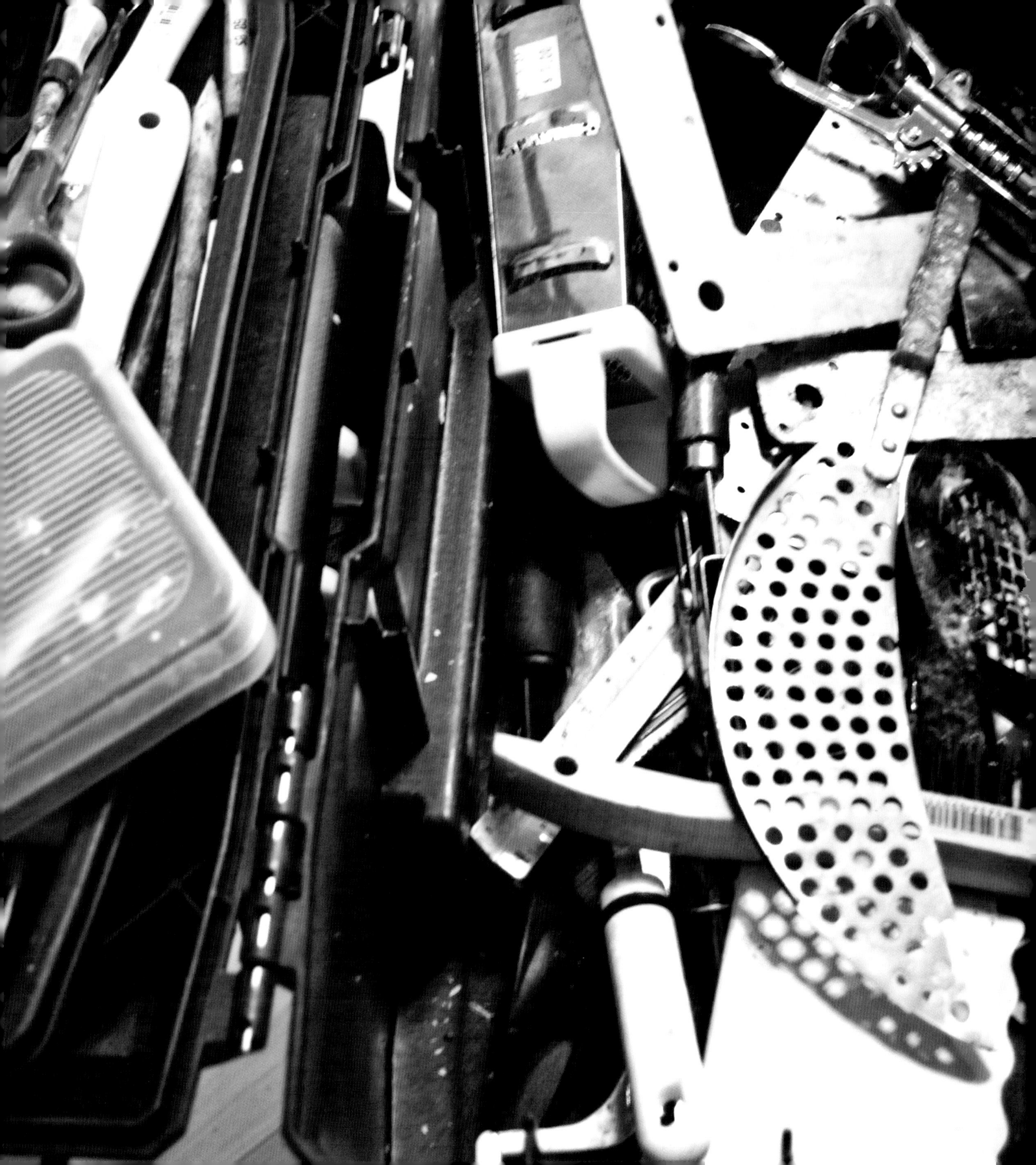

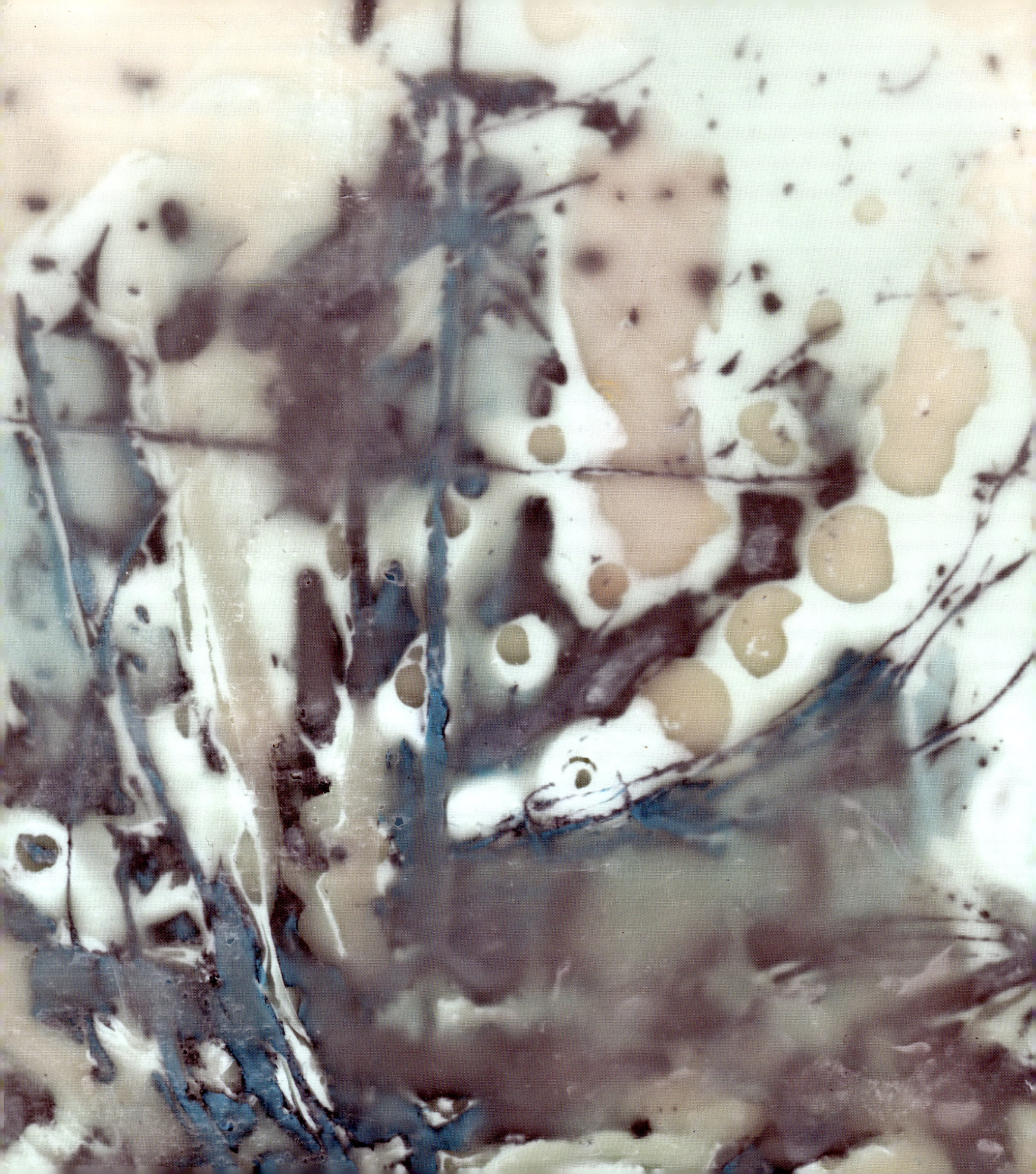

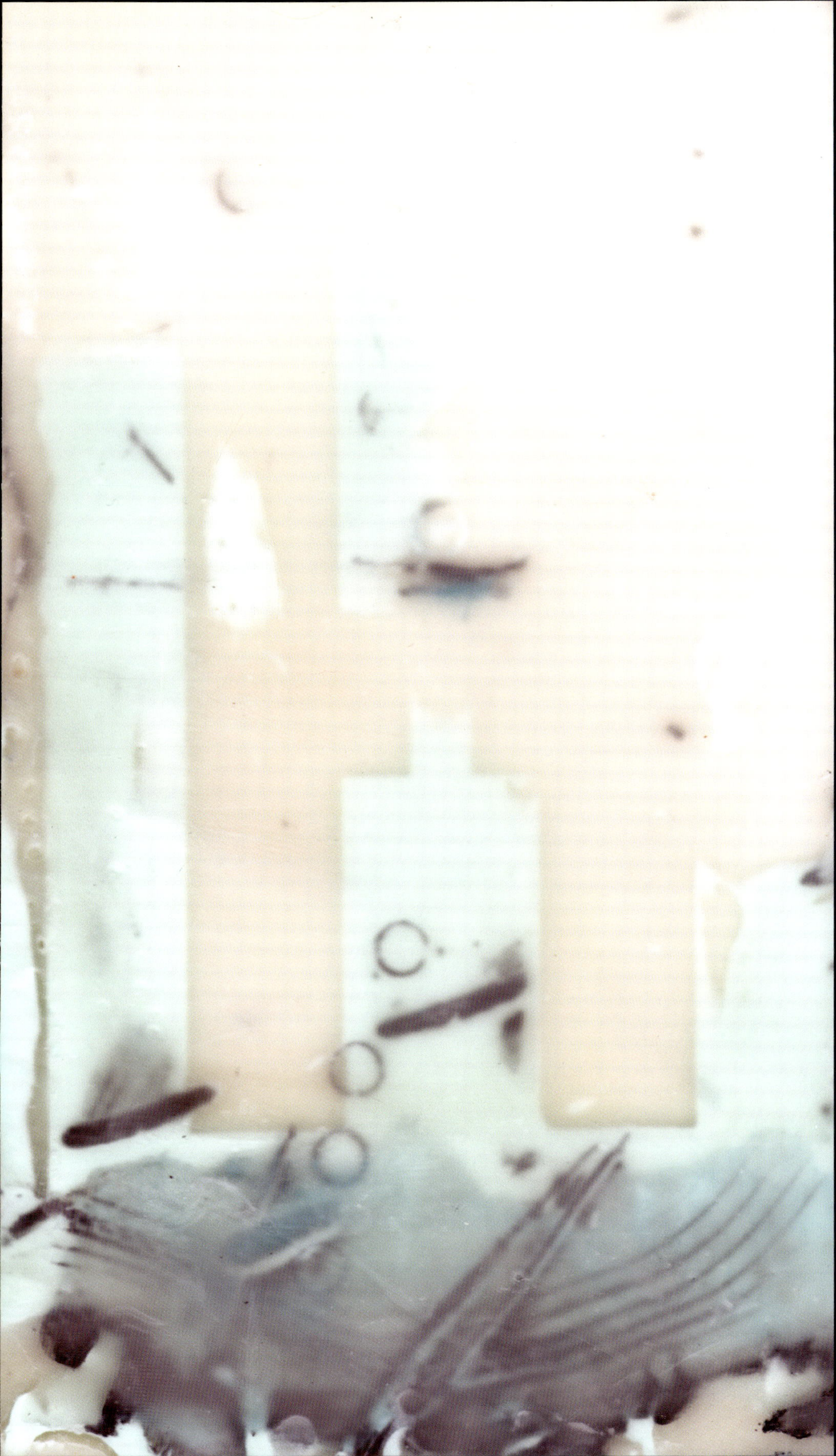

Surfing Penguin 2010
Encaustic on clayboard
8 x 8 in.

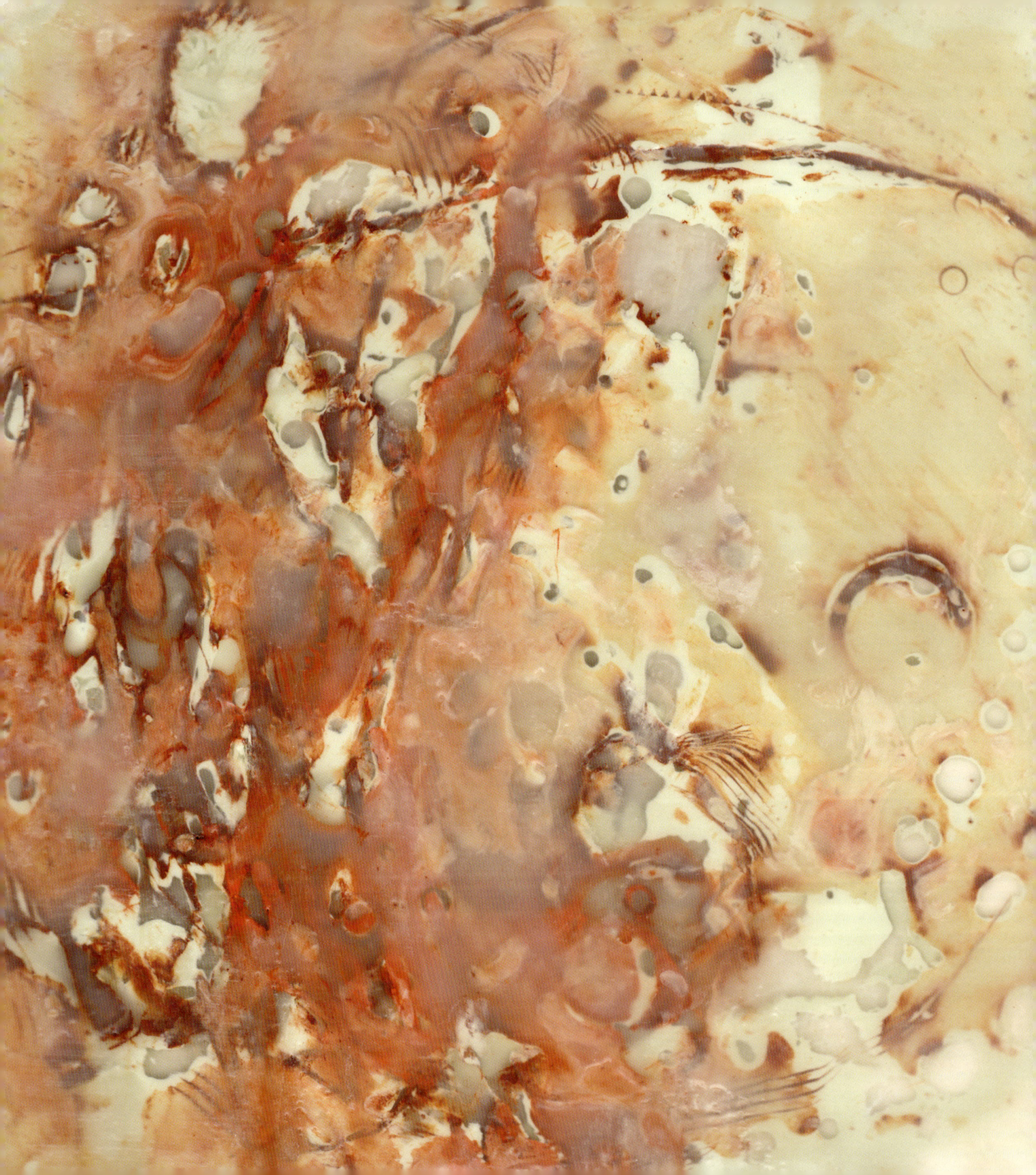

The Fisherman

The Fisherman 2010
Encaustic on clayboard
8 x 8 in.

Santa wants his presents back

Santa wants his presents back 2009
Encaustic on clayboard
8 x 8 in.

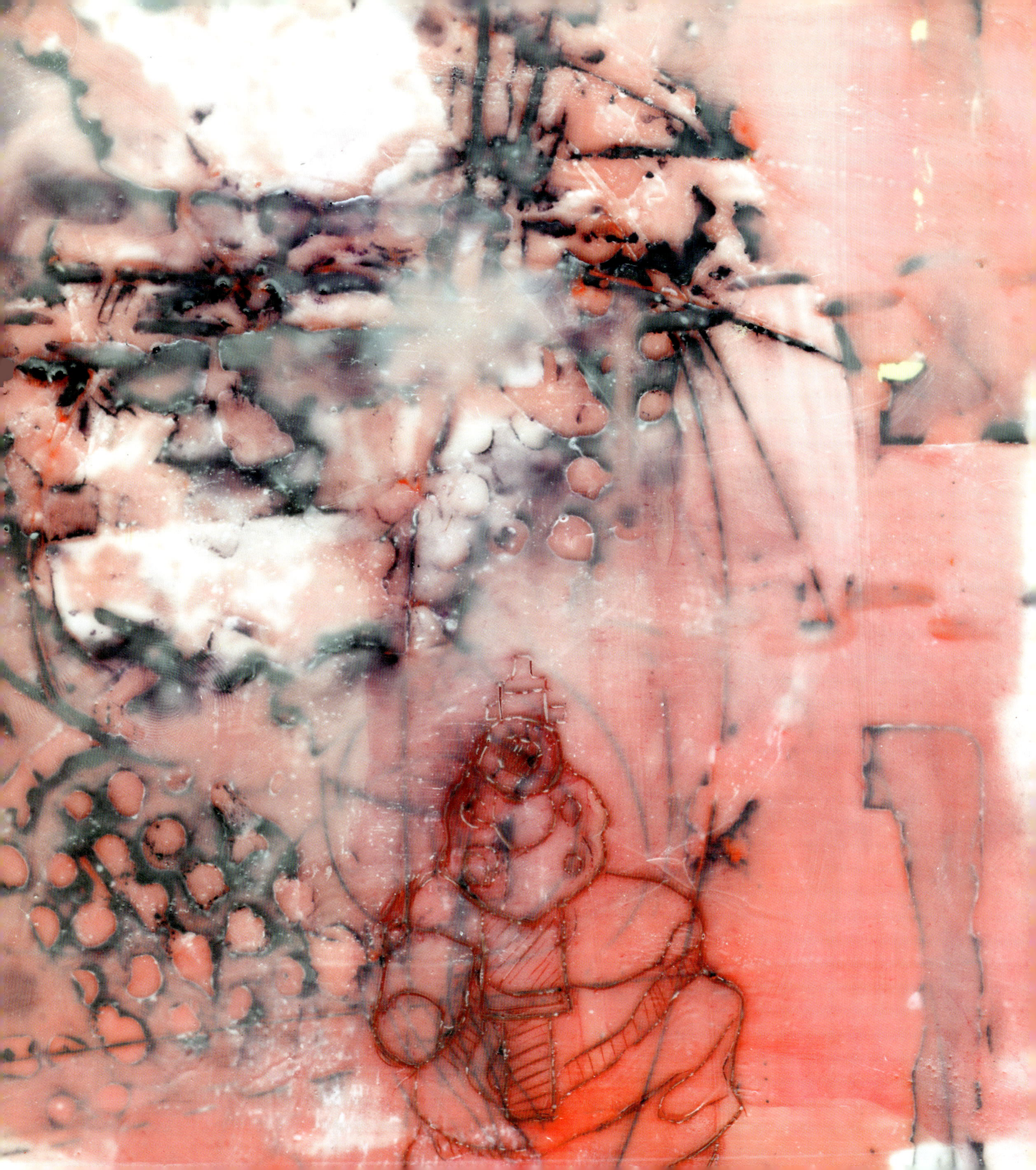

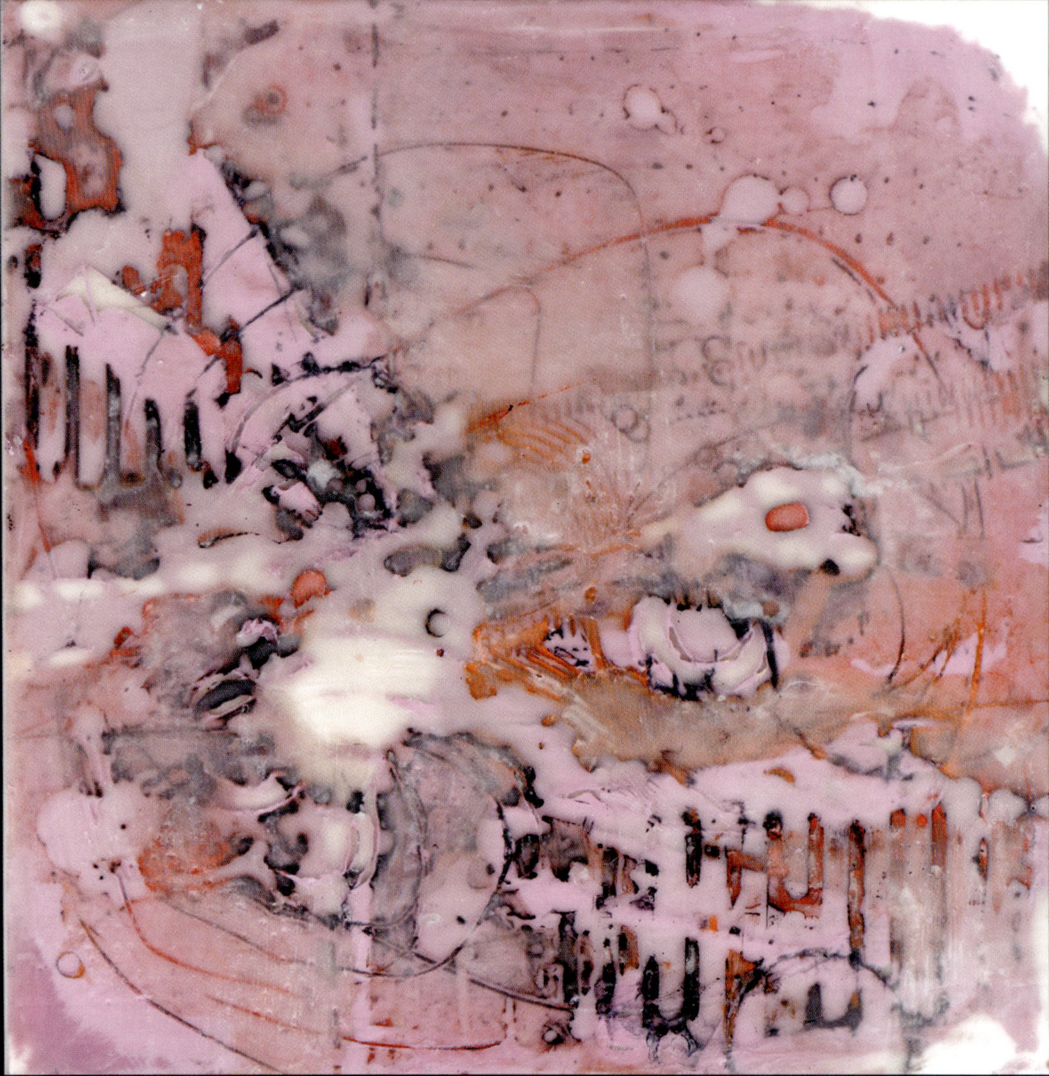

Red Eyed Phoenix
2010
Encaustic on clayboard
8 x 8 in.

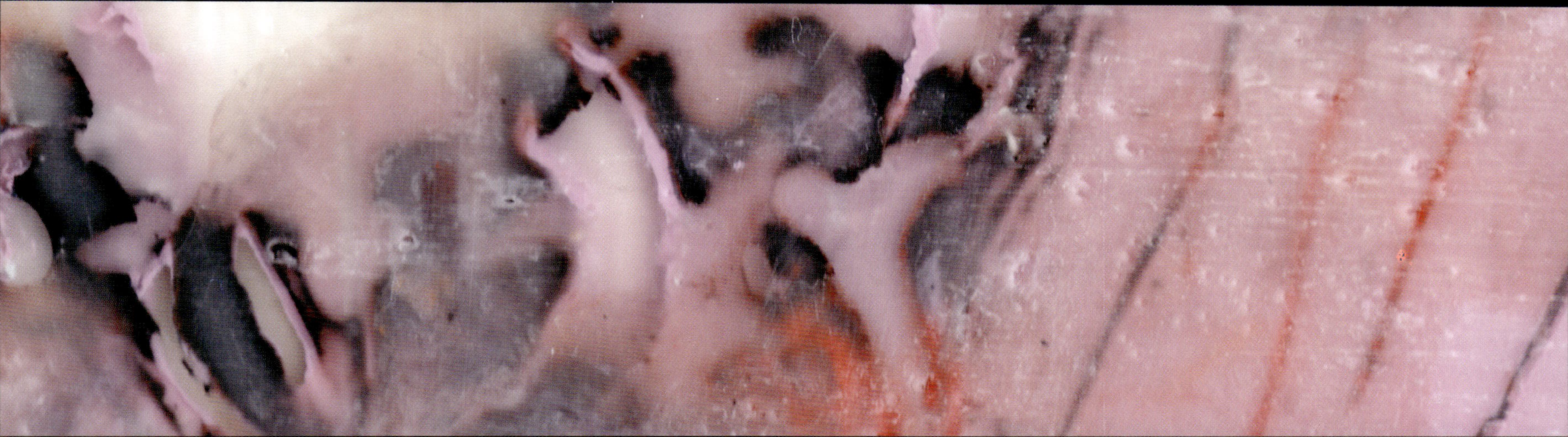

Red Eyed Phoenix

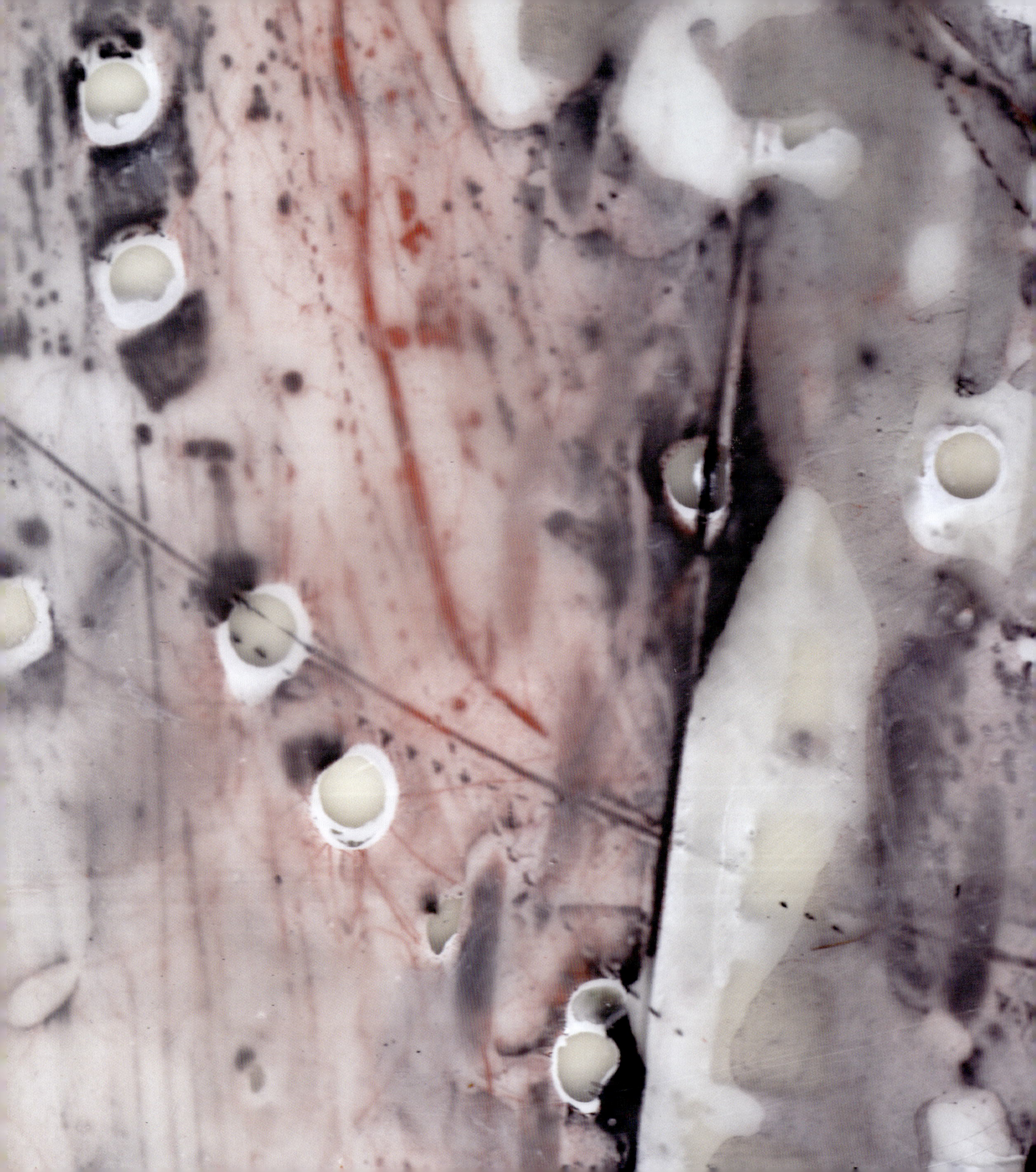

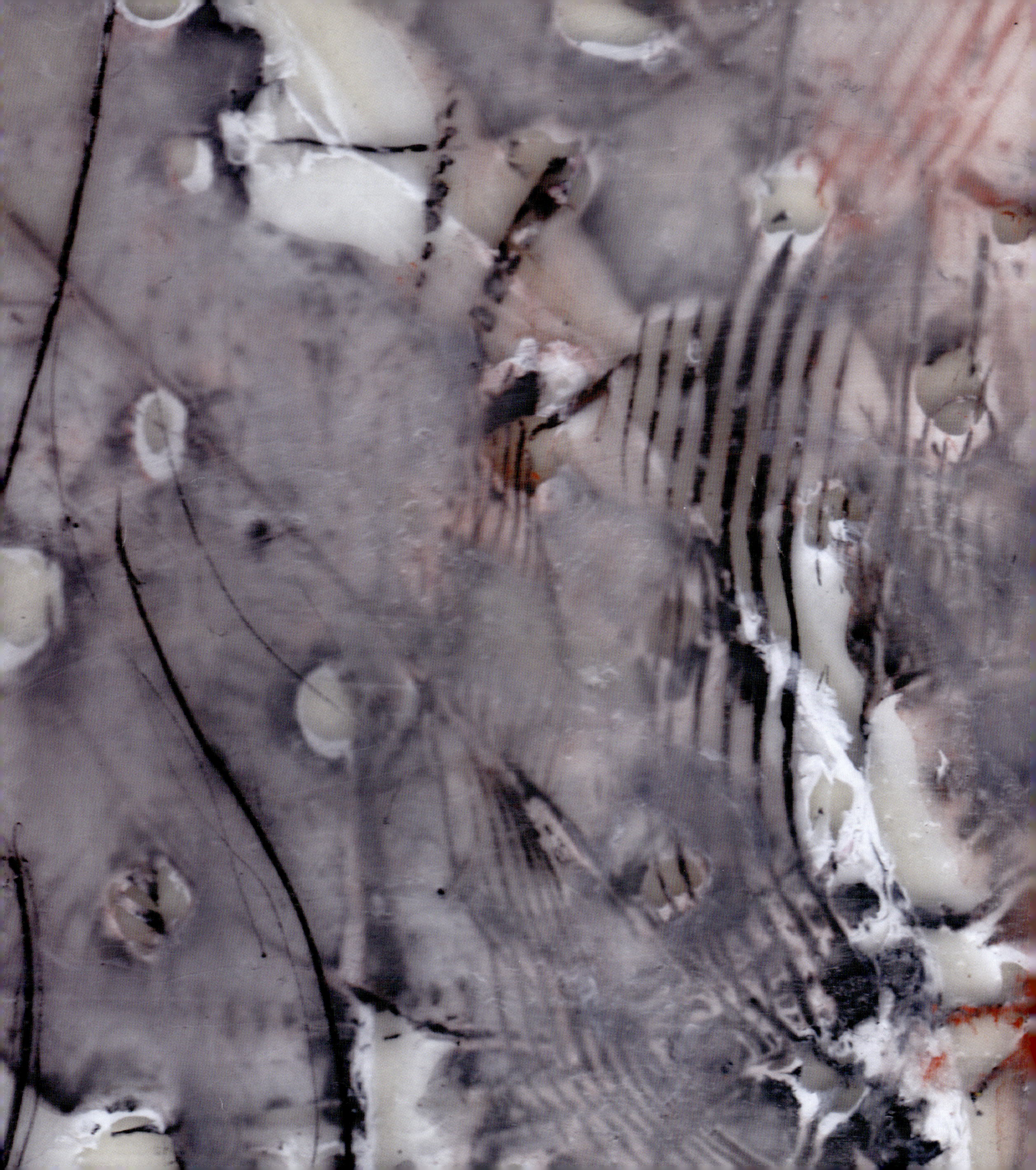

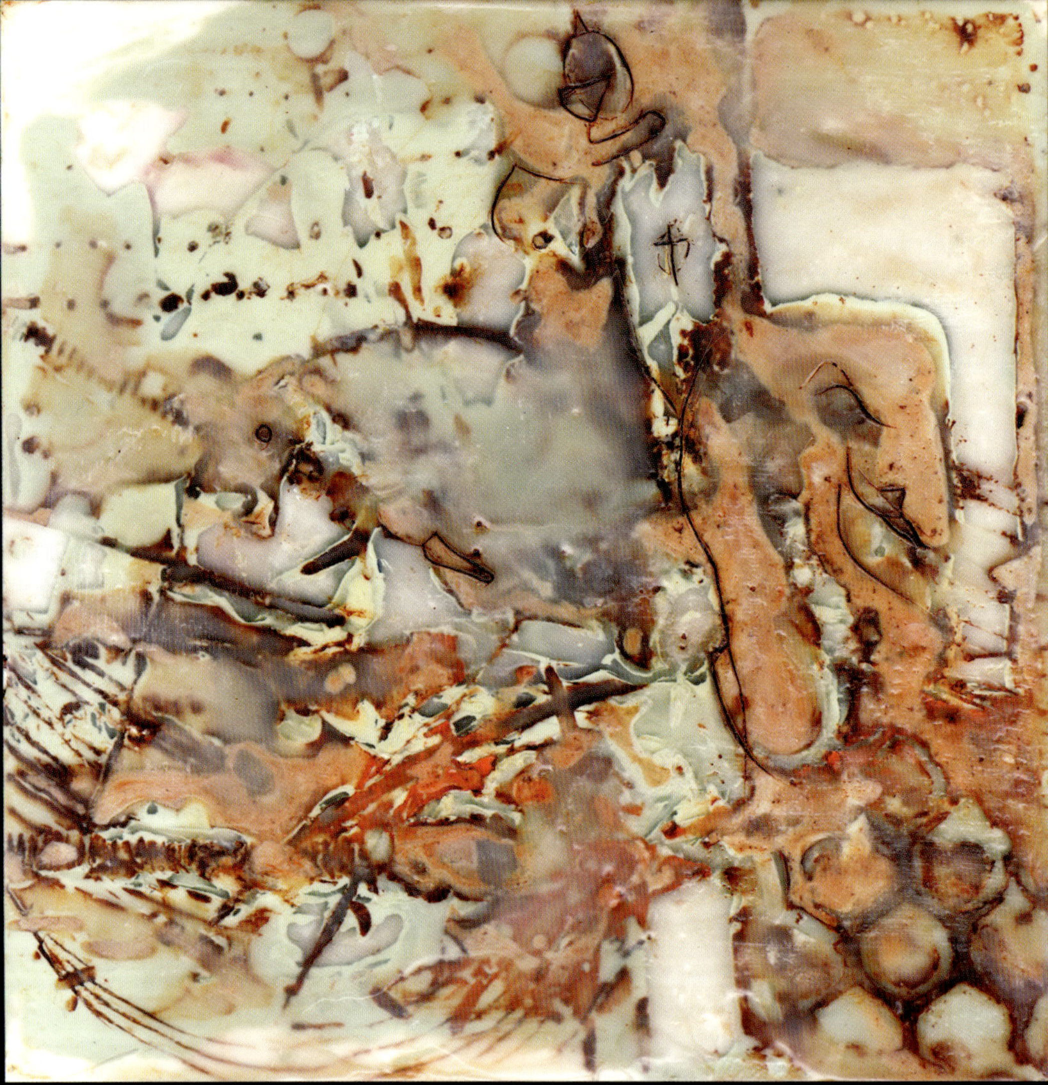

(previous page)
Wounded, Naked, & Cold (detail)
2010
Encaustic on clayboard
8 x 8 in.

knight lancing dragon while his scared horse jumps over the campfire
2010
Encaustic on clayboard
8 x 8 in.

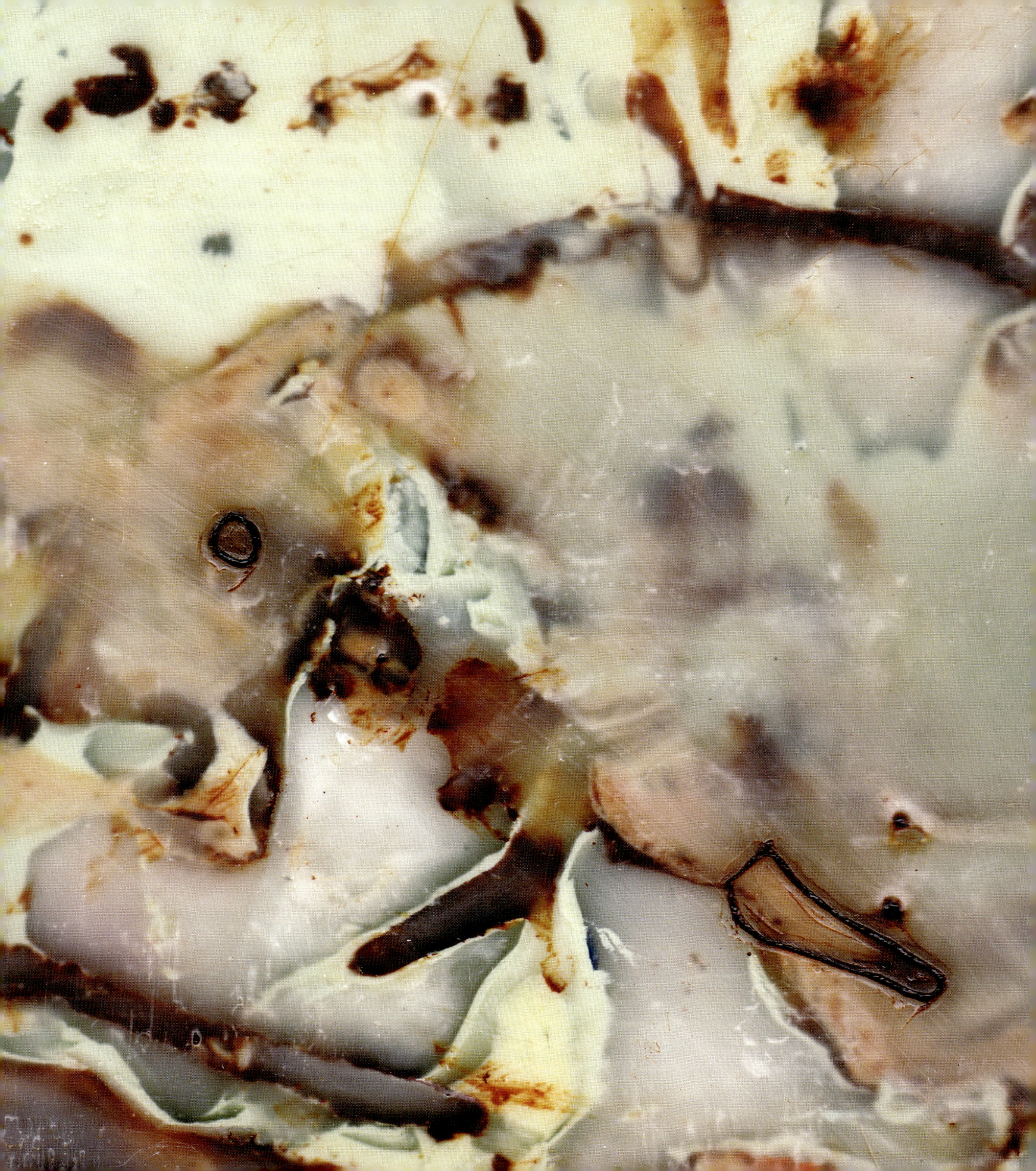

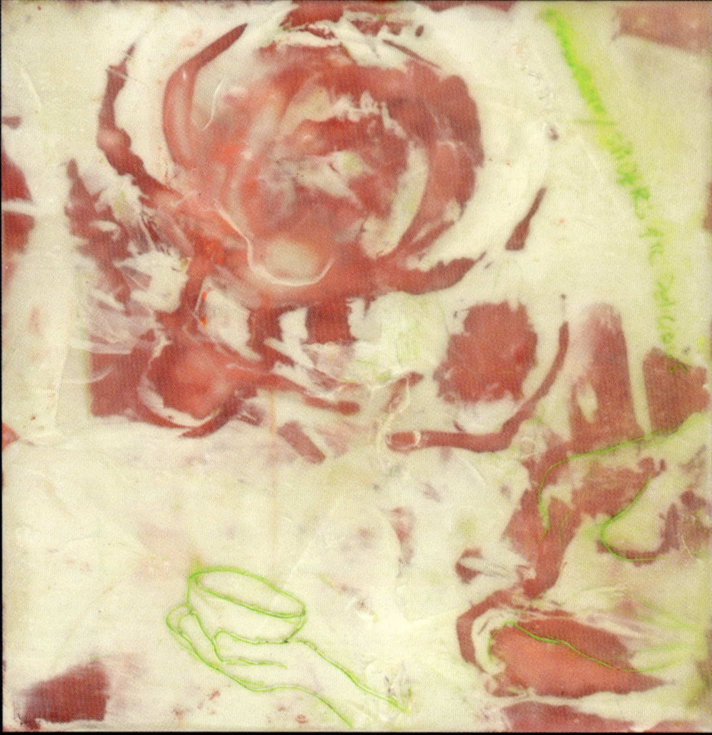

Strawberry Spiders are Delicious 2009
Encaustic on clayboard
8 x 8 in.

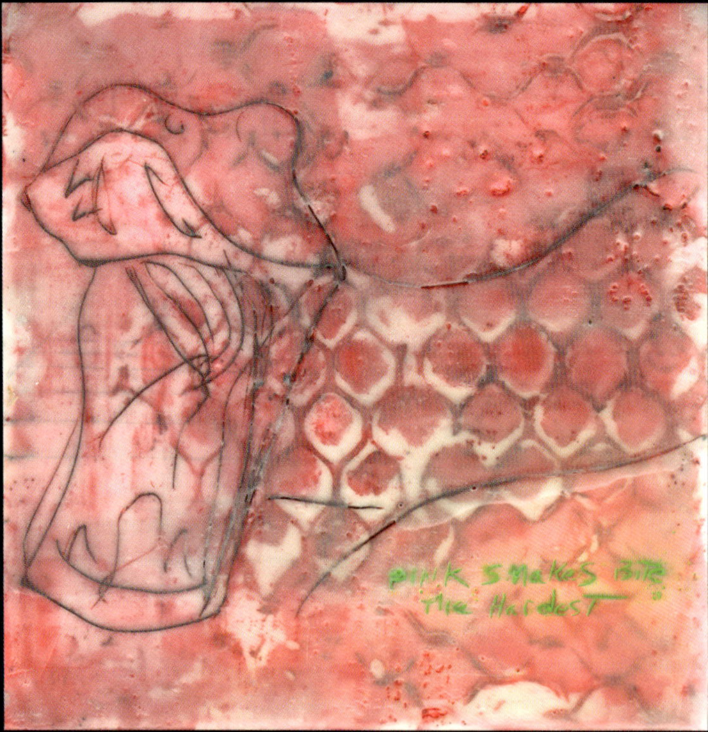

Pink Snakes Bite the Hardest 2009
Encaustic on clayboard
8 x 8 in.

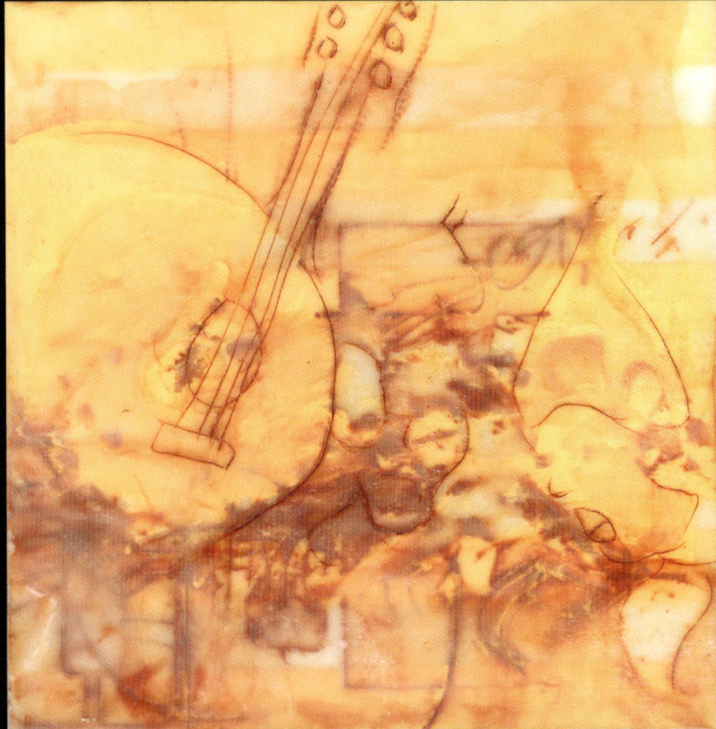

Prodigal son with hair on fire jamming with alien and guitar 2009
Encaustic on clayboard
8 x 8 in.

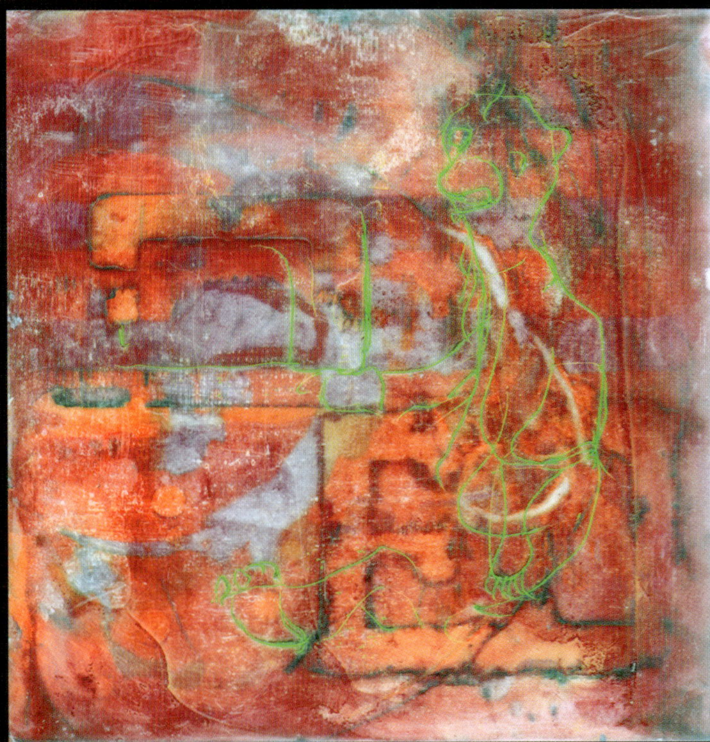

Sewing Sun-Bear 2009
Encaustic on clayboard
8 x 8 in.

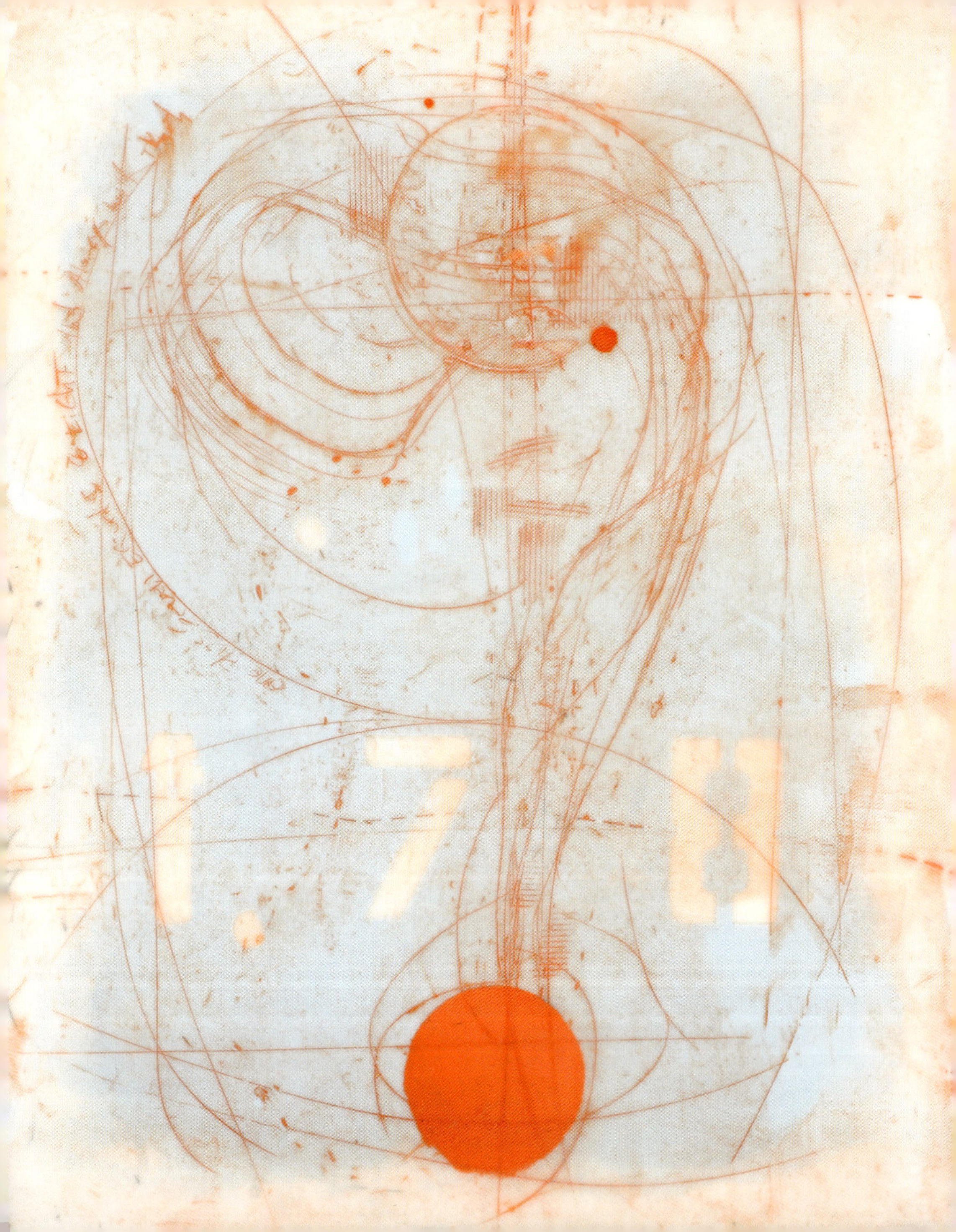

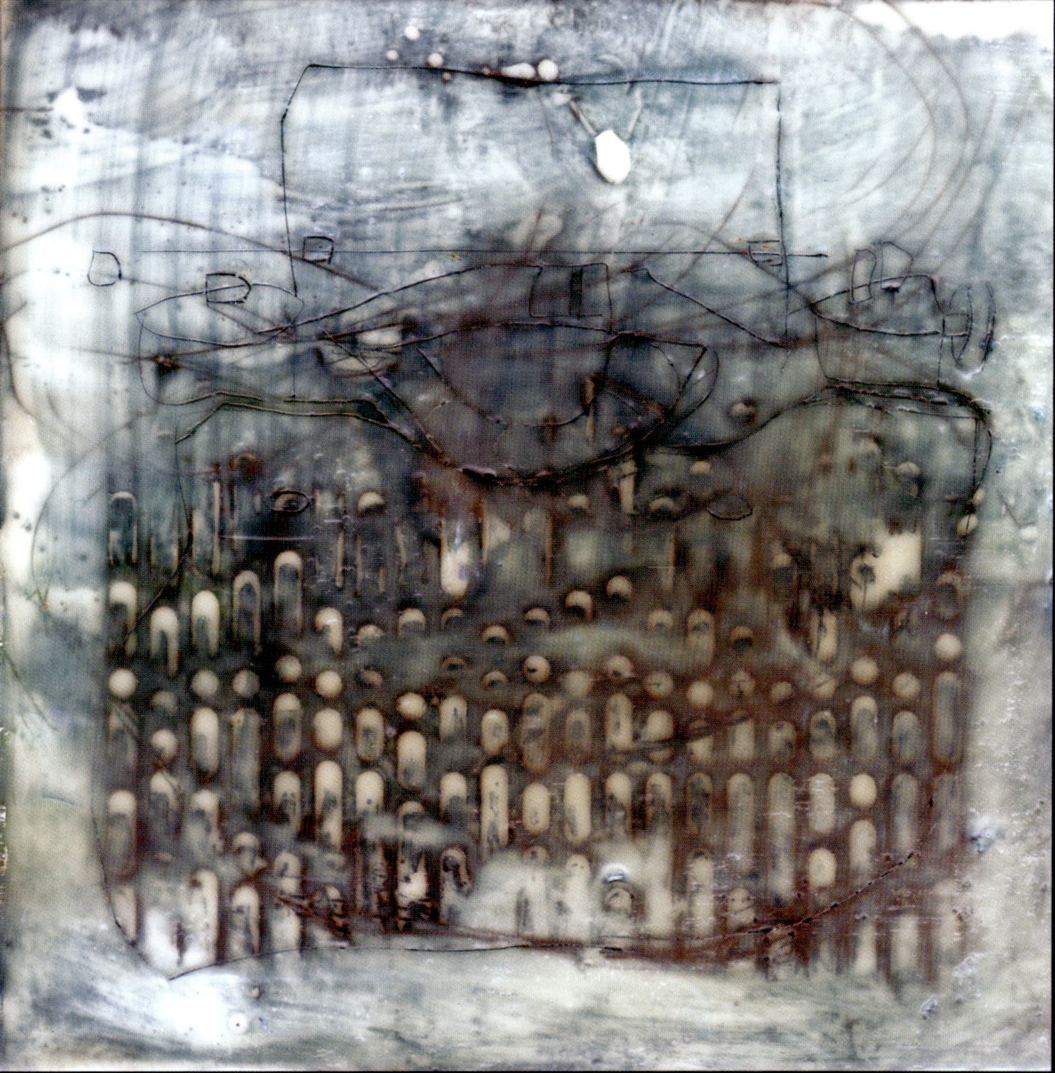

Spirit Leaving Body 2009
Encaustic on clayboard
20 x 16 in.

Typewriter 2009
Encaustic on clayboard
8 x 8 in.

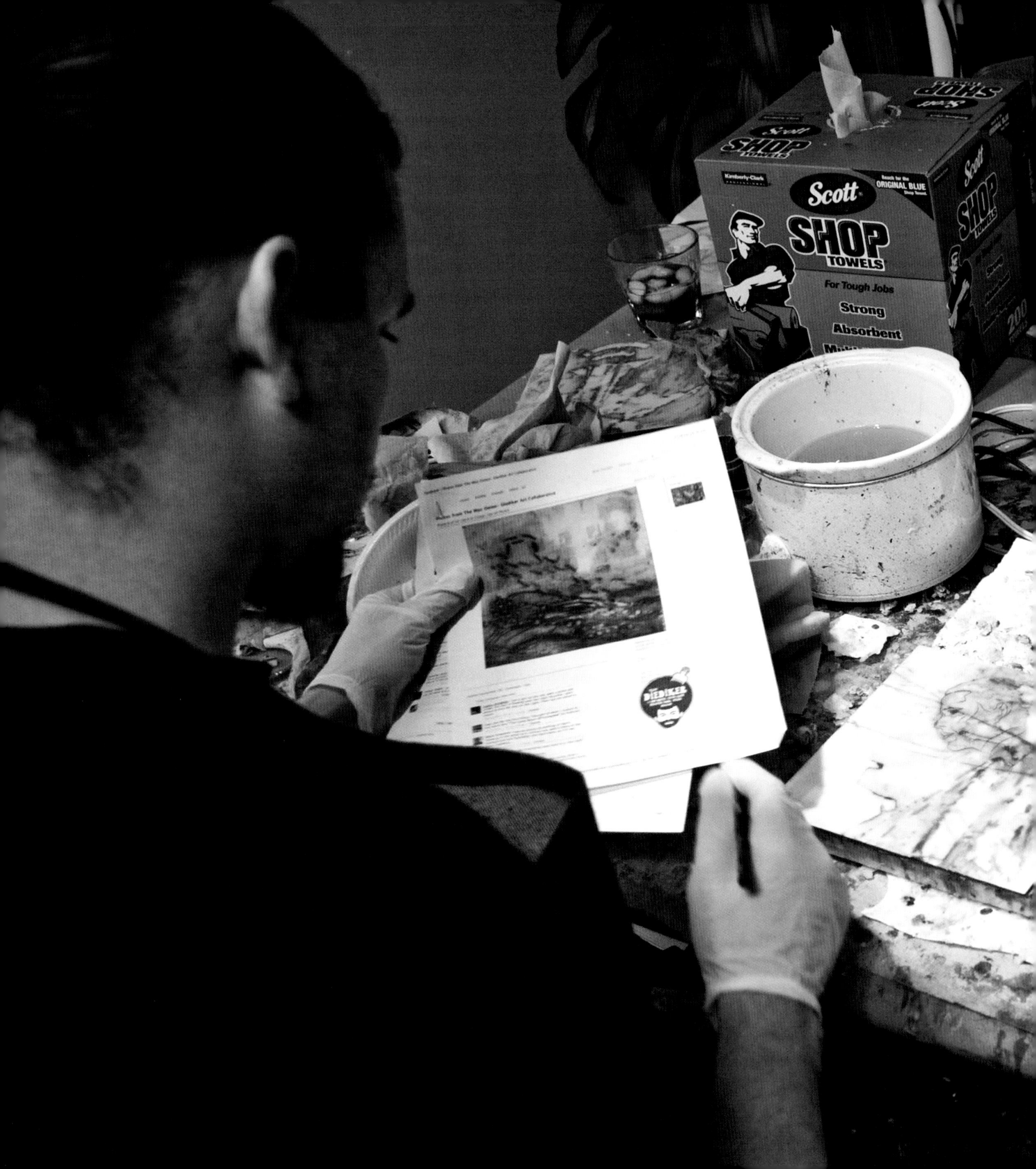
Kimberly-Clark
ORIGINAL BLUE
Scott
SHOP
TOWELS
For Tough Jobs
Strong
Absorbent

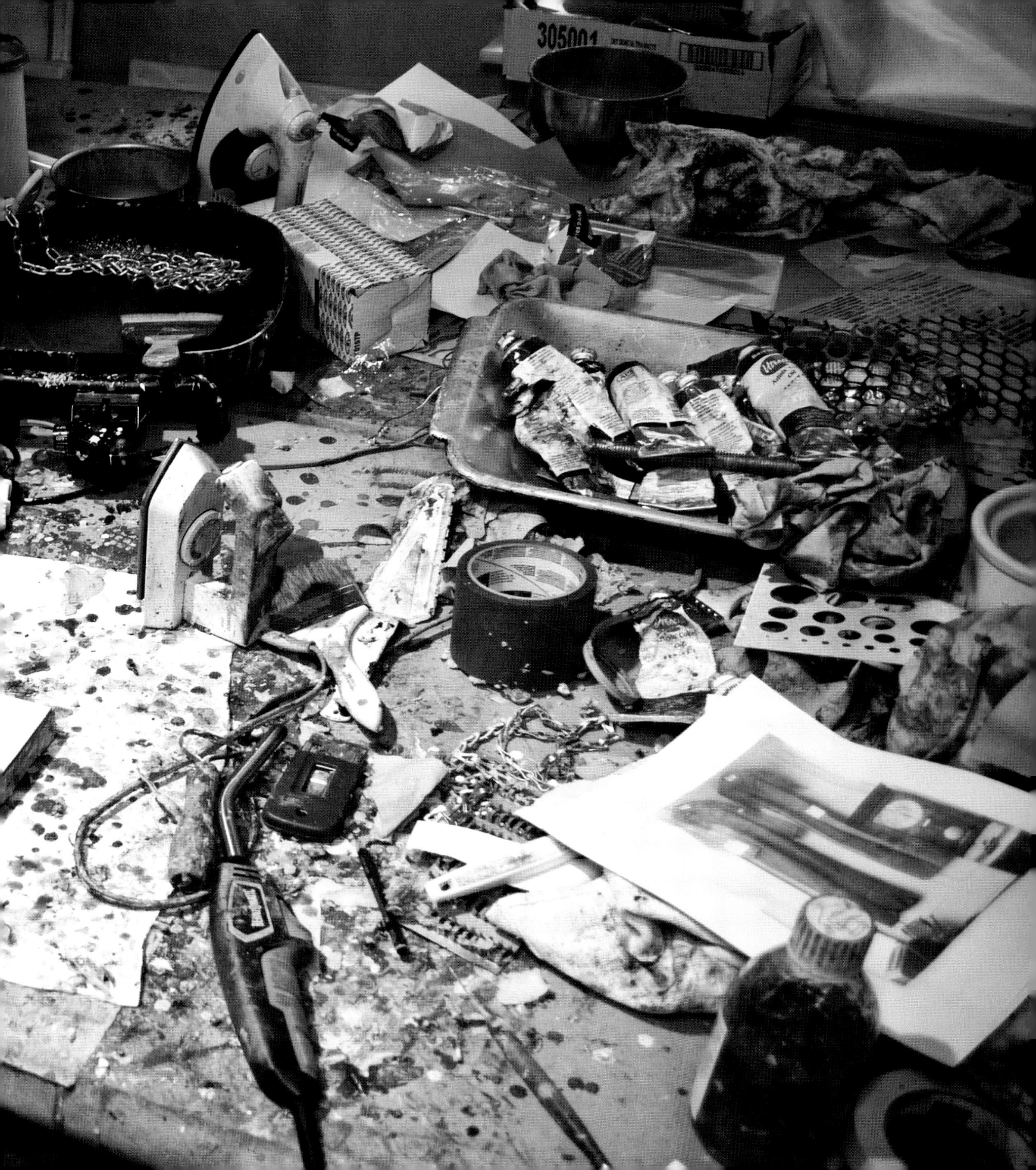
305001

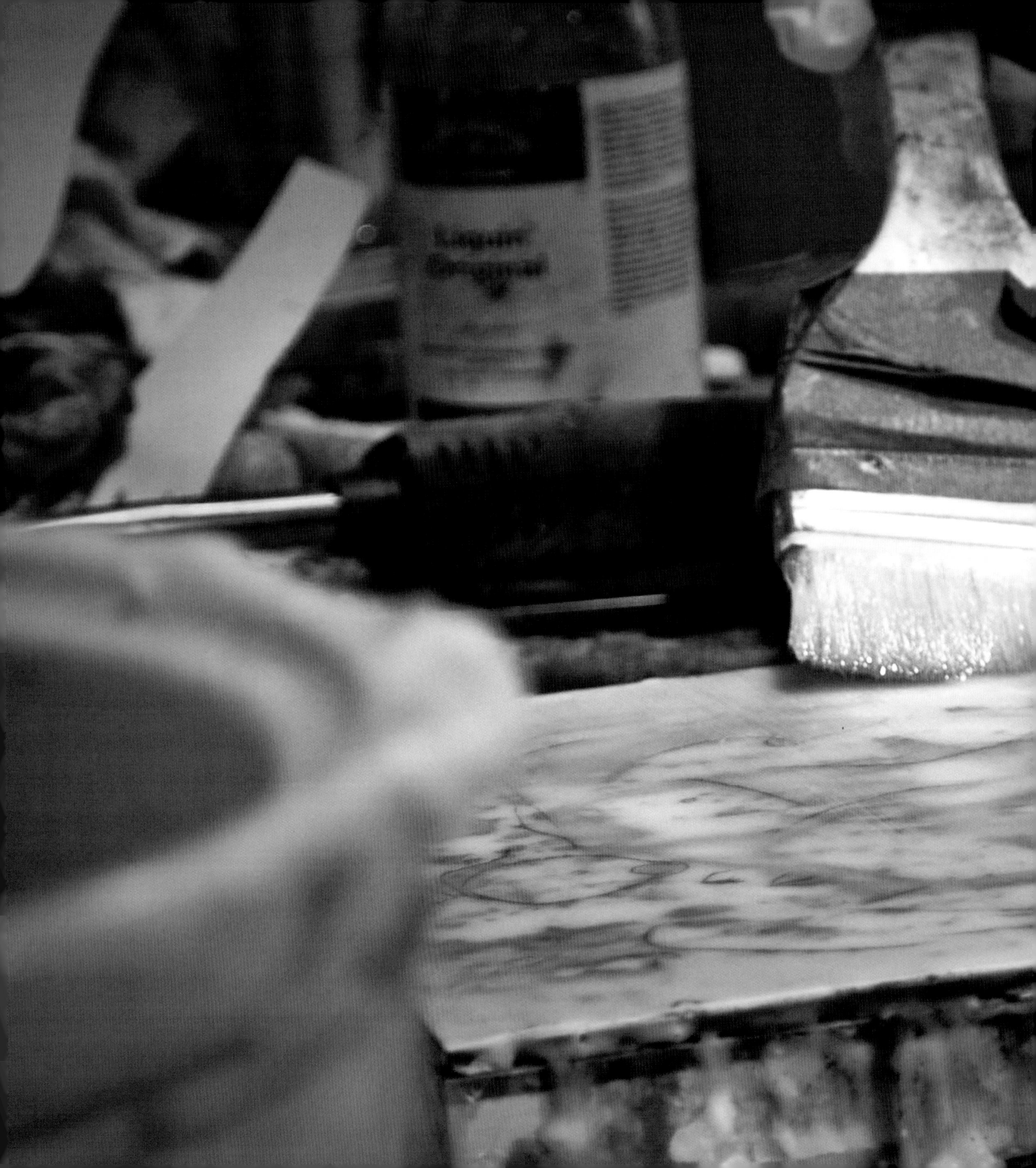

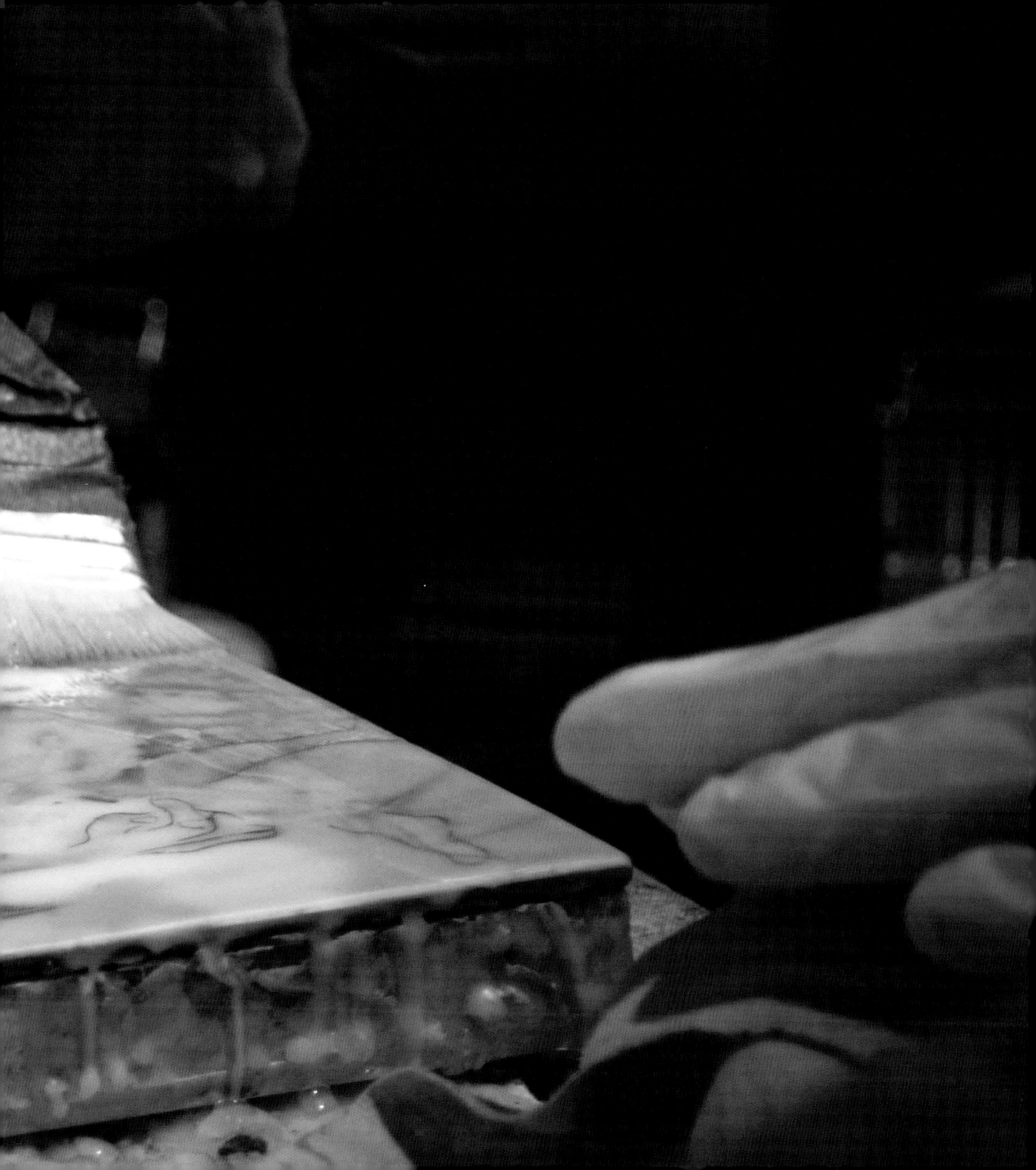

CHAPTER 6

Under the Influence

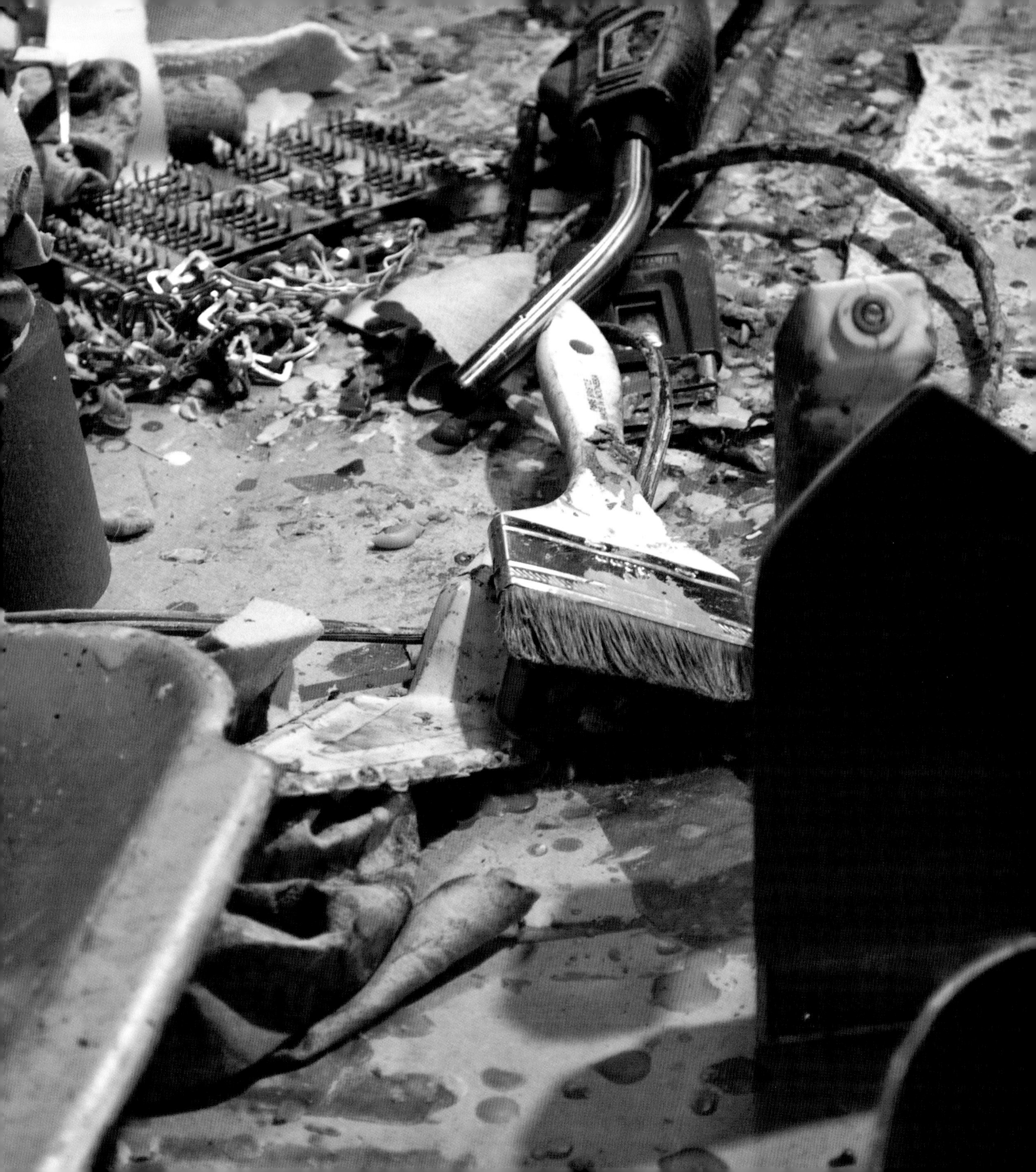

Other works
by

DIEDIKER

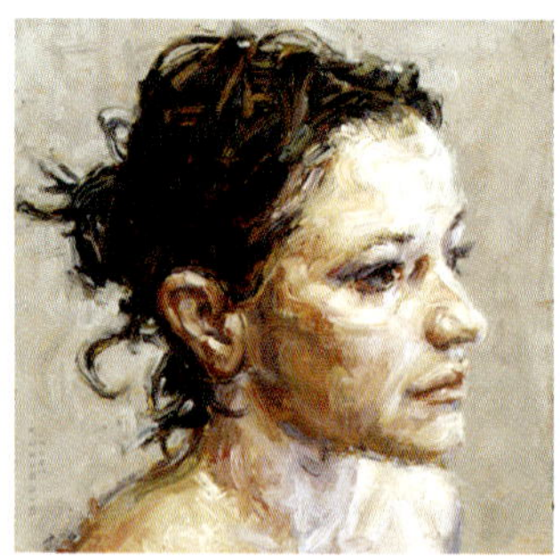

Under the Influence

Diediker's interest in working with the encaustic medium originated during a visit to Santa Fe, New Mexico. While touring the city's galleries with some of the students he teaches at the Bridge Academy of Art, an institution of which he is a founding member, Diediker came across an encaustic piece that sparked his creative curiosity. "I just knew that the medium would be great for exploring surfaces, that it would allow me to stack and suspend pigment to unique effect," says Diediker. In that moment, a glimmer of opportunity presented itself to Diediker, who embarked on a journey – both literal and figurative – that took him away from his traditional studio work and towards the more abstract medium of beeswax.

To some, this might seem like quite a departure, but Diediker explains that it's not really a departure at all. In his traditional paintings, Diediker employs a classical approach with impressionistic application. Most of his prior work has rendered realistic images with an emphasis on the interplay of light on varied surfaces. "I really enjoy the vast array of mark-making that suggest an image but are still paint," says Diediker. "It's about the surface." Diediker's A Prayer for those in Traffic is evidence of his love for interesting surfaces and interplay of light.

"It's a synergistic hybrid of an acrylic under-painting topped with a more refined oil painting, which reveals intriguing surface interplay that is more interesting than the subject on its own." This intense dedication to creating compelling surfaces spills over into his work in encaustics. "I became interested in the encaustic medium because it seemed like a natural extension of my love for creating interesting surfaces," he says. "The path feels very similar to me. The same rules still apply, as far as composition, form, turbulence, and movement."

..."it's not really a departure at all"...

Andrea Head Study 2002
Oil on Linen
14 x 14 in.

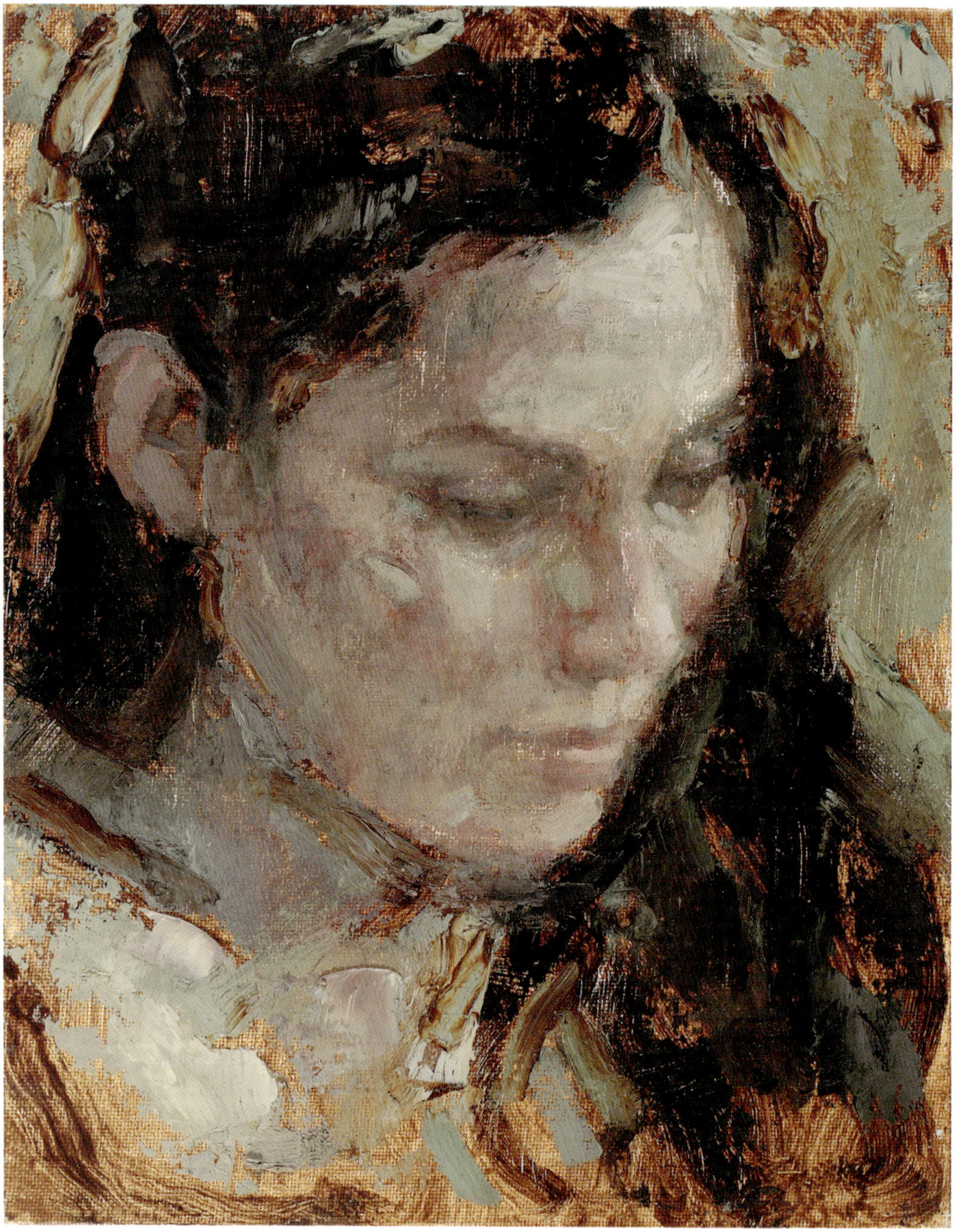

Kinsi Head Study
2009
Oil on Linen
10 x 8 in.

He cites the masters of the realistic image – Vermeer, Van Eyck, and Rembrandt – as major influences, though his work also reveals Van Gogh's significant influence. Diediker has said that he considers Vermeer's The Milkmaid to be a perfect painting for its composition, flawless color, and subject. "In traditional oil painting, the nature of the medium allows you to layer the oil to produce extremes of light and dark," says Diediker. "In The Milkmaid, the colors are very dark, and Vermeer takes great pains to perfect his dry-on-dry rendering." Diediker, who originally viewed The Milkmaid on exhibit in Amsterdam, was riveted by Vermeer's craftsmanship. "While smaller in size, his composition and color balance stand head and shoulders over every painting in that room," he says.

While Diediker appreciates oil paint for its ability to layer colors to dramatic levels of darkness, lightness, opacity, and surface depth, his work in encaustics has led him to appreciate the medium's interplay with sunlight. "There is no pigment on the lightest parts of the encaustic plates, there is only the light passing through the beeswax and onto the white clay at the base of the plate," says Diediker. "It allows for very nice transitions of color and form. There is no way to attain the same quality of surface depth in other mediums." Diediker yields himself to the nature of the medium to get the best possible surface quality,without obstructing the passage of light through the medium. "My concern is to enhance the beauty of the medium," he says, a characteristic which marks his traditional work as well.

Kinsi Head Study

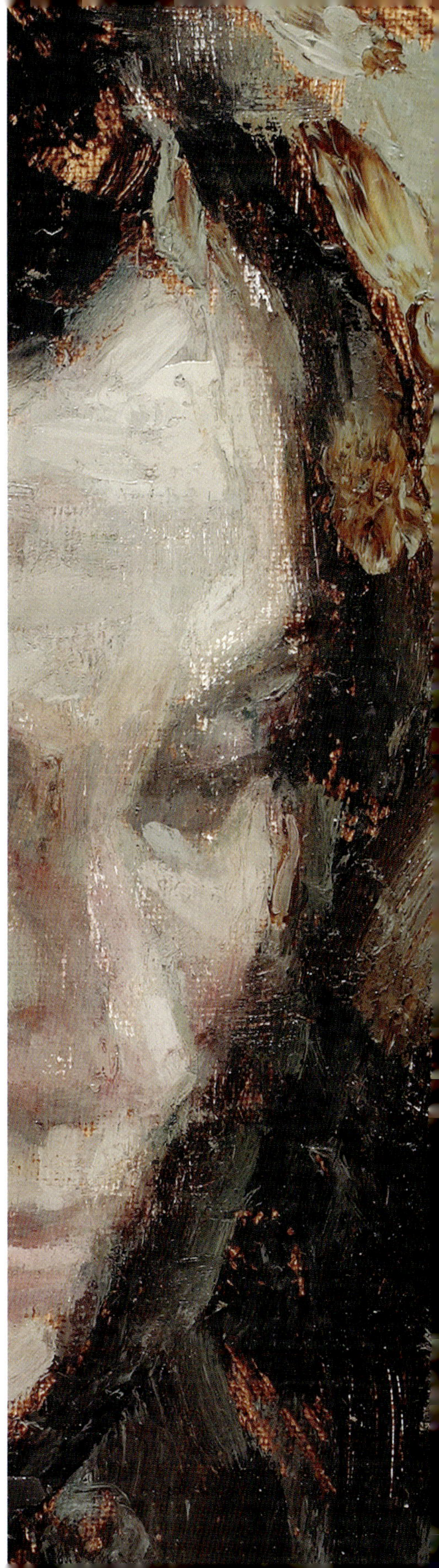

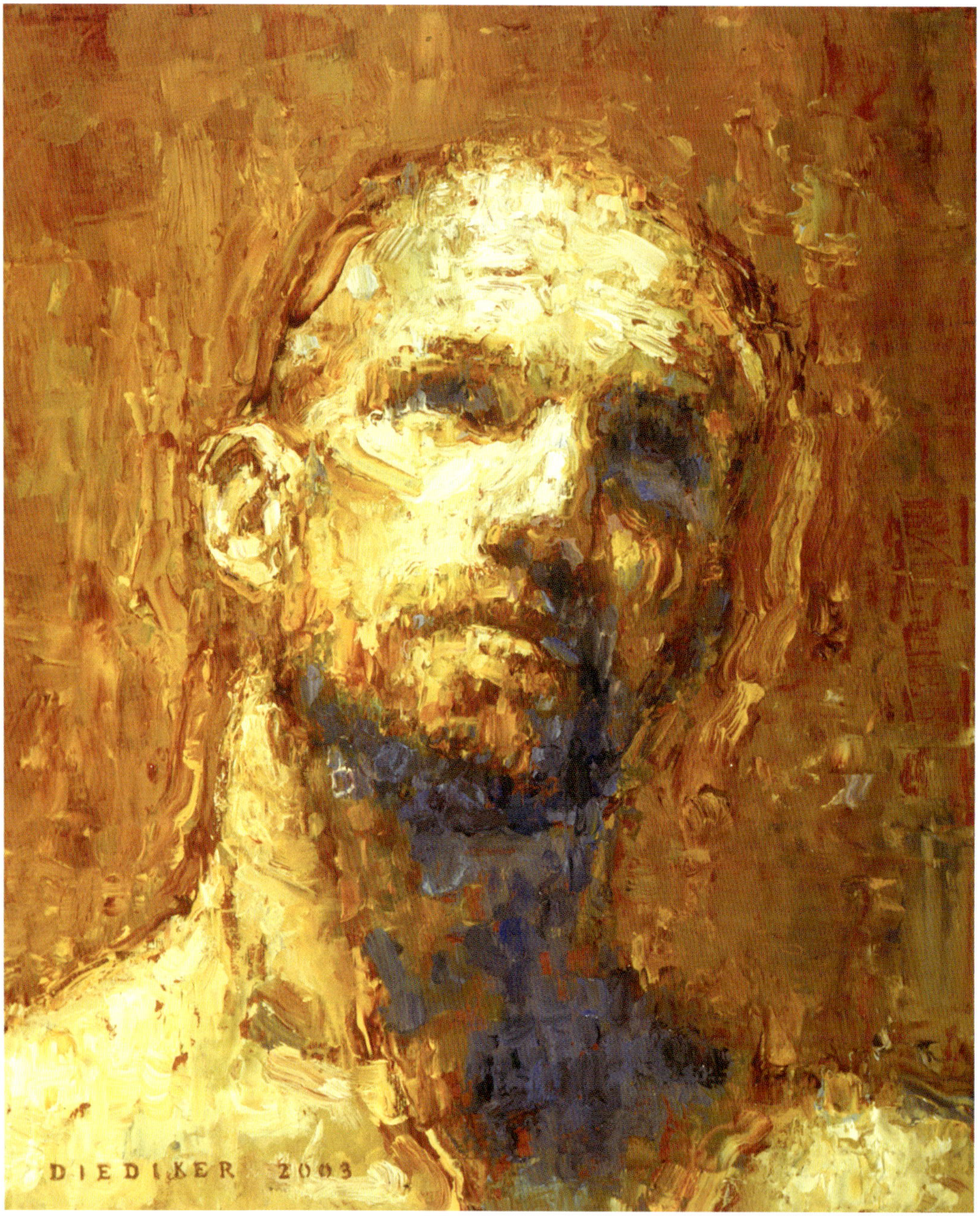

Conversion of Aaron Turner
2004
Oil on Linen
13 x 11 in.

Under the Influence

He offers another richly saturated master work as a sound vehicle for connecting his love of painting to his love for encaustics: Van Eyck's Arnolfini Wedding. "While I love the Arnolfini Wedding for its amazing color saturation and refinement, the utter complexity of the image doesn't come through until you're viewing the painting at very close range. That's when you see Van Eyck's mastery in composing and painting every detail, every inch of canvas," he says. "I enjoy working with encaustics for their chance abstractions, which are the opposite of Van Eyck's controlled images. But the beauty is still there for the viewing. You have to look closely at the encaustic plates in order to appreciate their delicacy and beauty."

"All the things that I've learned from the old masters can still be applied to my work in encaustics," notes Diediker. "When I'm thinking of a color scheme or trying to make an interesting surface, when I'm rendering a small part of one of my traditional pieces... I'm trying to make everything about those few square inches seem interesting," says Diediker. "I'm trying to give them depth with my glazes and under-painting." He applies the same approach to his encaustic work, taking pains to honor the differing nature of the medium. "It may seem like the final product looks vastly different from my traditional work, but the artistic process is exactly the same for each," he says.

"I hope that my past collectors will realize that my encaustic work is not a departure from painting," says Diediker. "In fact, the encaustics will probably be a limited series. Once I complete it, I'll return to my traditional painting with renewed vigor and an improved perspective."

"All the things that I've learned from the old masters can still be applied to my work in encaustics."

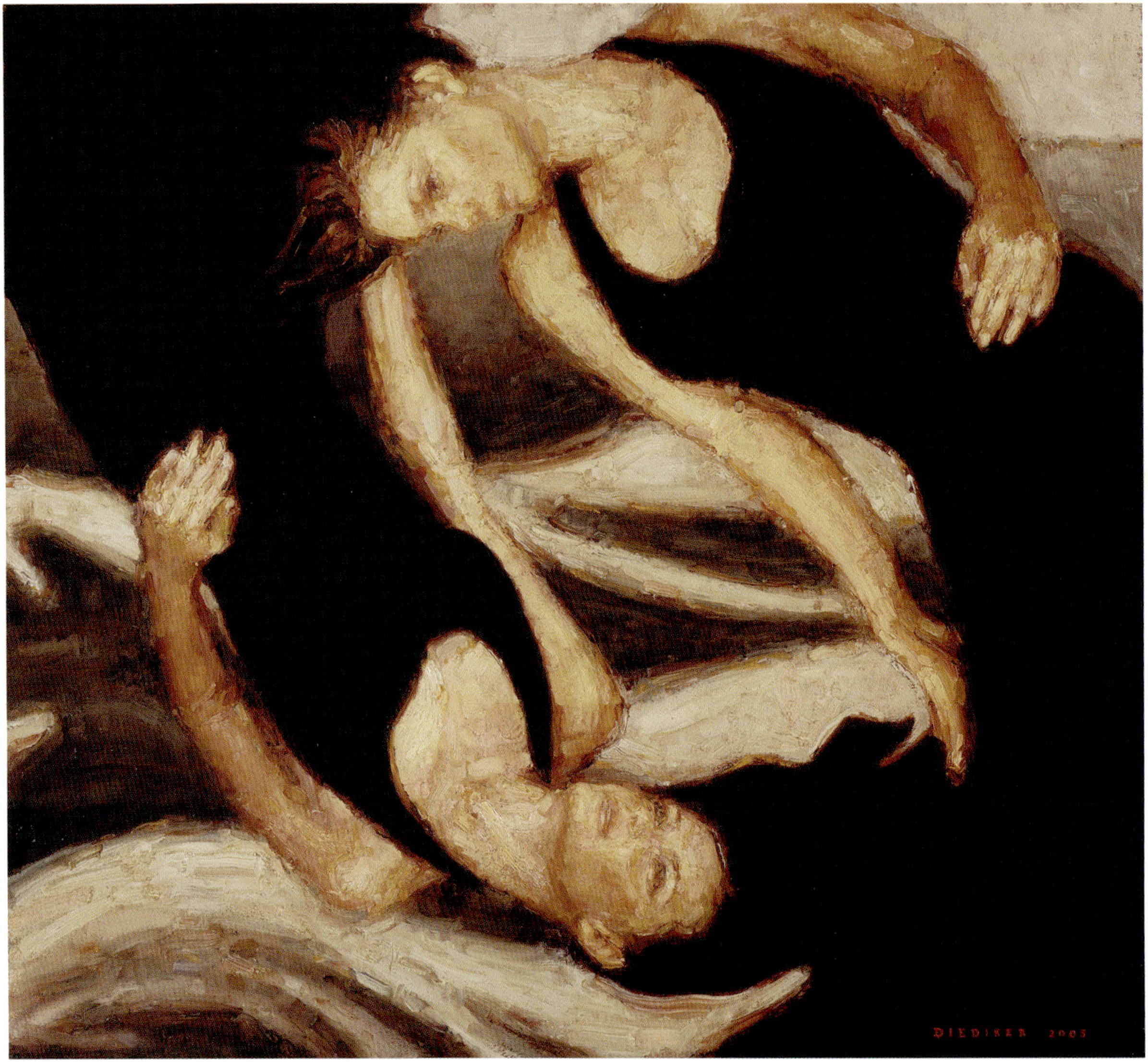
DIEDIKER 2005

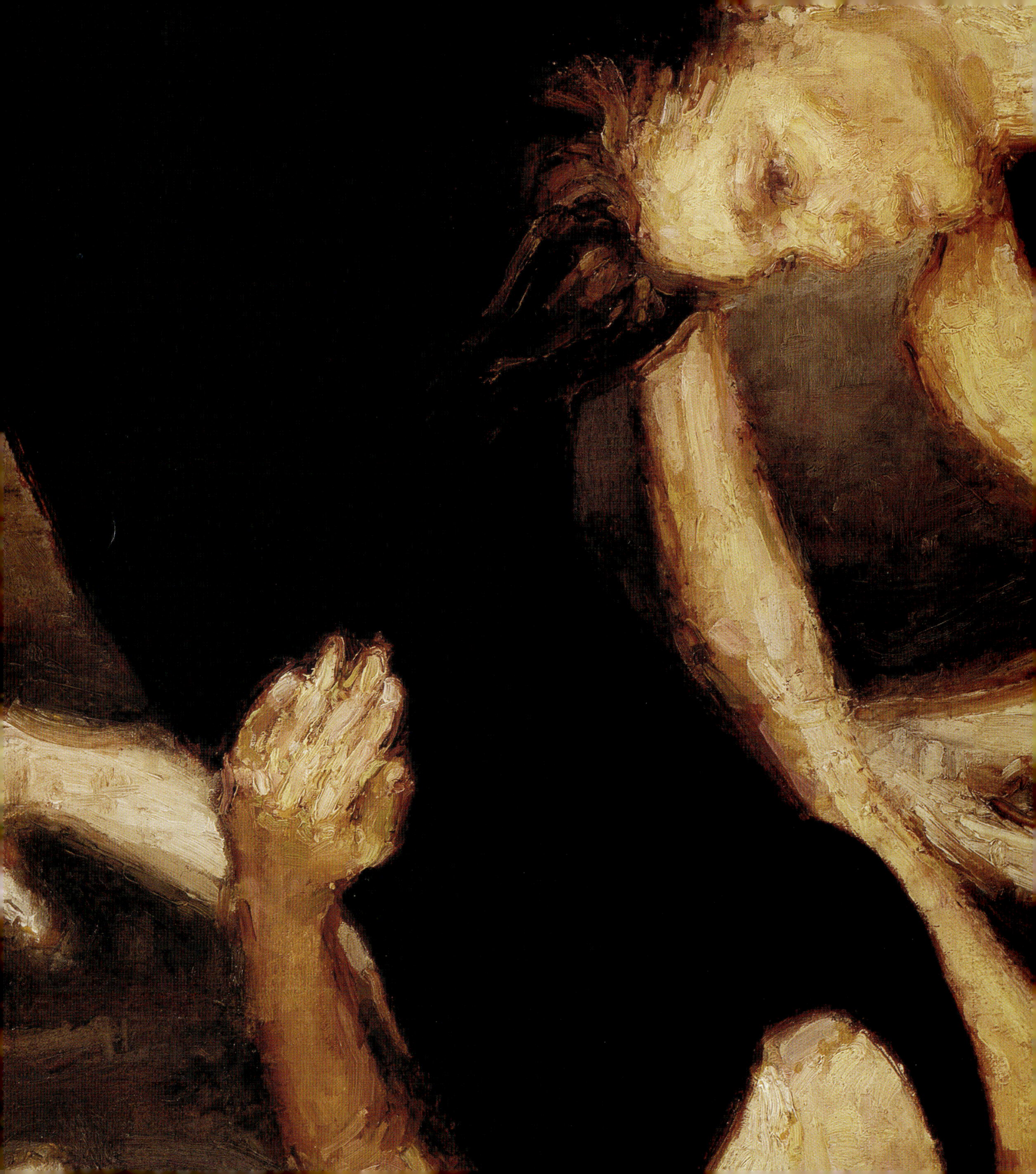

Tuesday

Tuesday
2003
Oil on Linen
51 x 34 in.

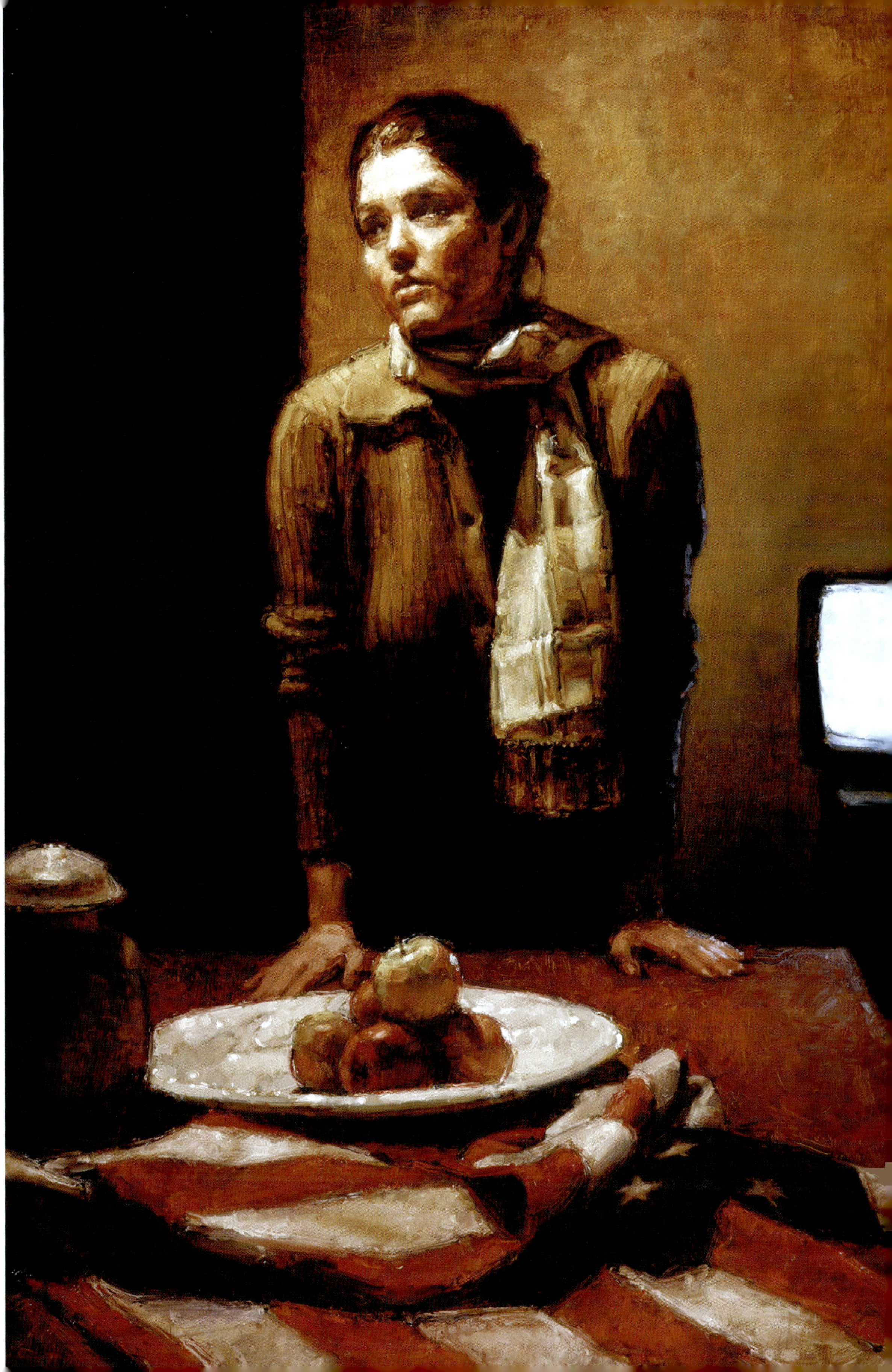

Guarding Destiny

Guarding Destiny
2006
Oil on Linen
64 x 50 in.

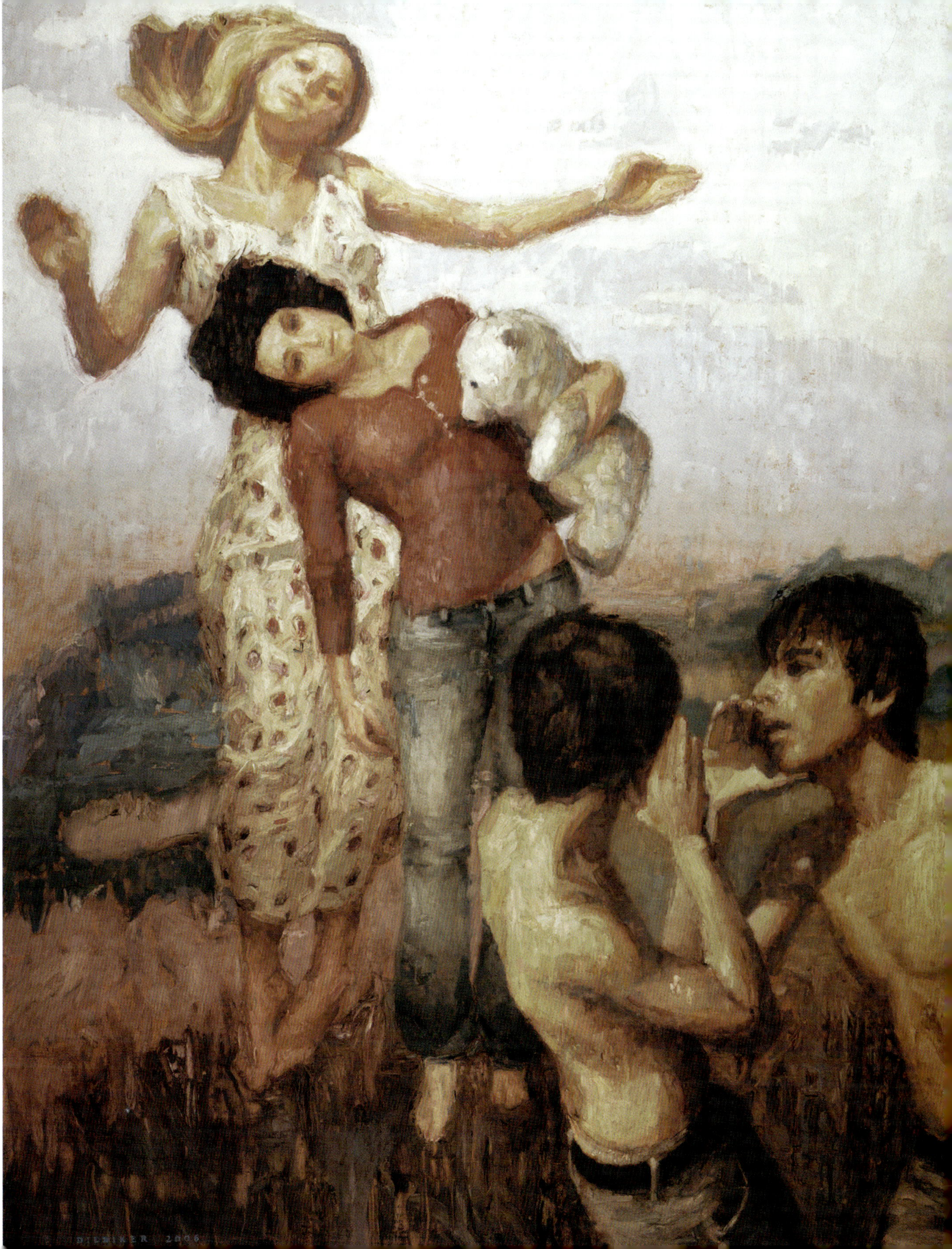

Red Chili

Red Chili
2005
Oil on Linen
30 x 20 in.

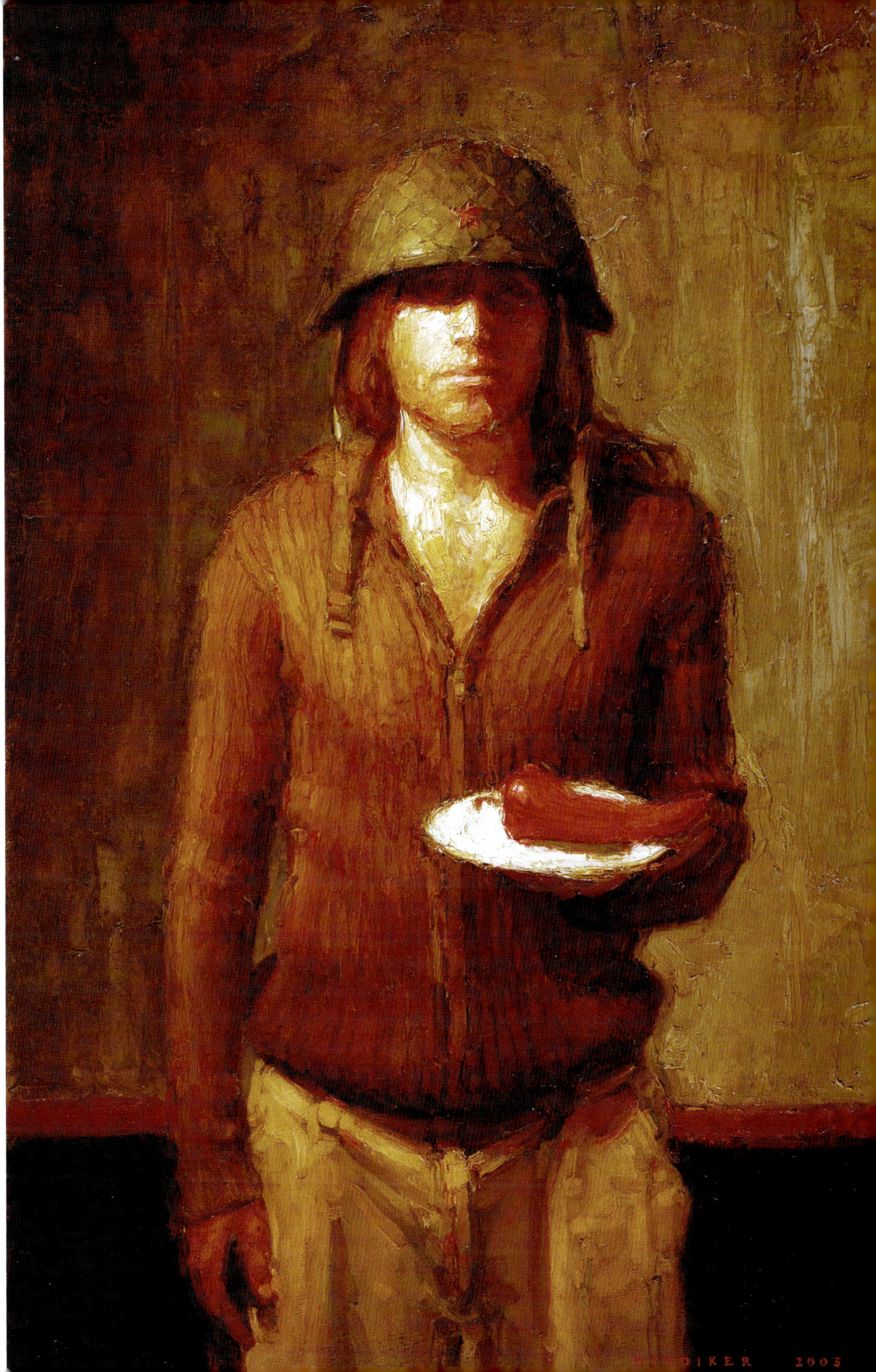

A Prayer for those in Traffic

A Prayer for those in Traffic
2007
Oil on Linen
24 x 16 in.

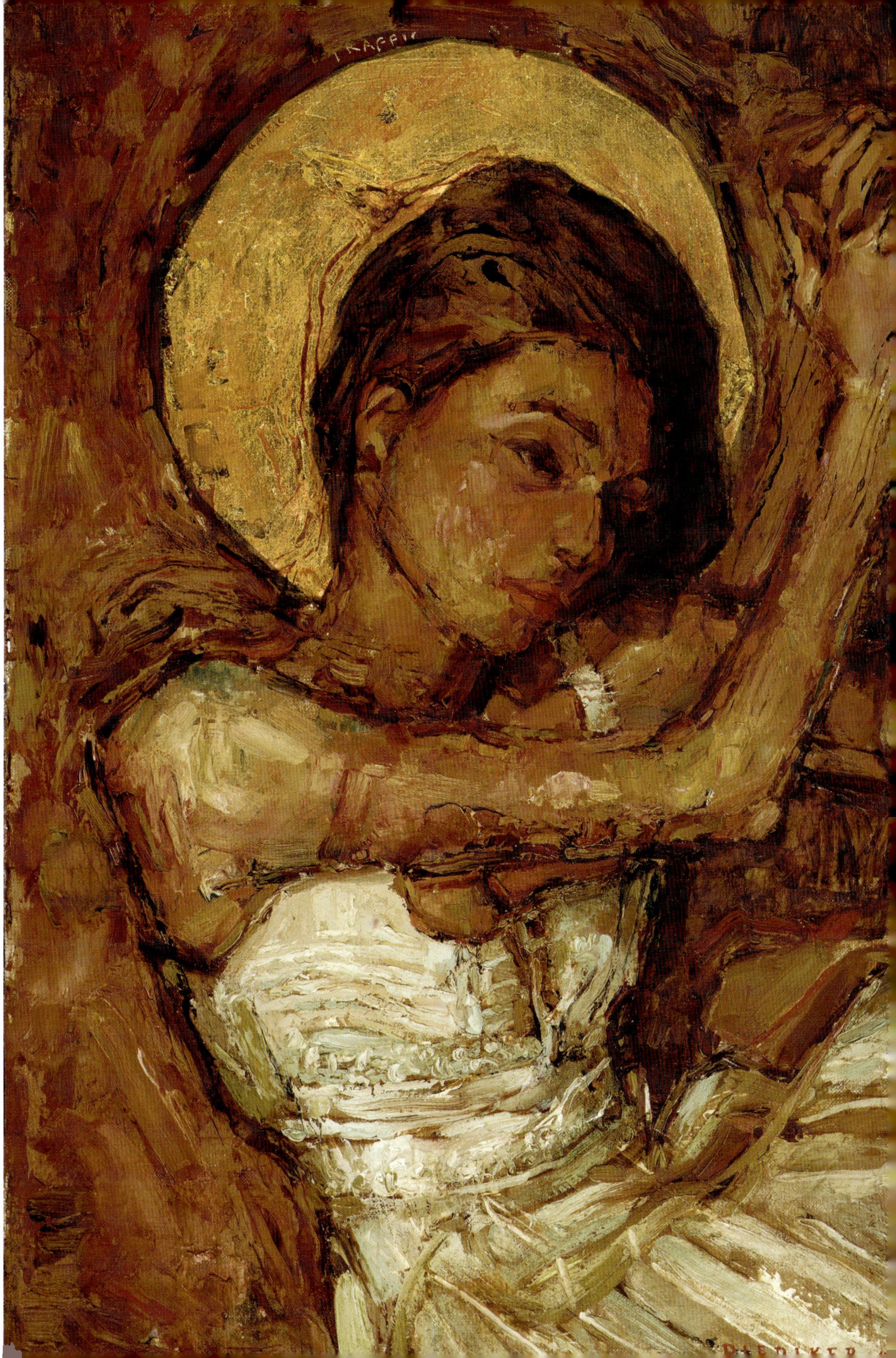

Ketchup

Ketchup
2003
Oil on Linen
60 x 50 in.

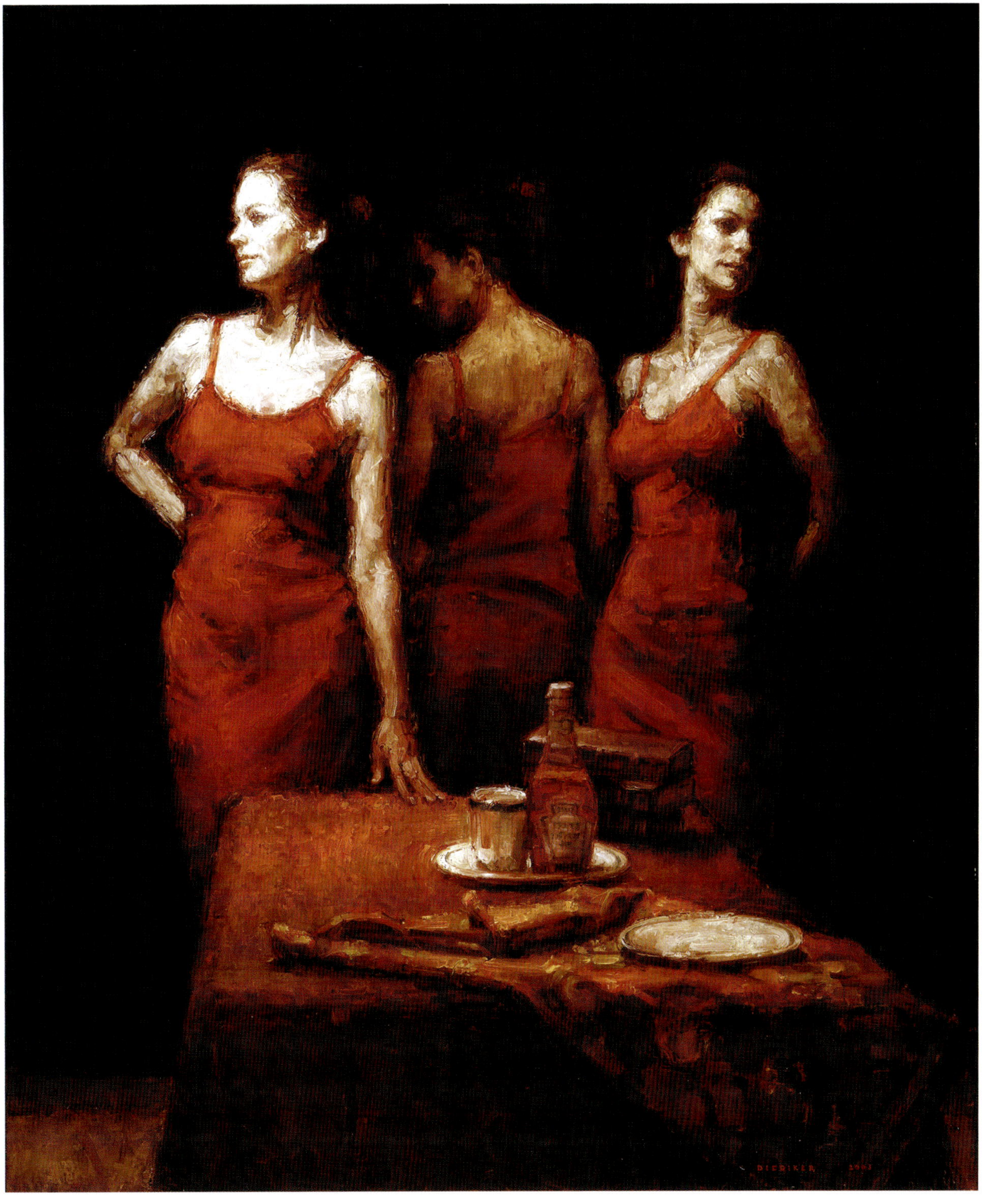

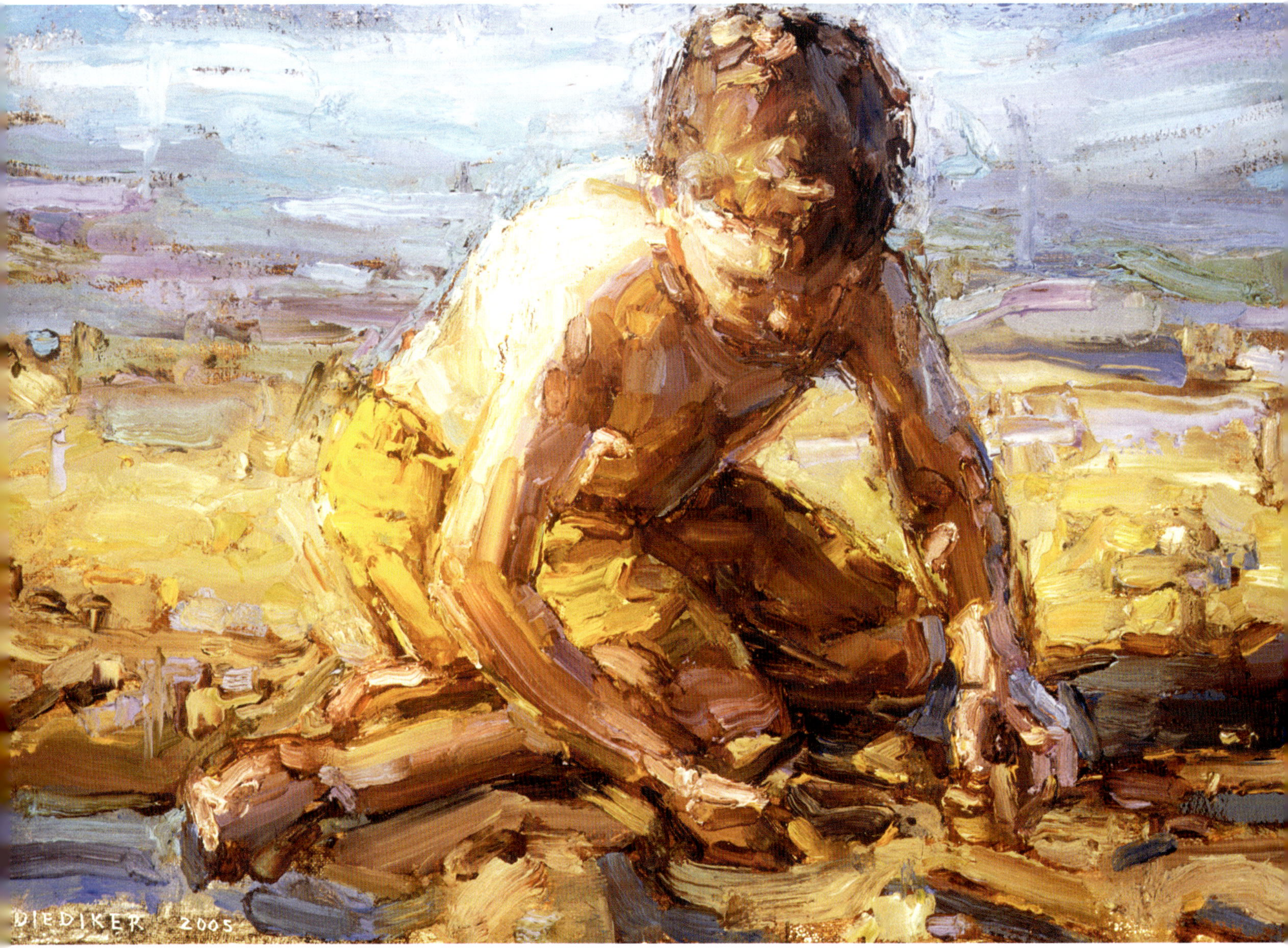

Boy Digging in Sand
2005
Oil on Linen
11.5 x 15 in.

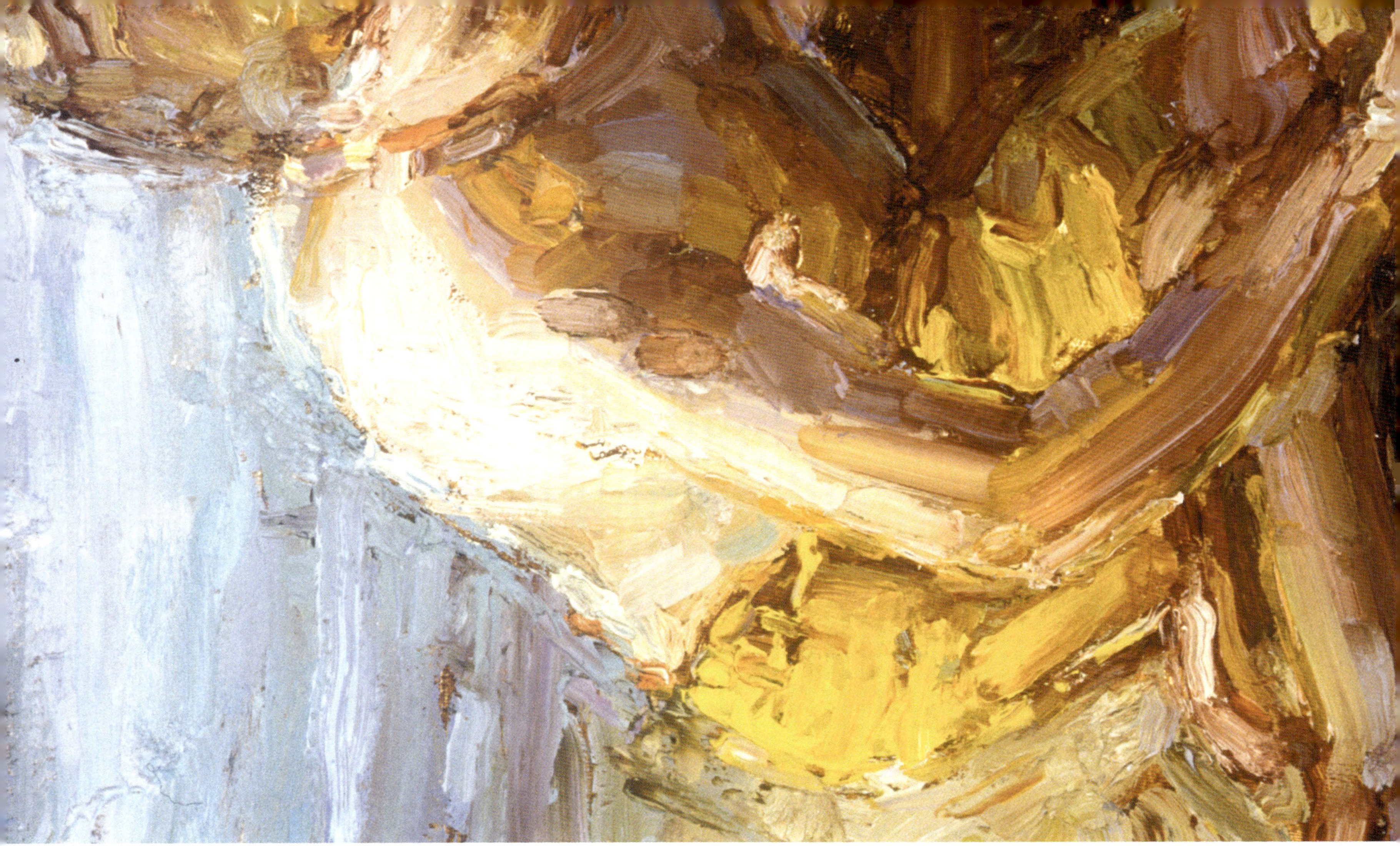

Boy Digging in Sand

Tim

Tim 2003
Oil on Linen
36 x 22 in.

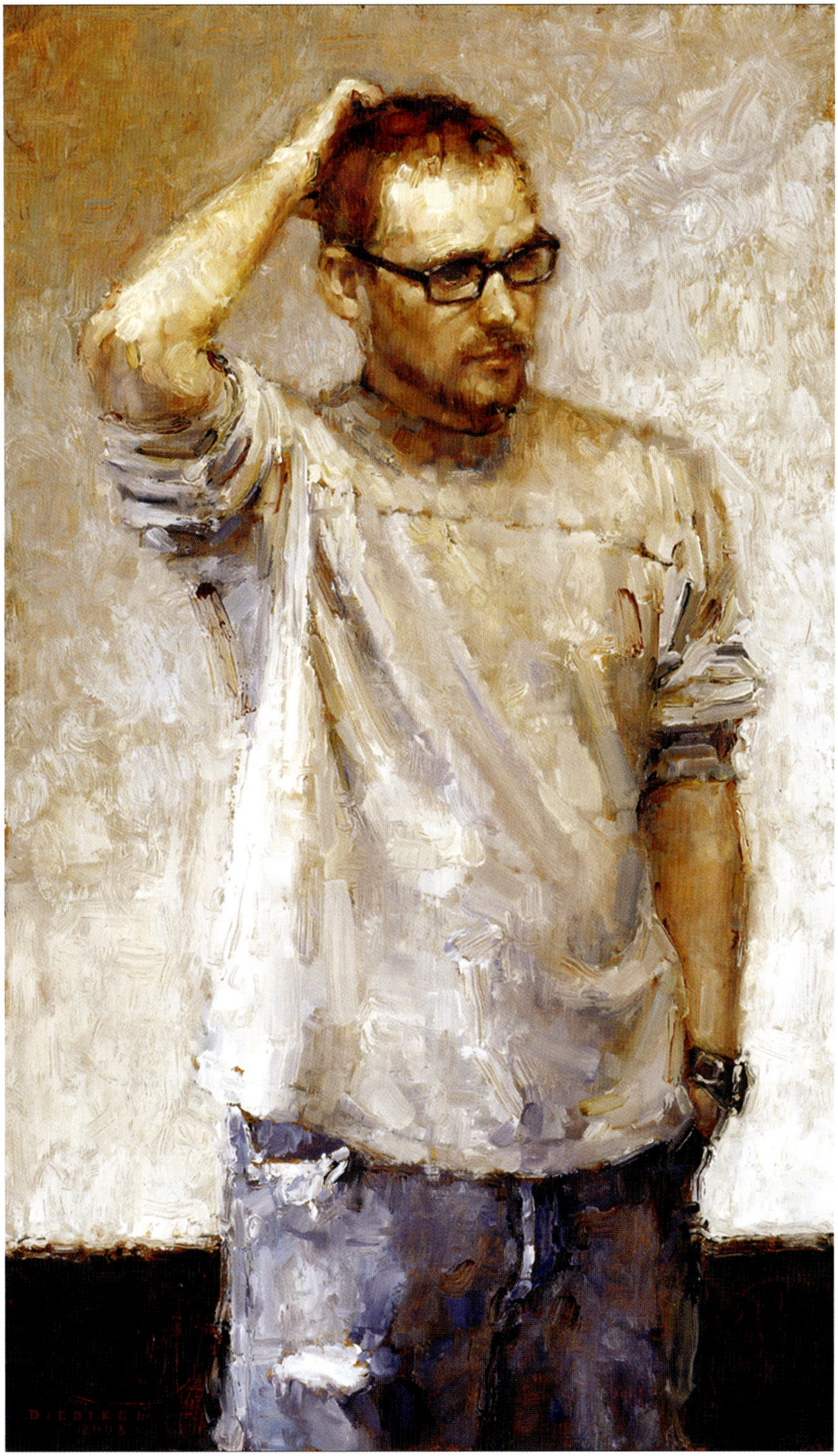

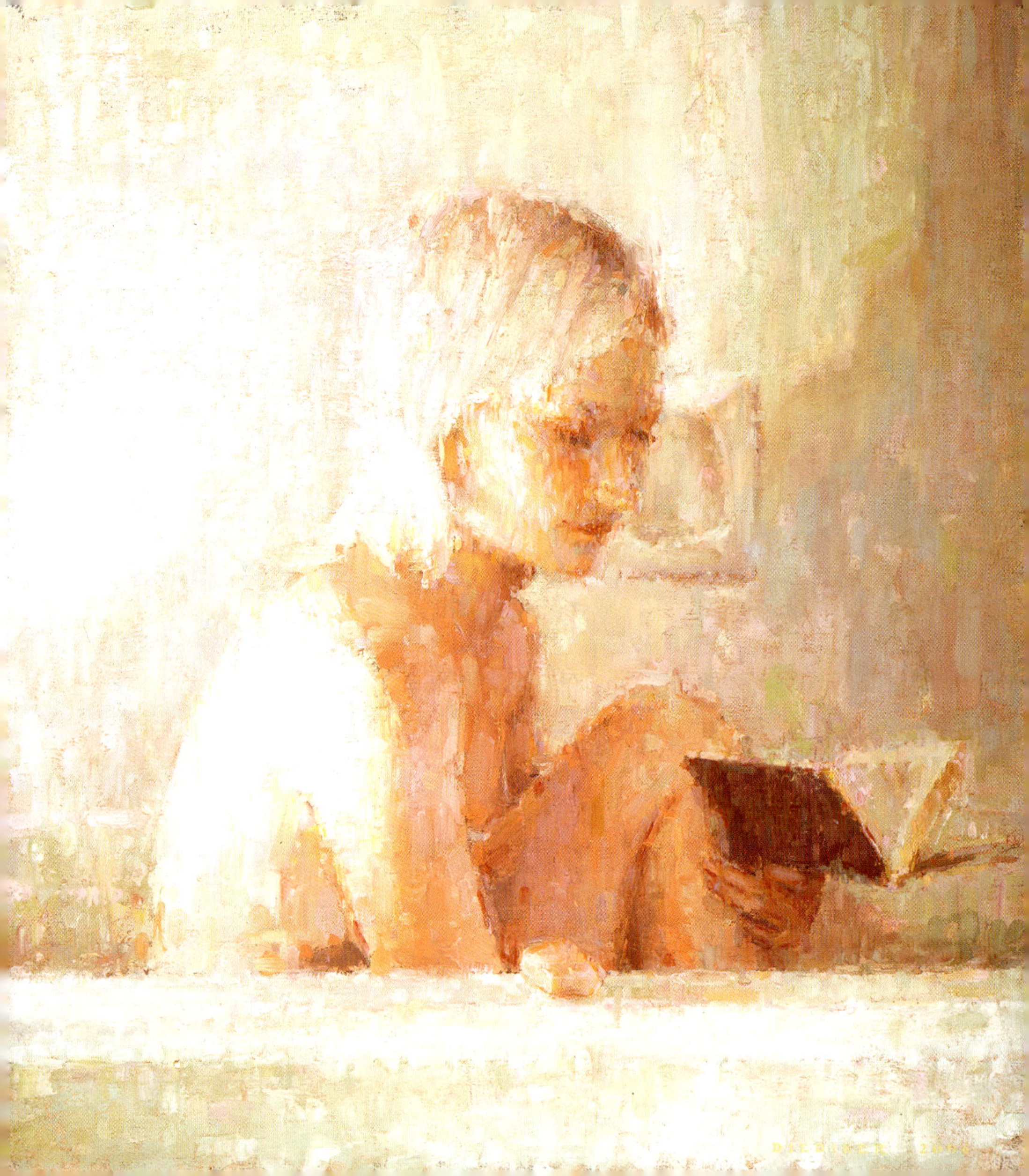

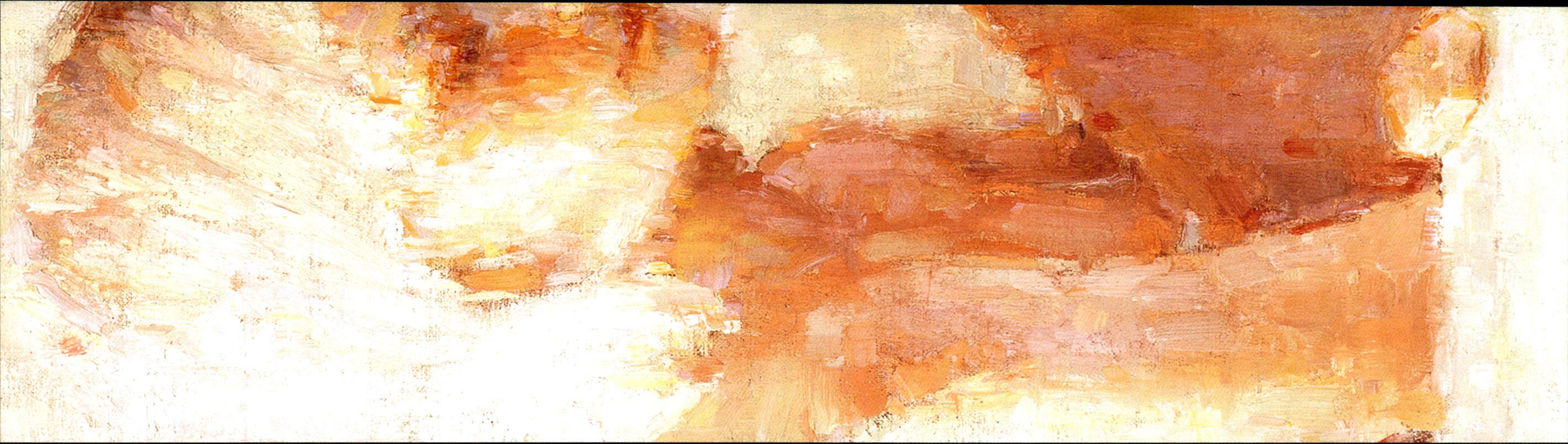

The Bath

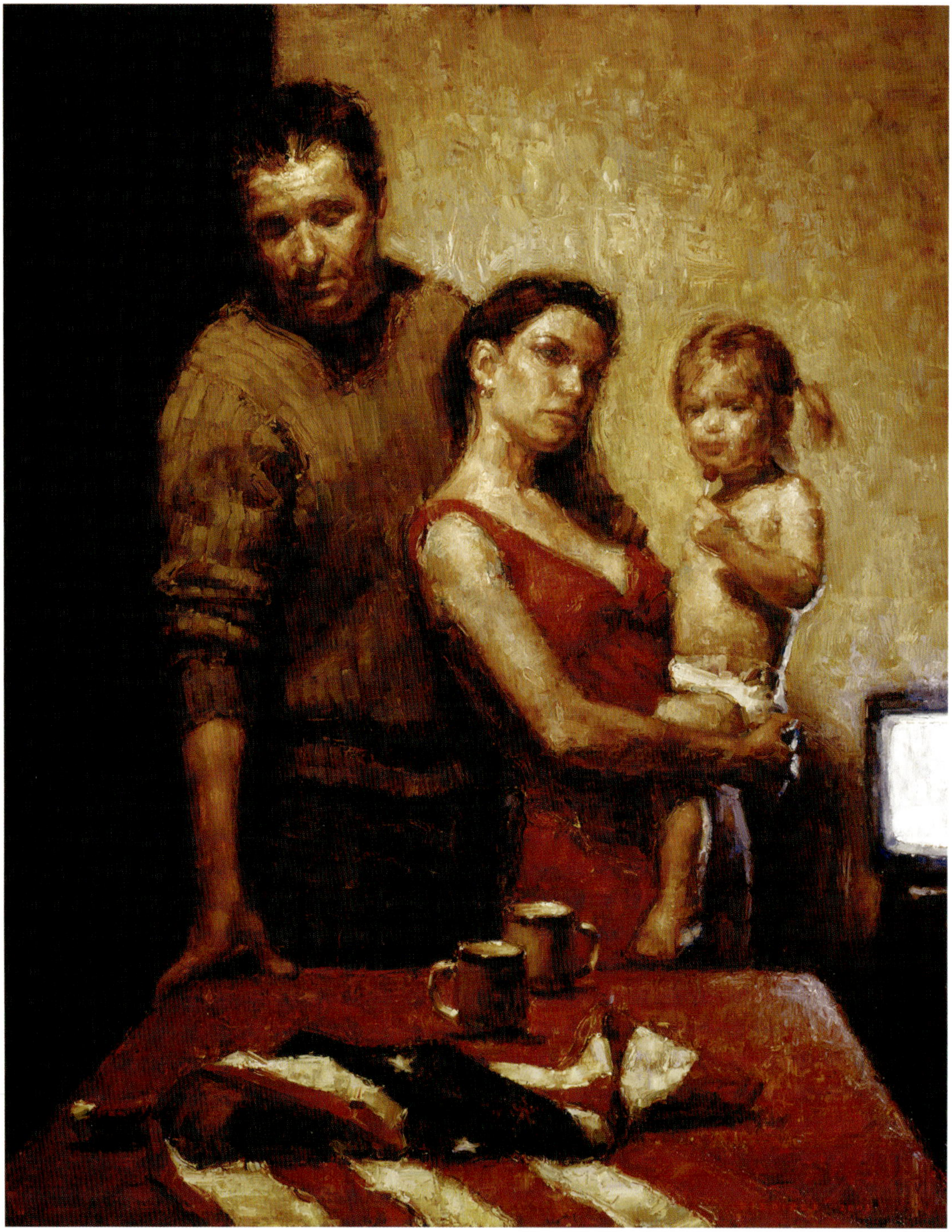

Tuesday II
2003
Oil on Linen
50 x 40 in.

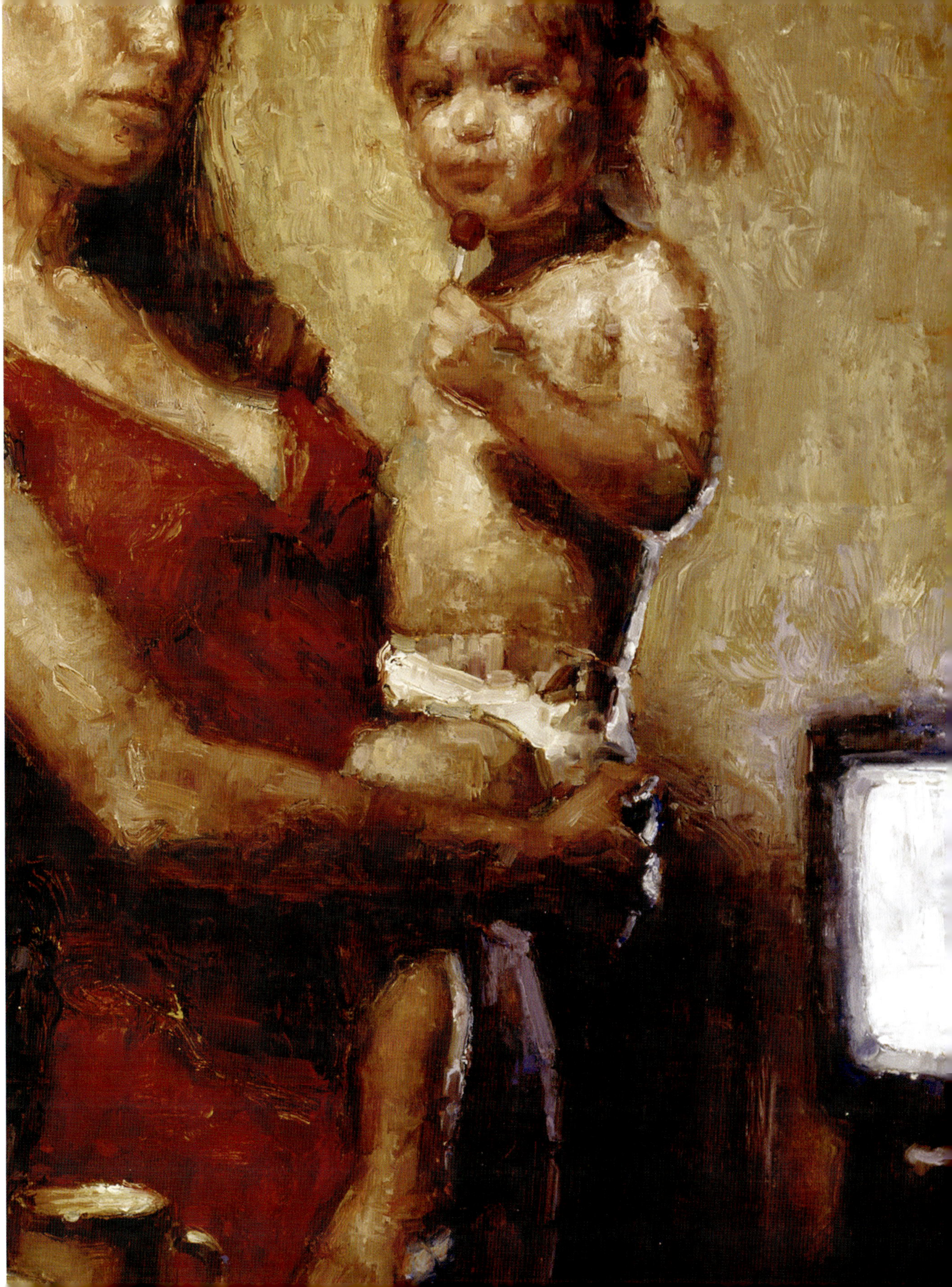

Sunday Afternoon

Sunday Afternoon 2005
Oil on Linen
30 x 27 in.

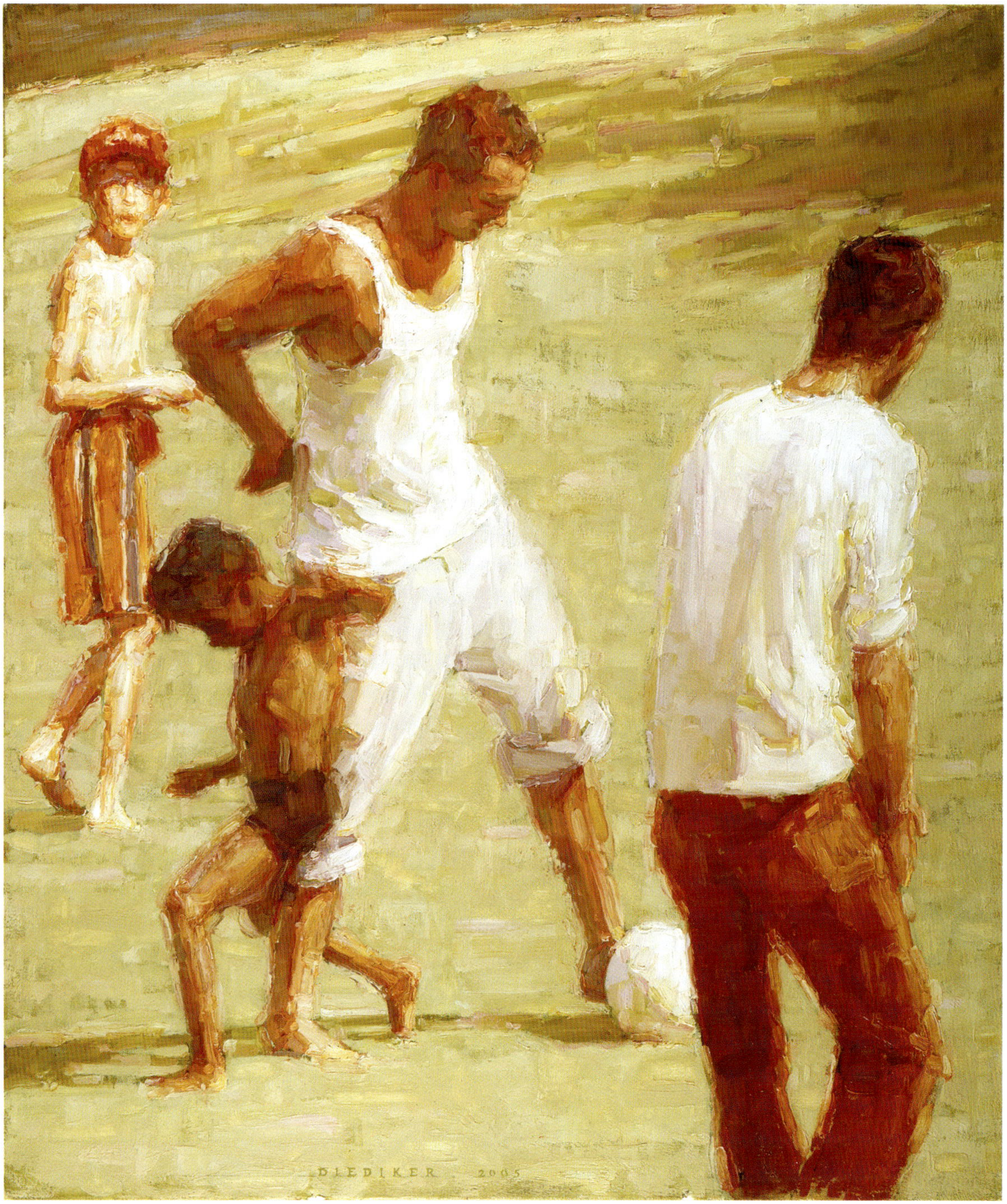
DIEDIKER 2005

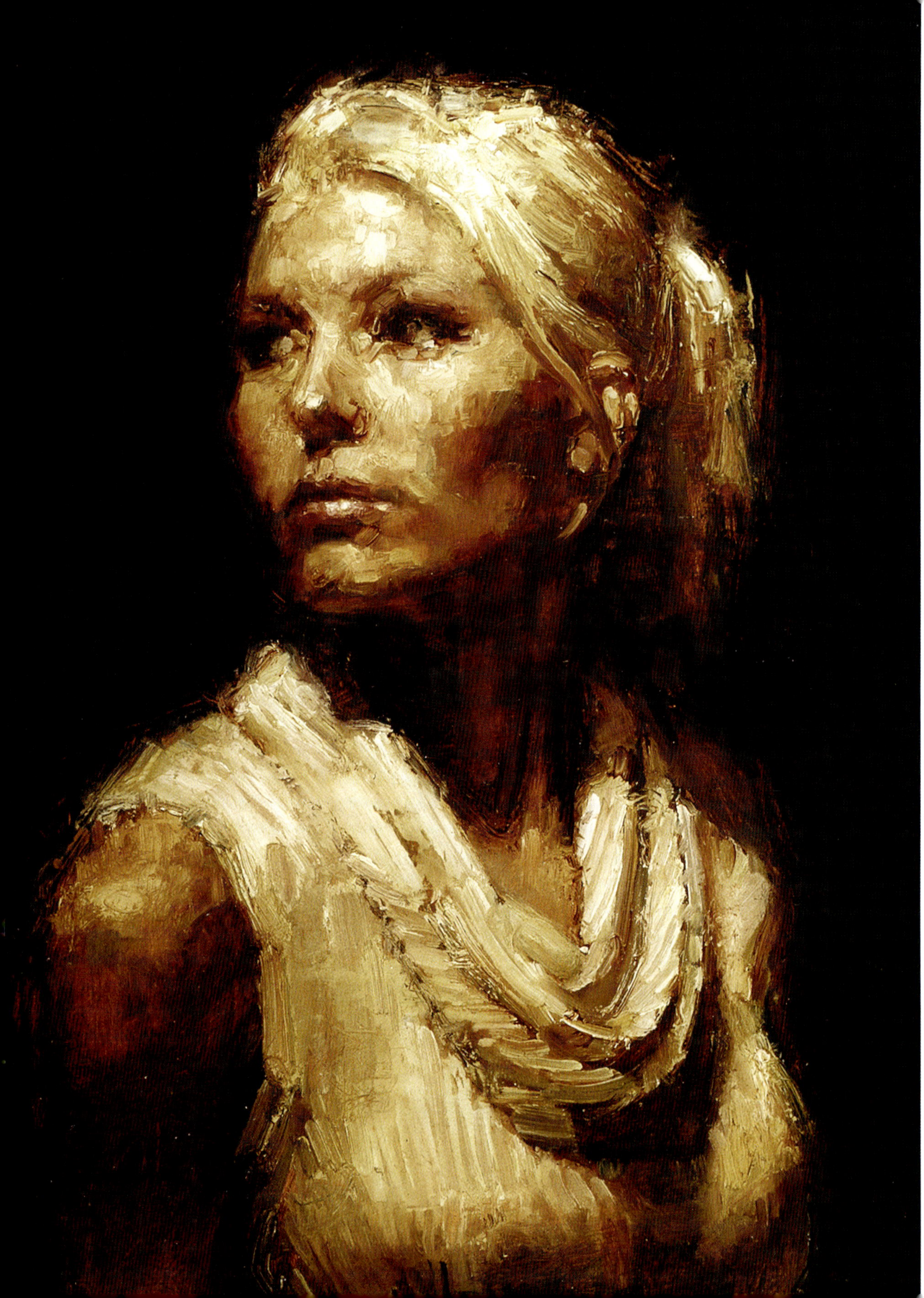

Evans Sisters
2003
Oil on Linen
50 x 36 in.

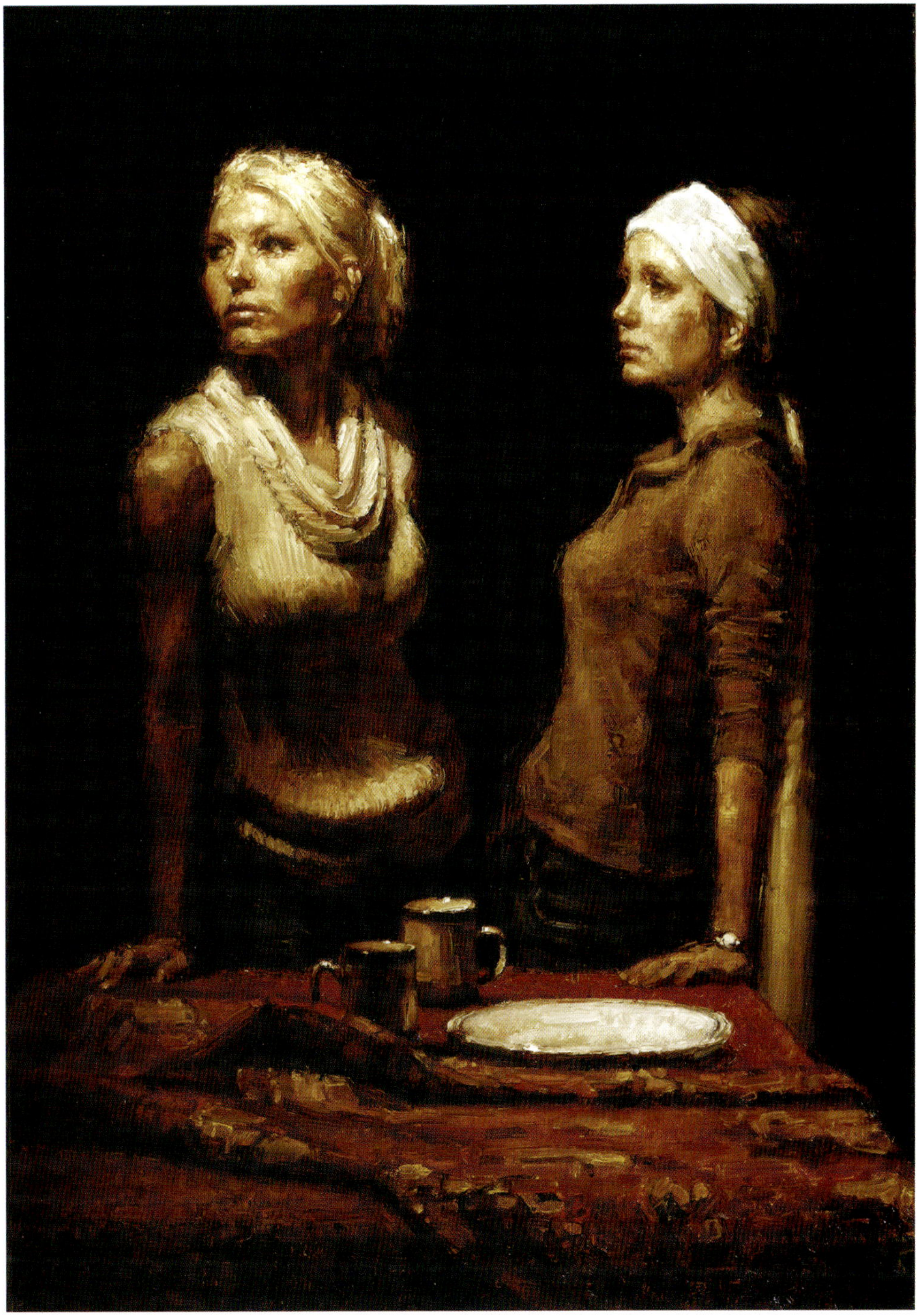

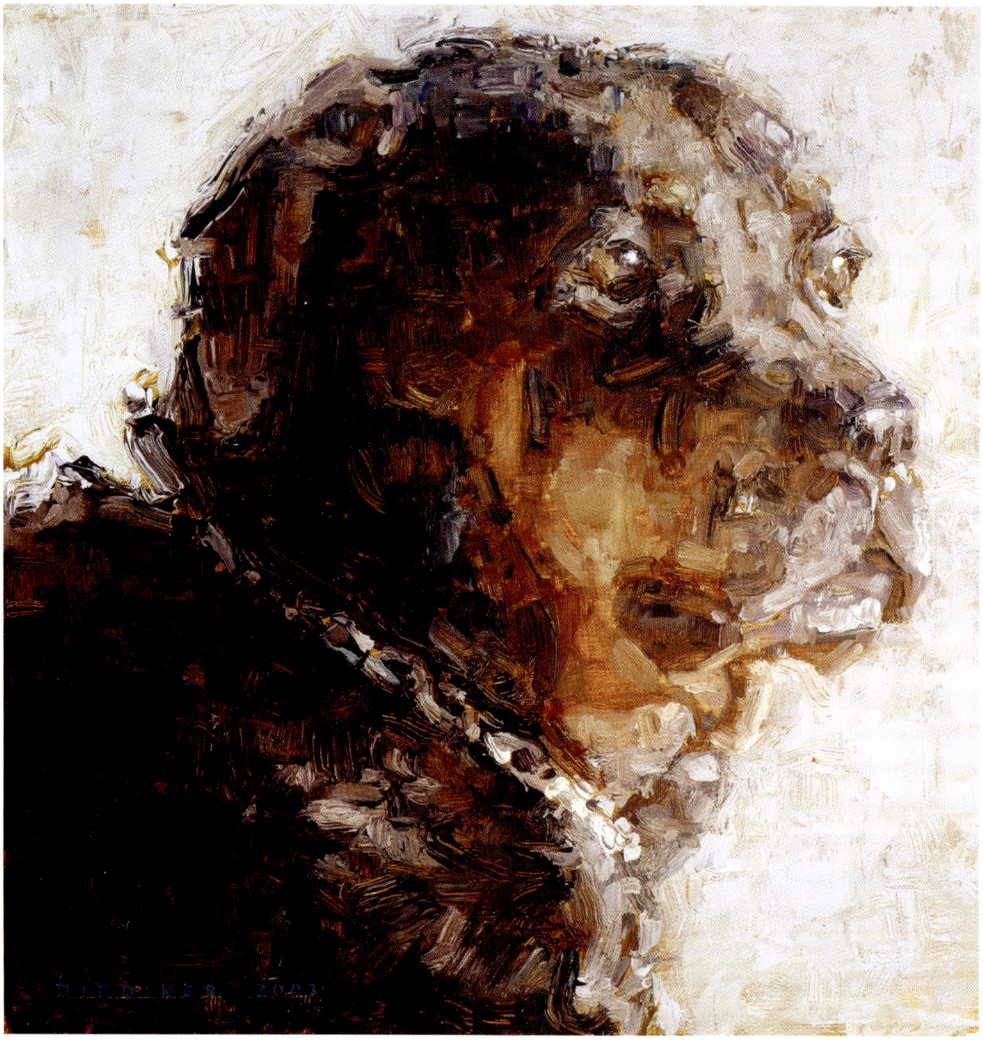

My Dog has Cancer
2003
Oil on Linen
13 x 12.5 in.

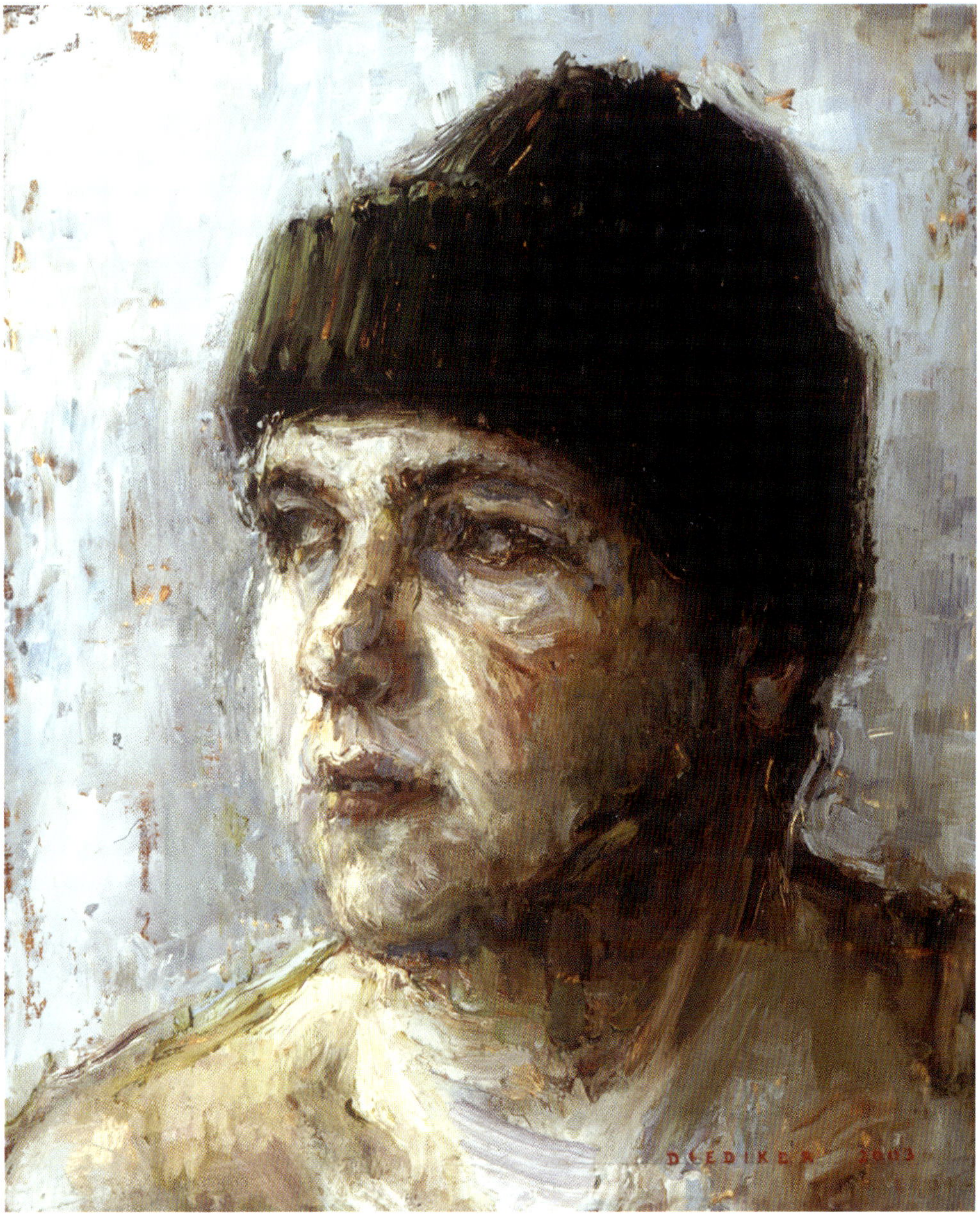

Jason
2003
Oil on Linen
13 x 11 in

Molly

Molly
2005
Oil on Linen
36 x 27 in.

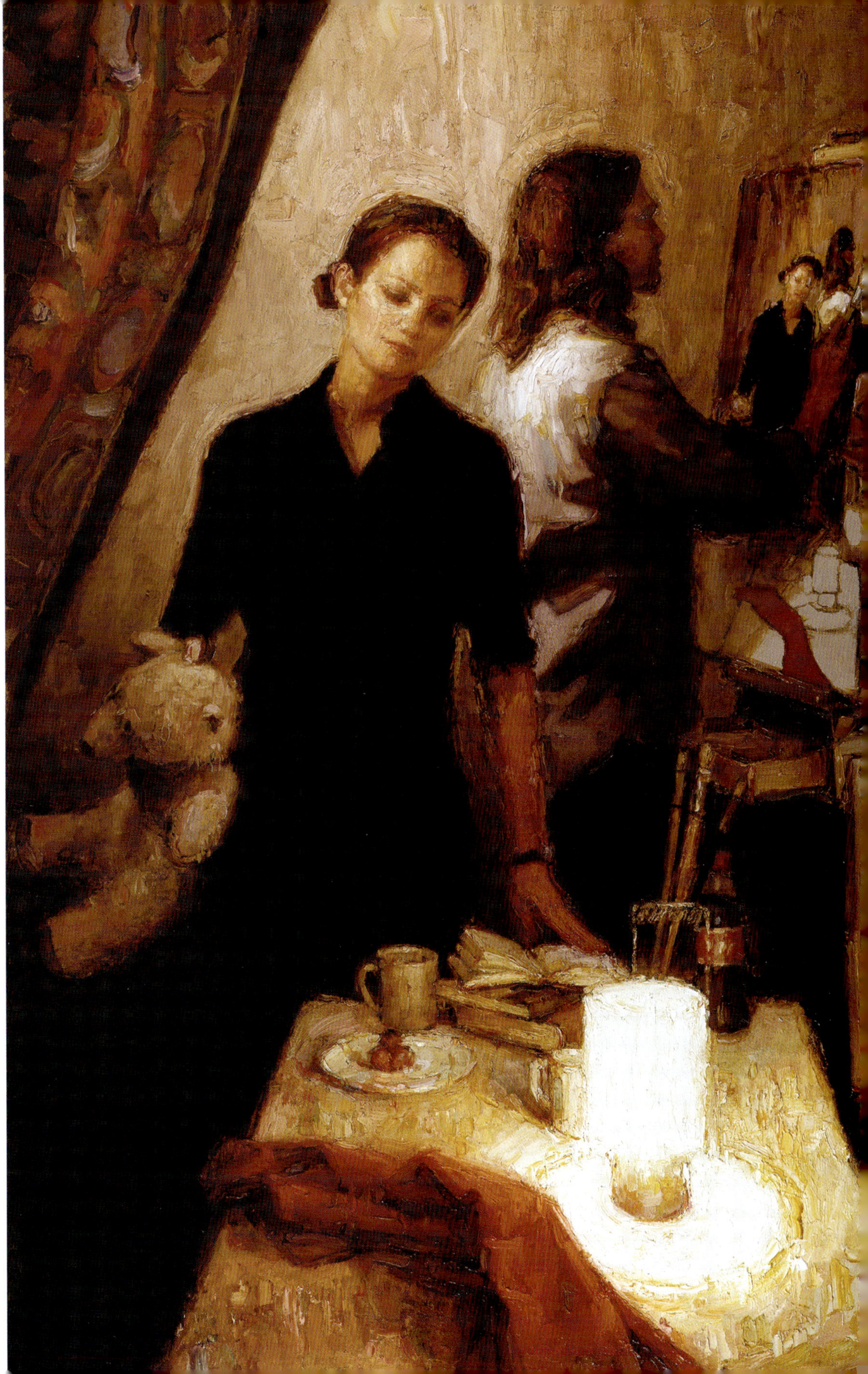

The Fall of Mr. Peepers

The Fall of Mr. Peepers
2006
Oil on Linen
50 x 34 in.

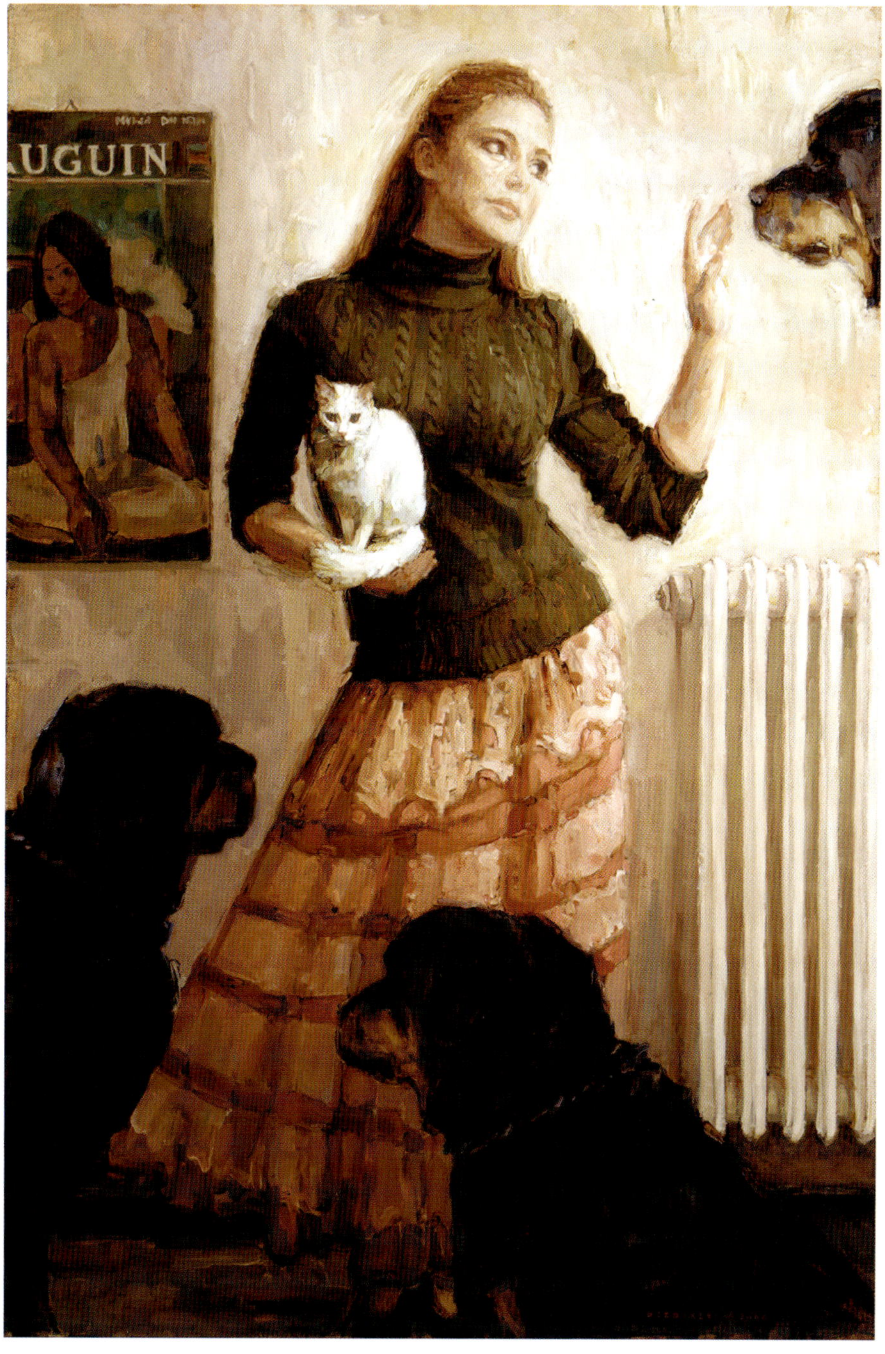
AUGUIN

Emily on Couch

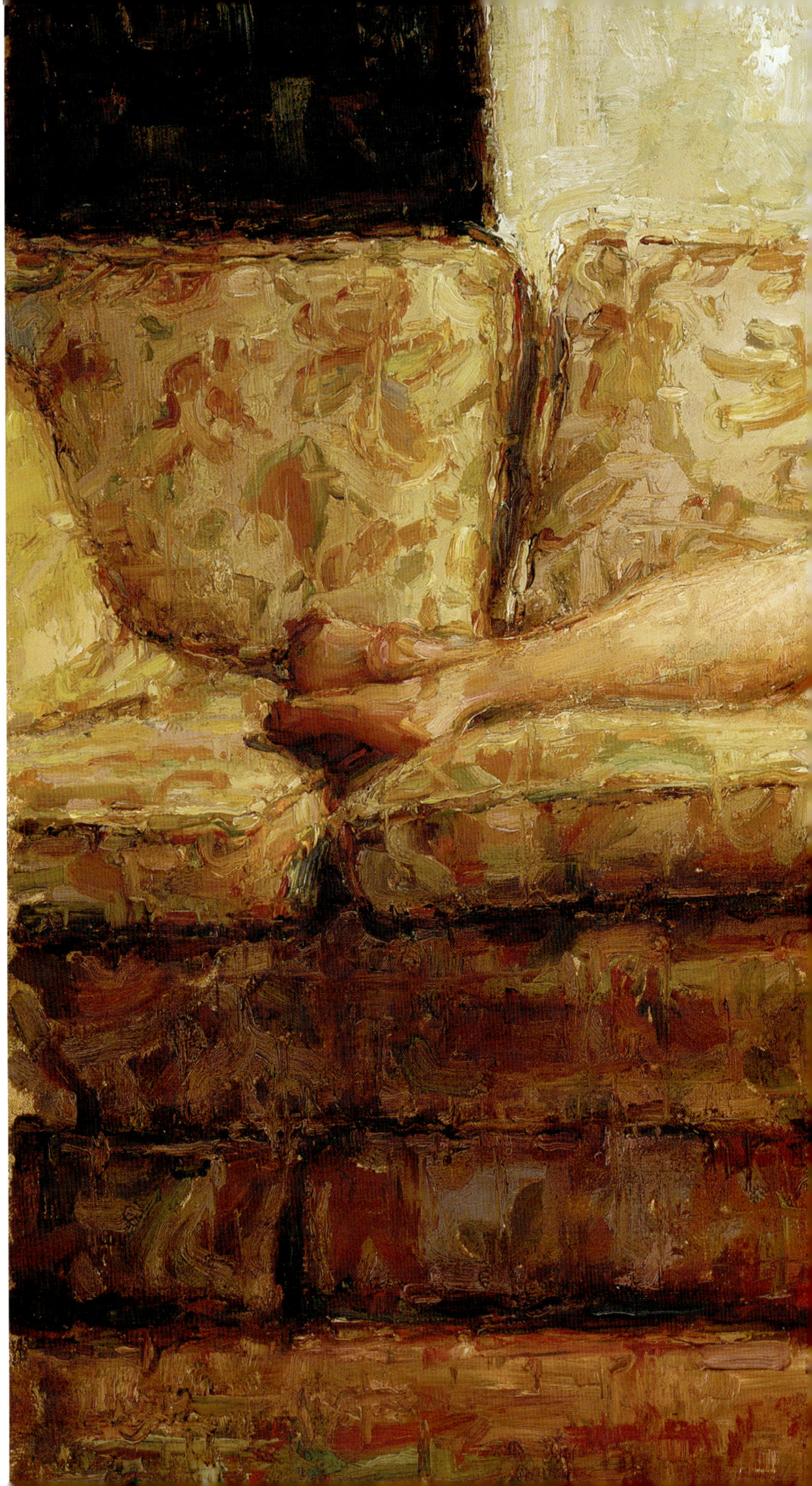

Emily on Couch 2005
Oil on Linen
27 x 33 in.

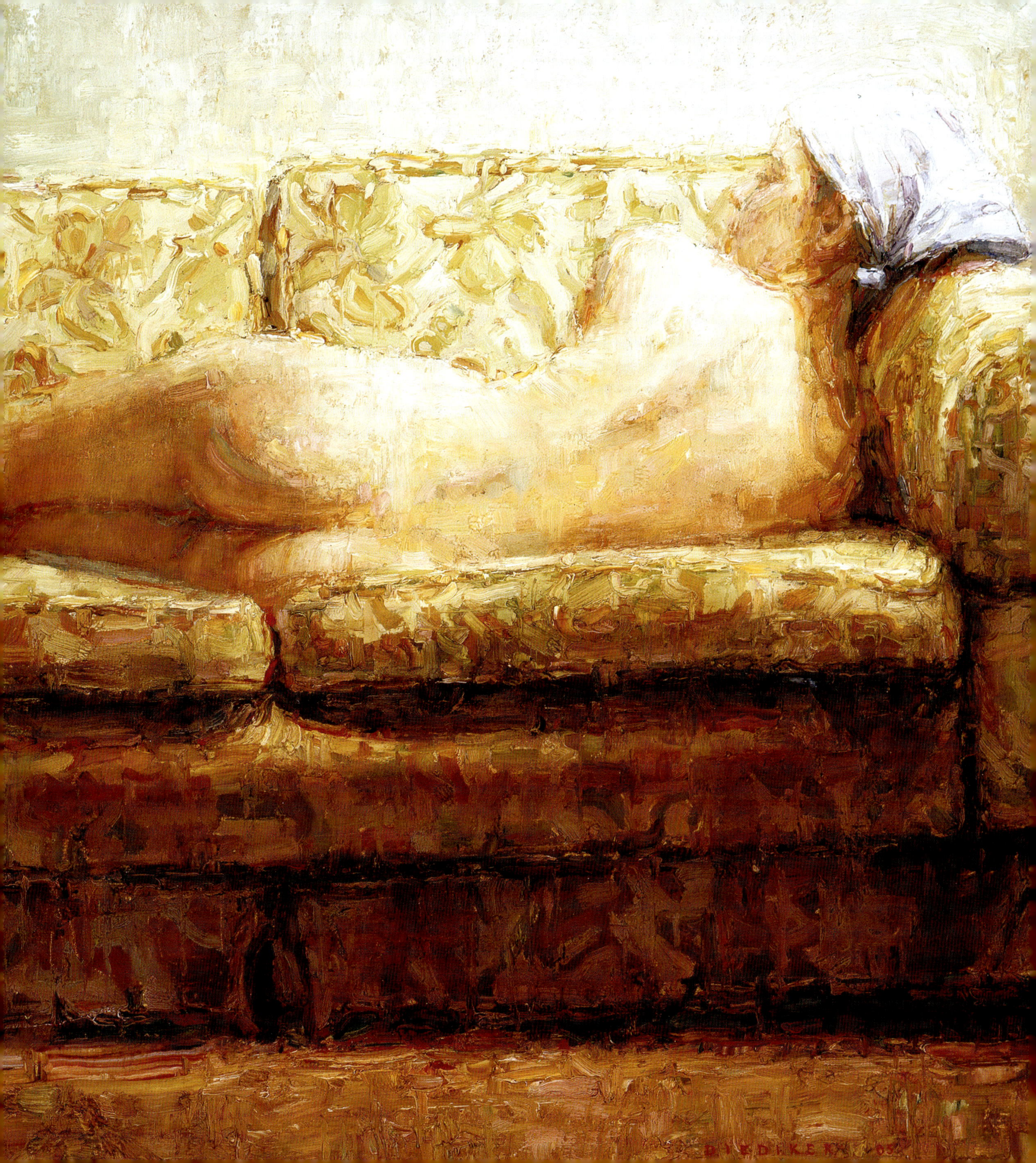

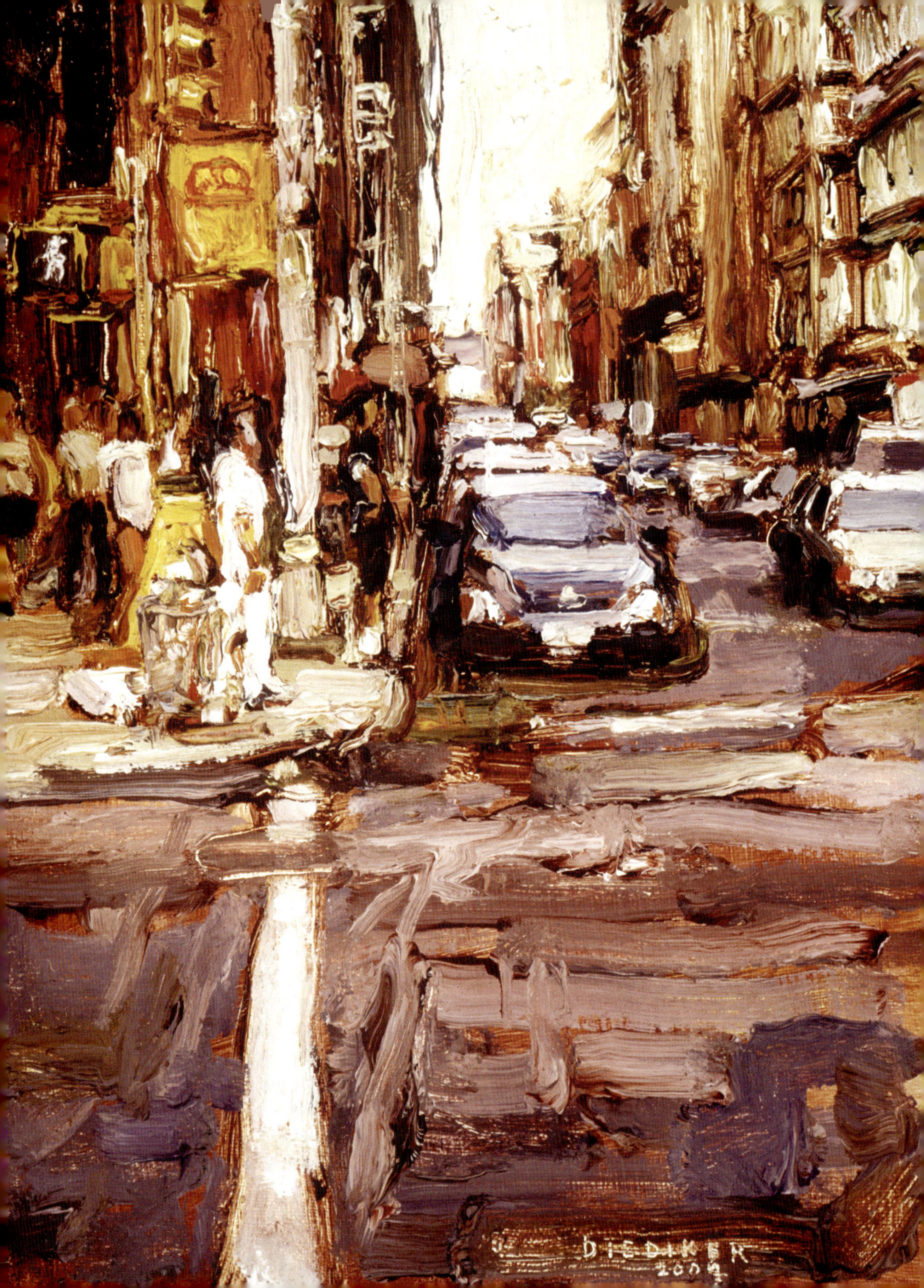

East on Canal

East on Canal
2004
Oil on Linen
12 x 9 in.

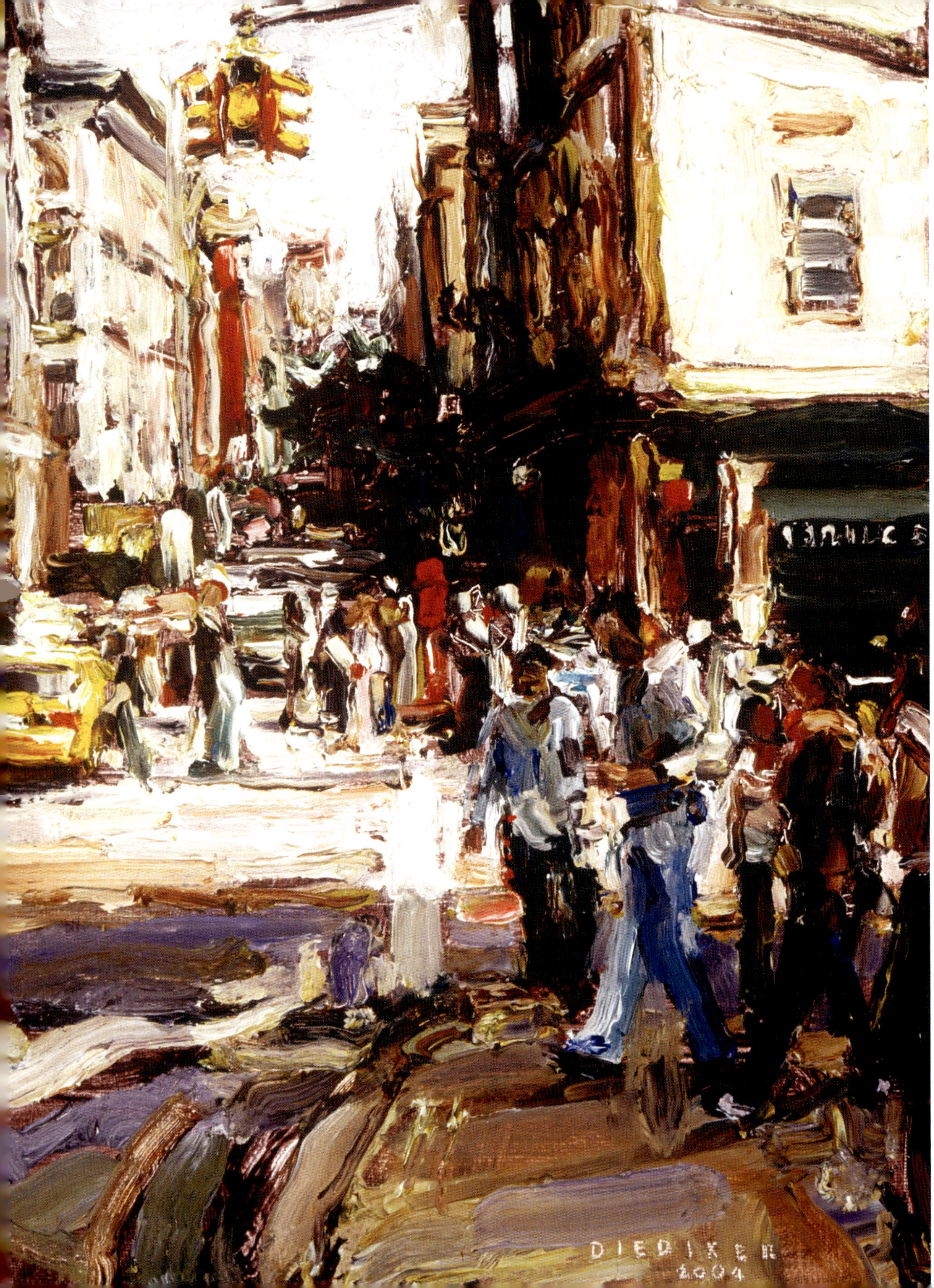
DIEDIKER
2004

Ben’s Pizza

Ben’s Pizza
2004
Oil on Linen
12 x 9 in.

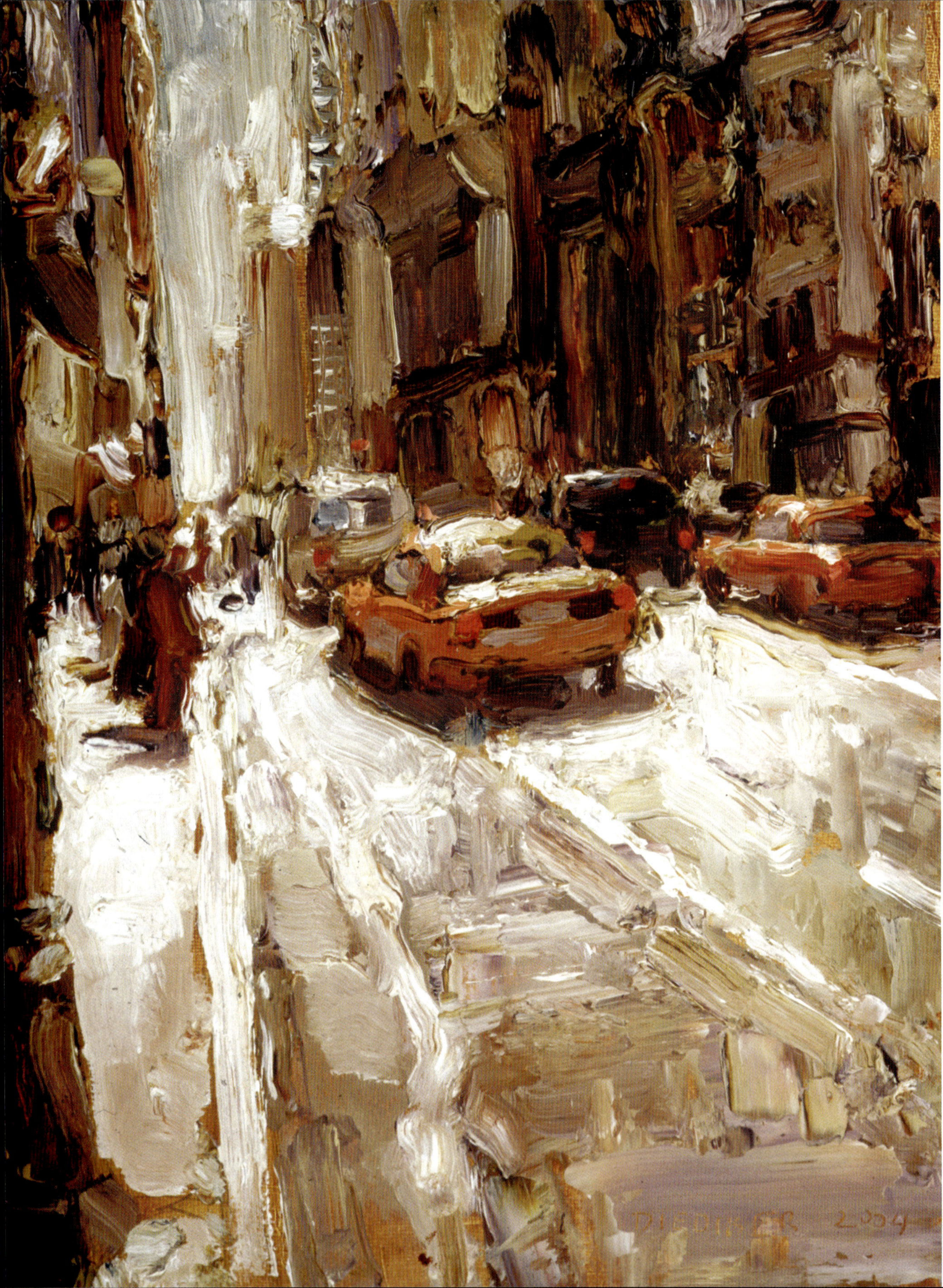
DIEDINER 2004

Cab on 5th

Cab on 5th
2004
Oil on Linen
12 x 9 in.

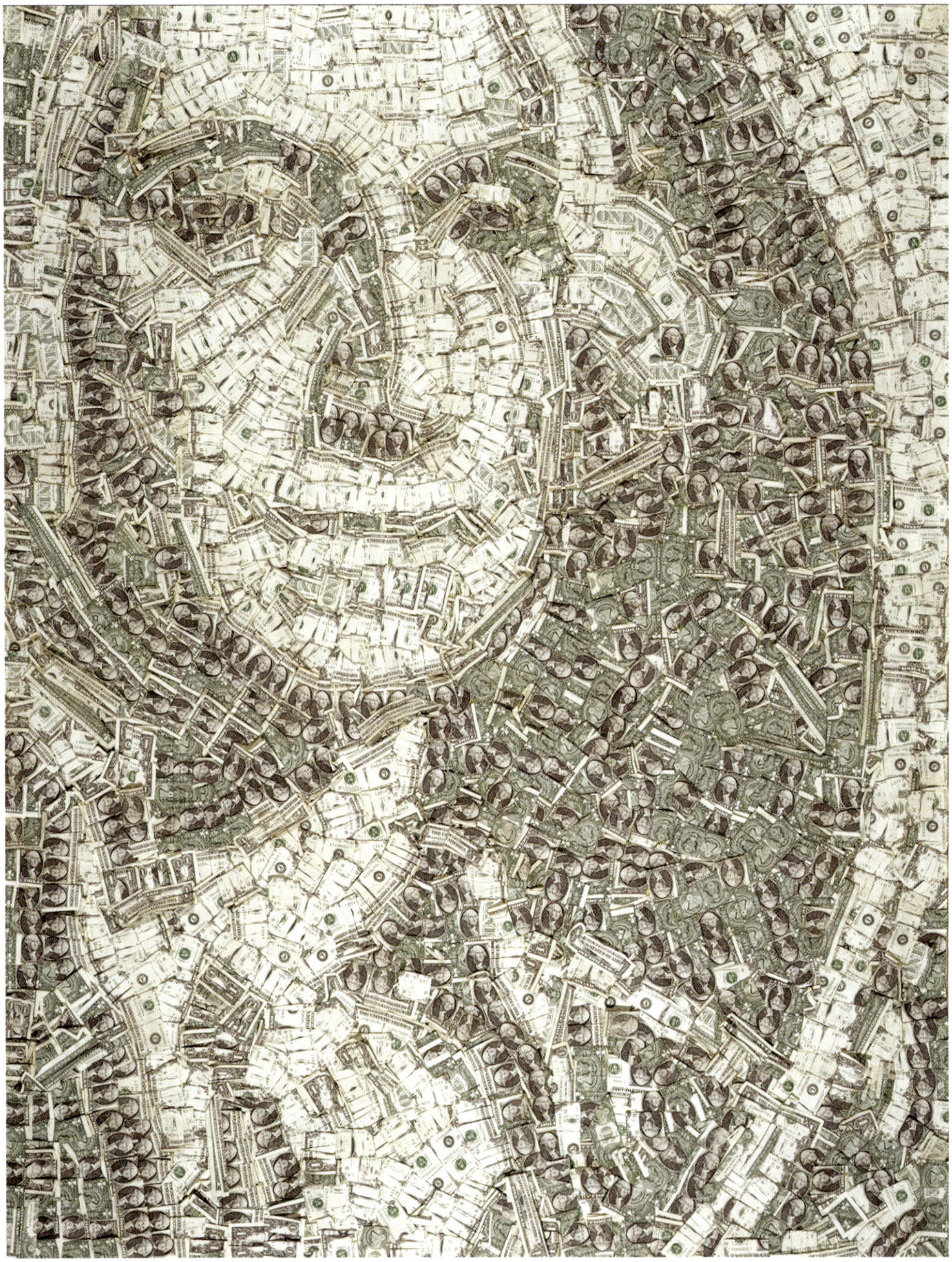

Washington 2005
US currency on Linen
64 x 51 in.

Washington

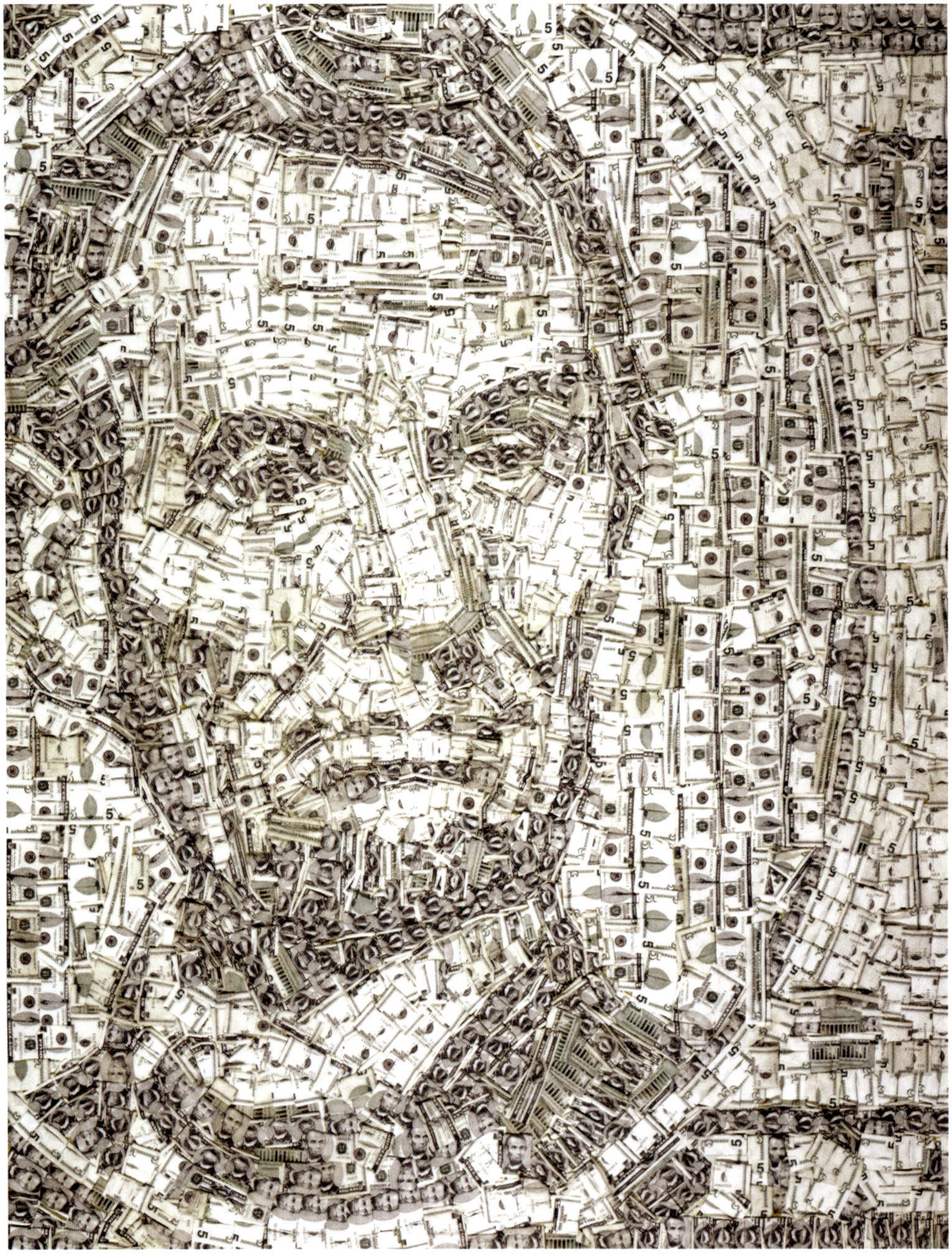

Lincoln 2007
US currency on Linen
64 x 51 in.

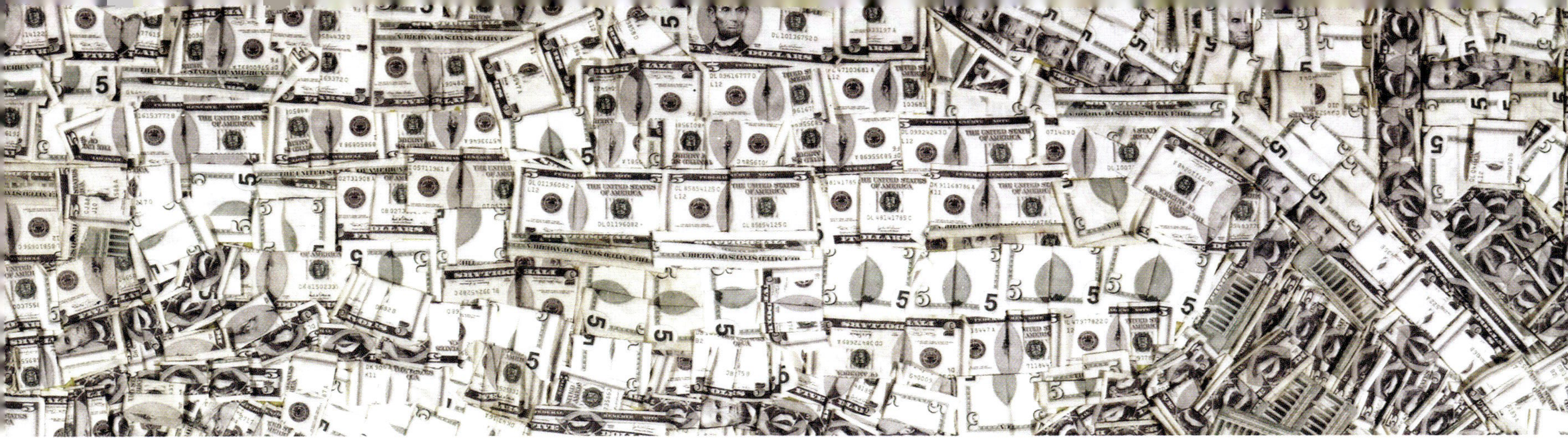

Lincoln

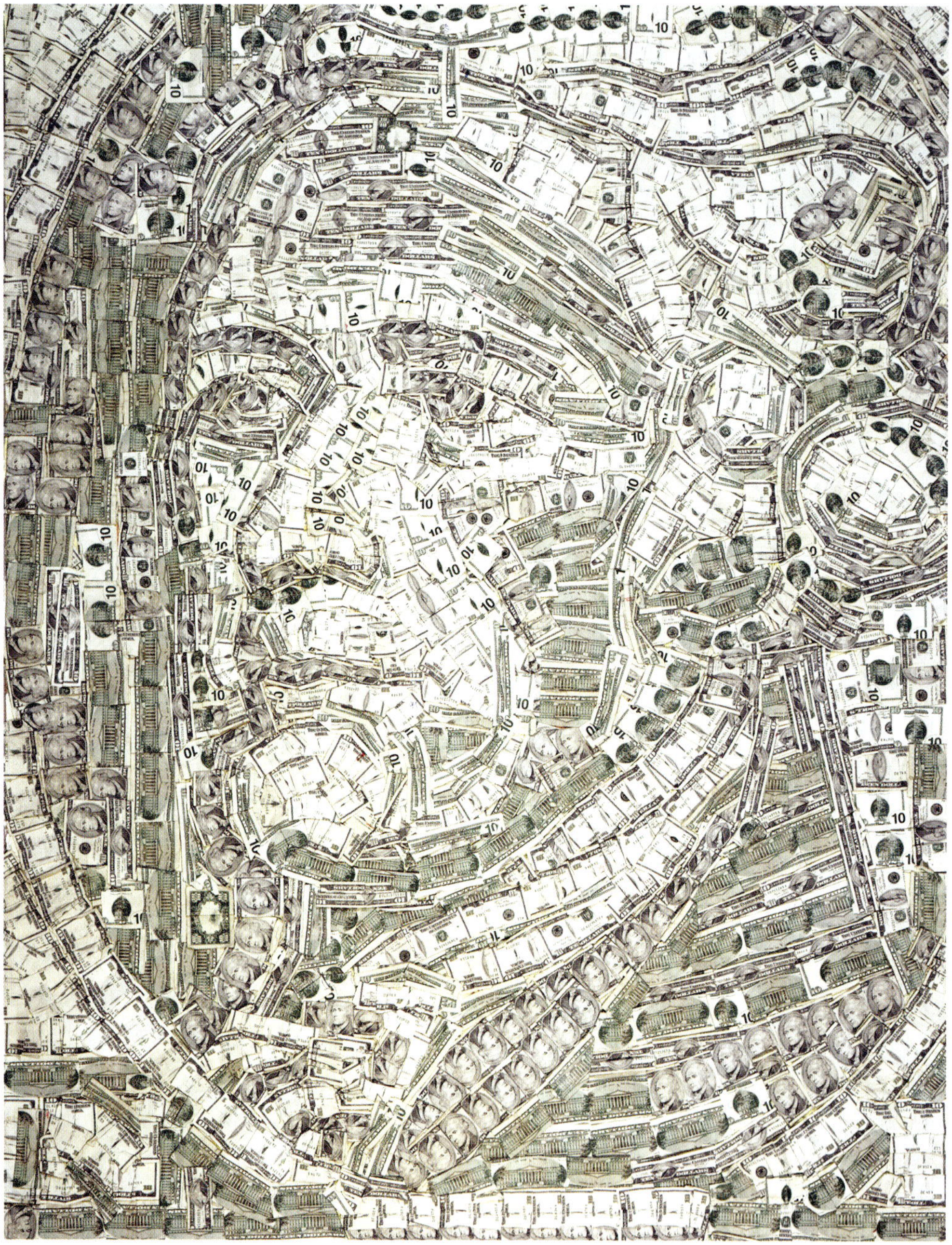

Hamilton 2008
US currency on Linen
64 x 51 in.

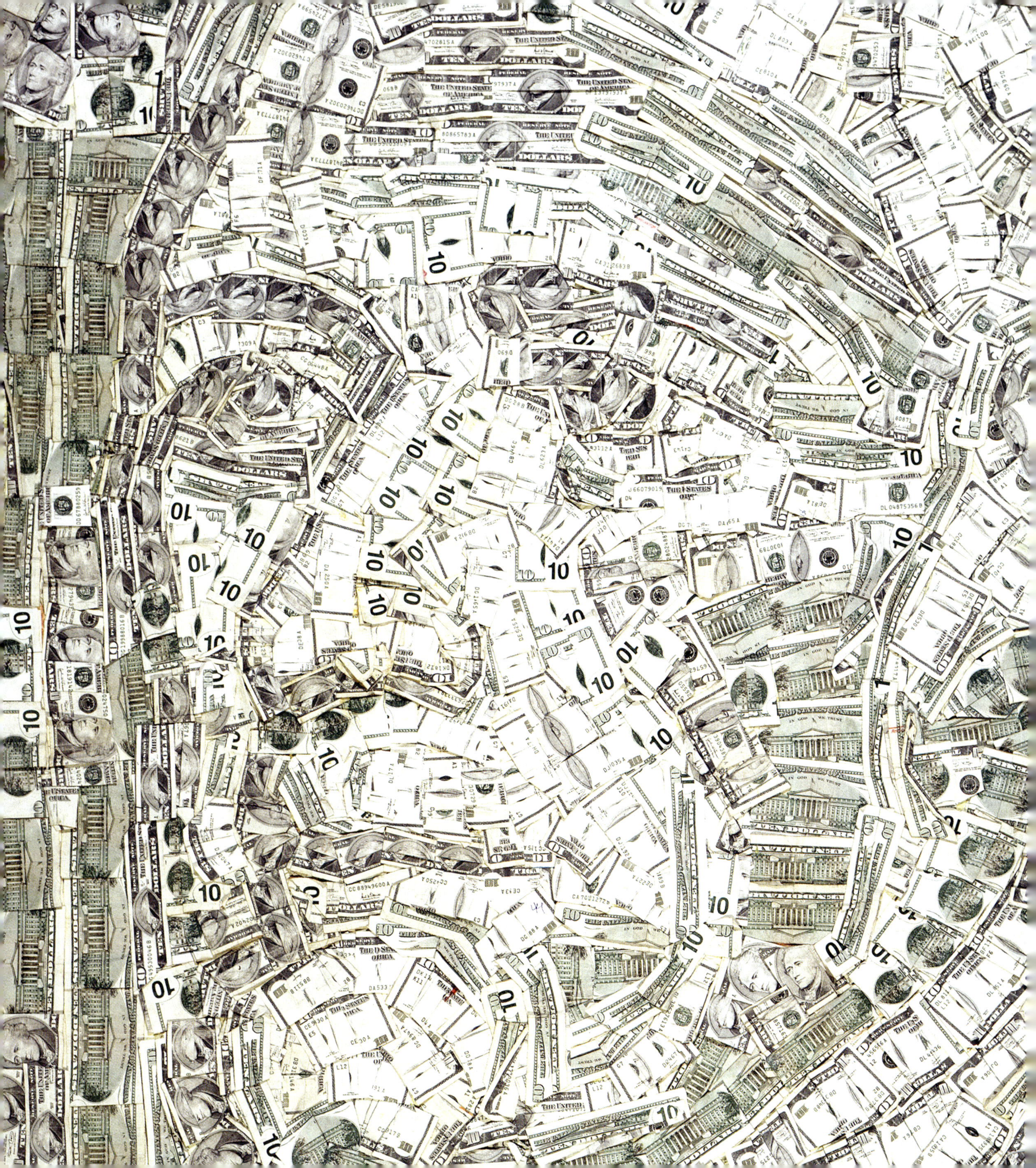

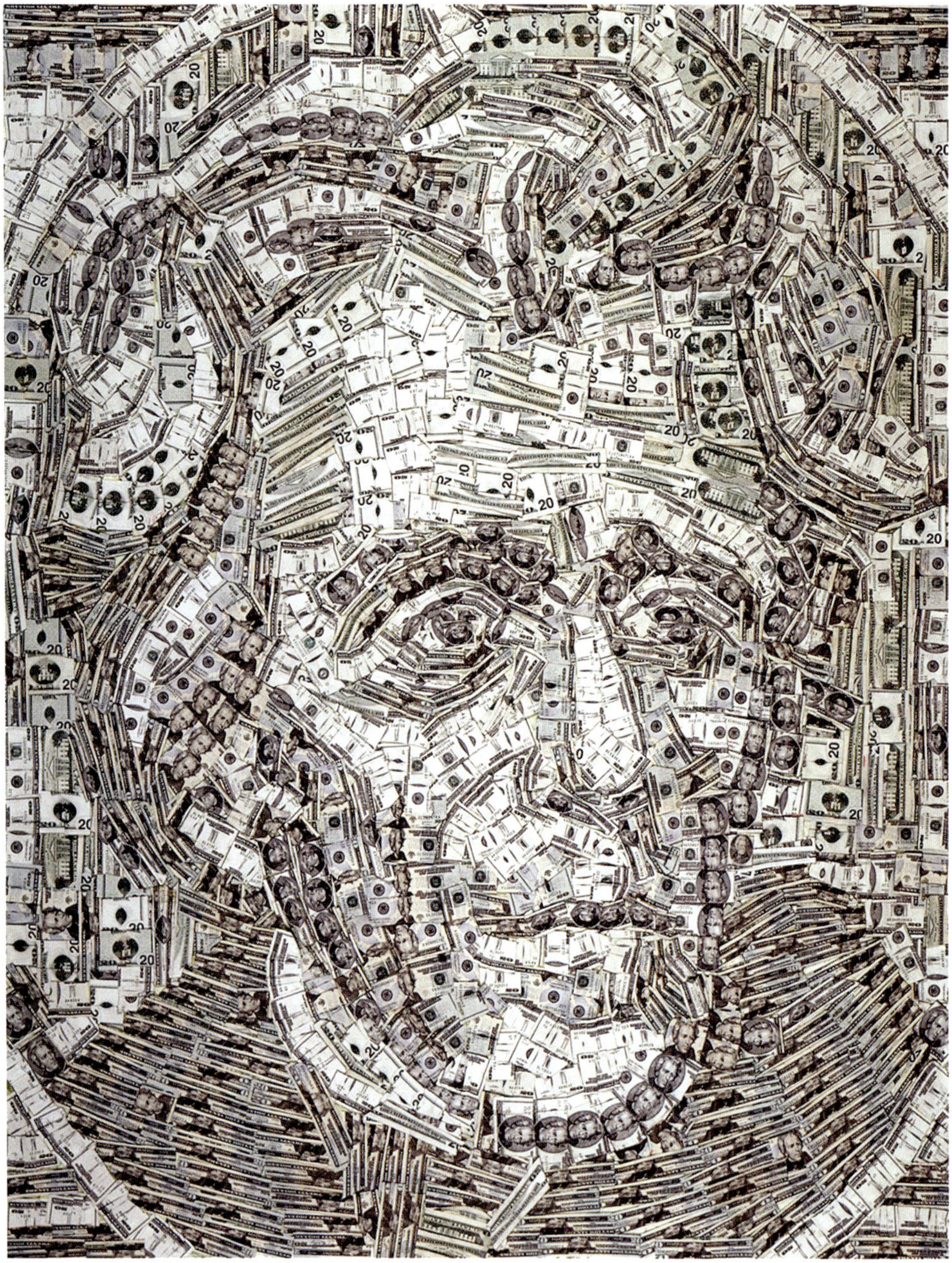

Jackson 2008
US currency on Linen
64 x 51 in.

"... If I had to describe it, I'd say I paint with a classical approach followed by impressionistic application..."

Sean Diediker

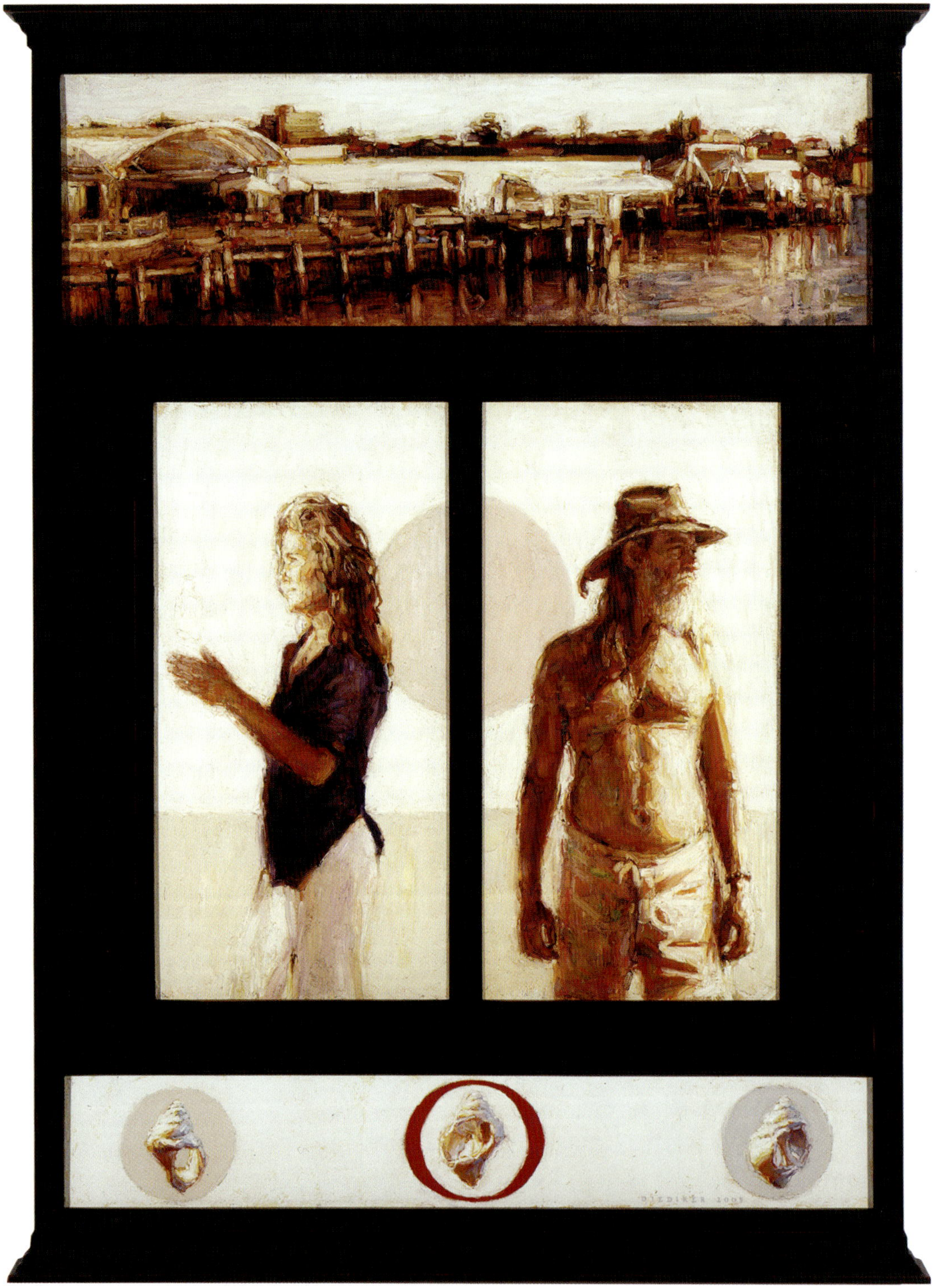

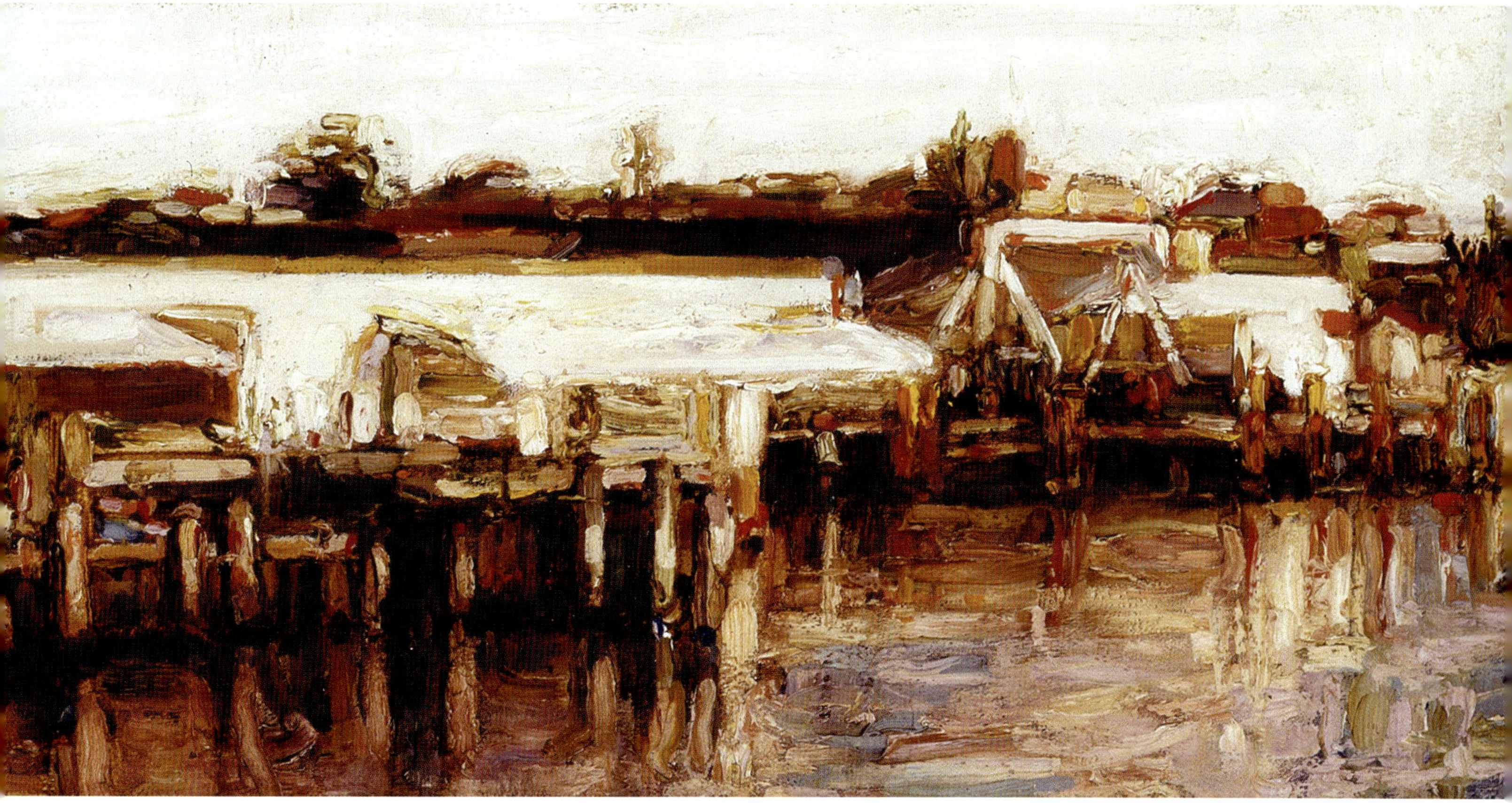

Sherlock

Sherlock 2005
Oil on Linen
64 x 51 in.

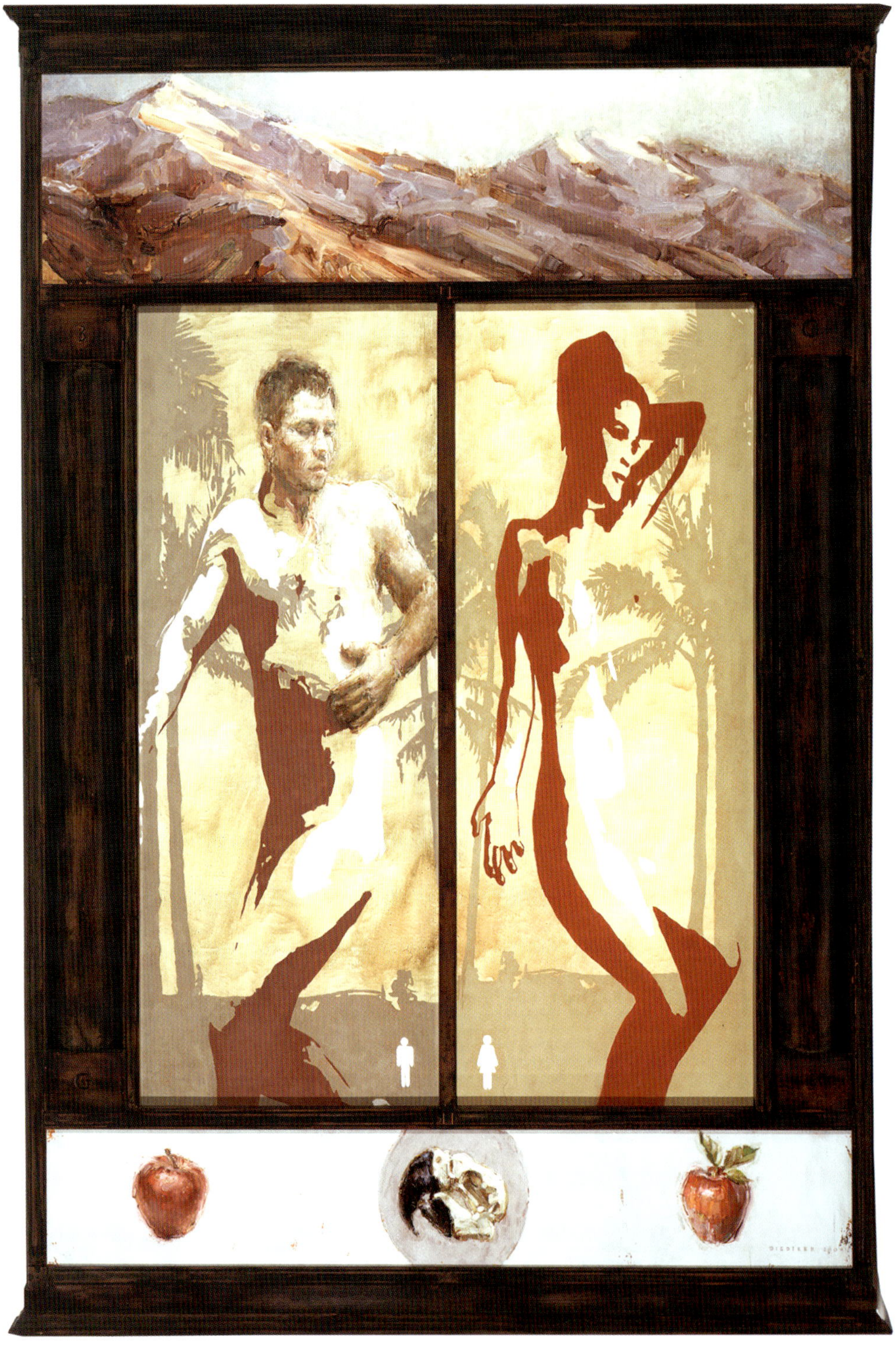

The Serpent Beguiled Me III 2004
Oil on Linen
90 x 52 in.

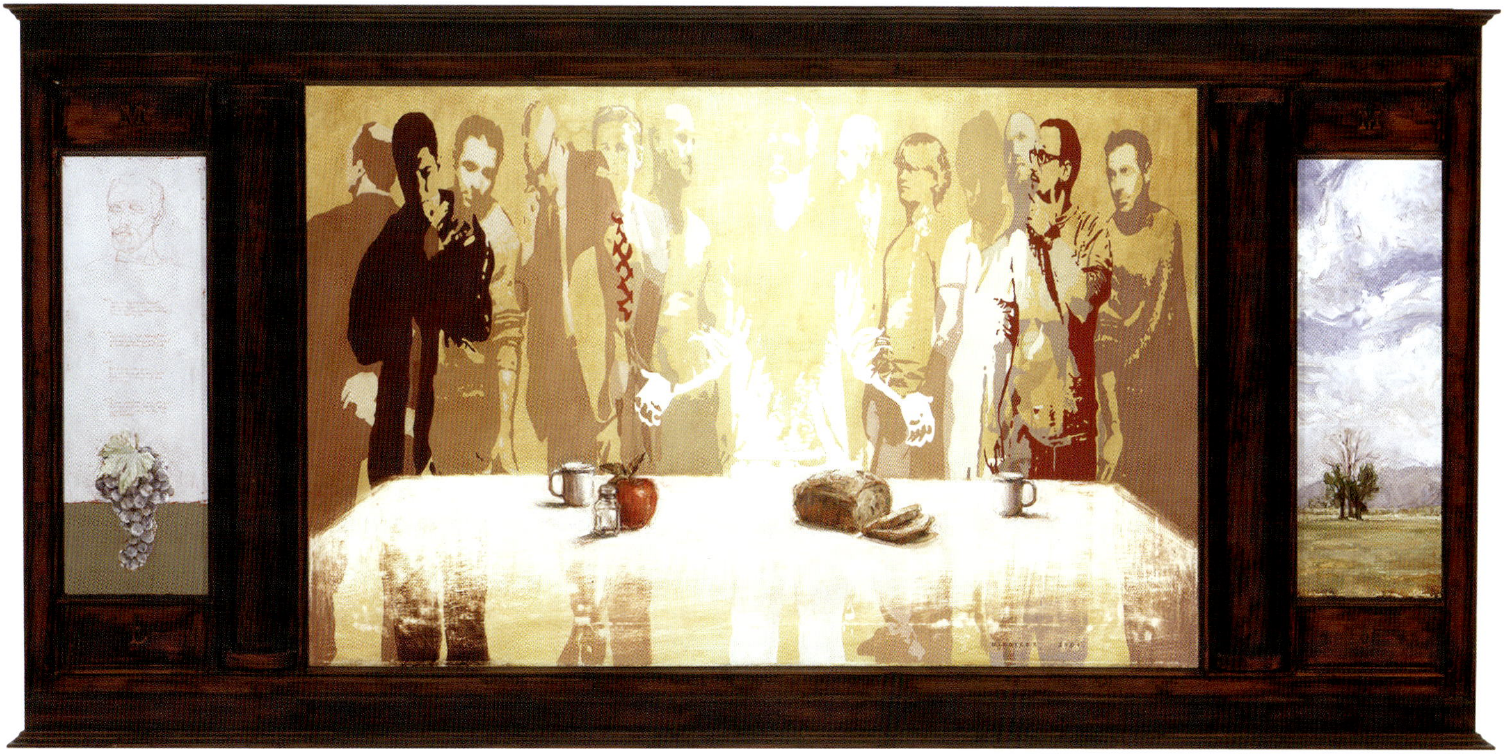

The Last Supper 2004
Oil on Linen
52 x 108 in.

Road to Cortez

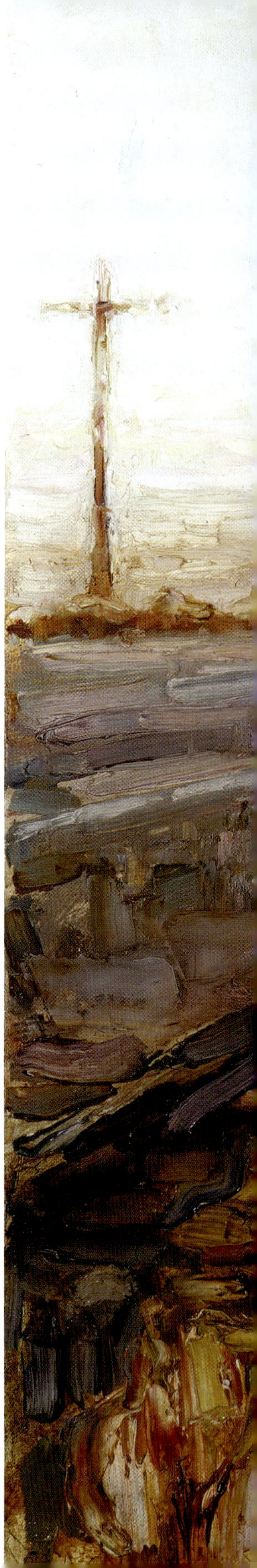

Road to Cortez 2004
Oil on Linen
31 x 34 in.

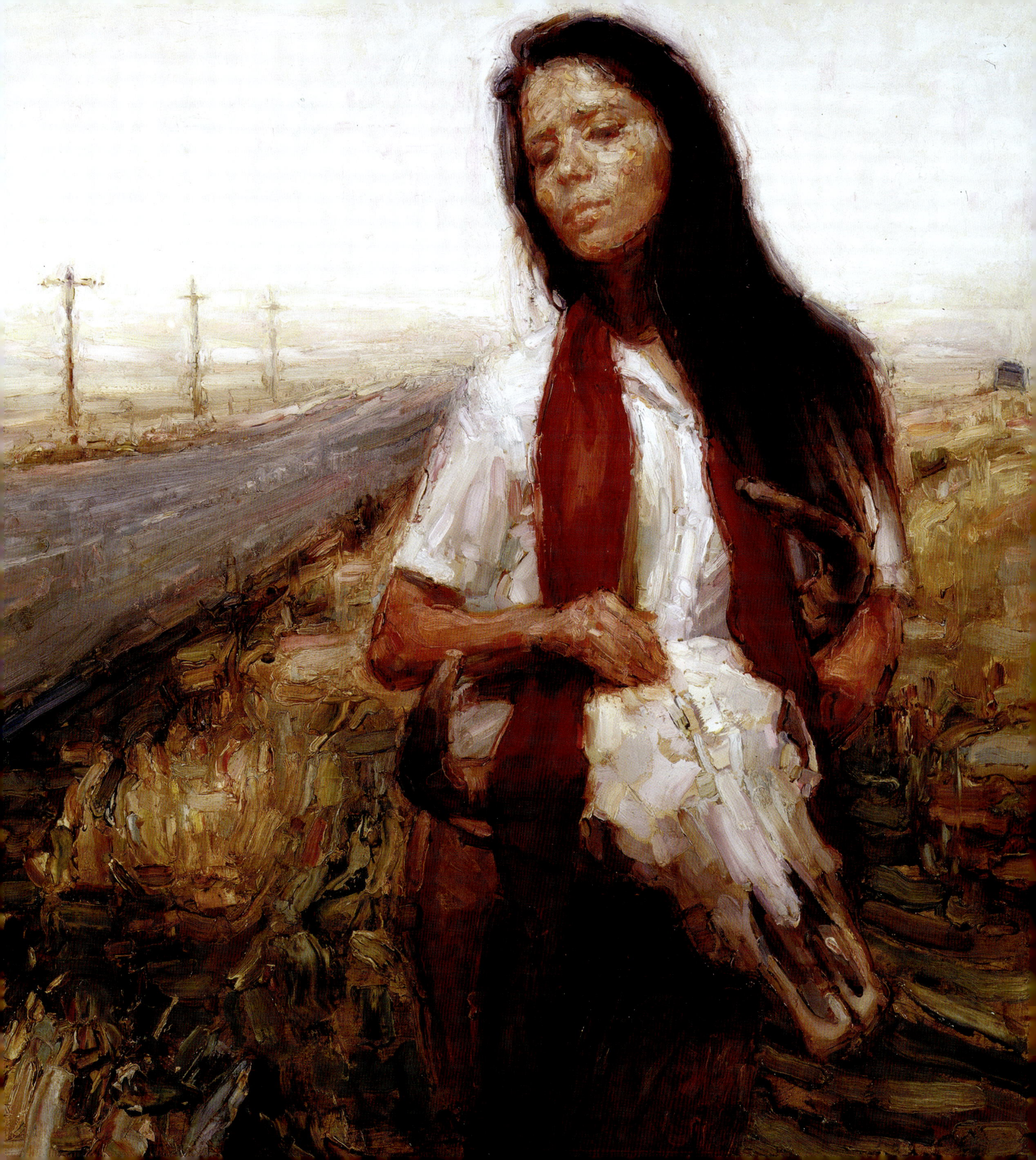

Ben

Ben
2009
Oil on Linen
20 x 16 in.

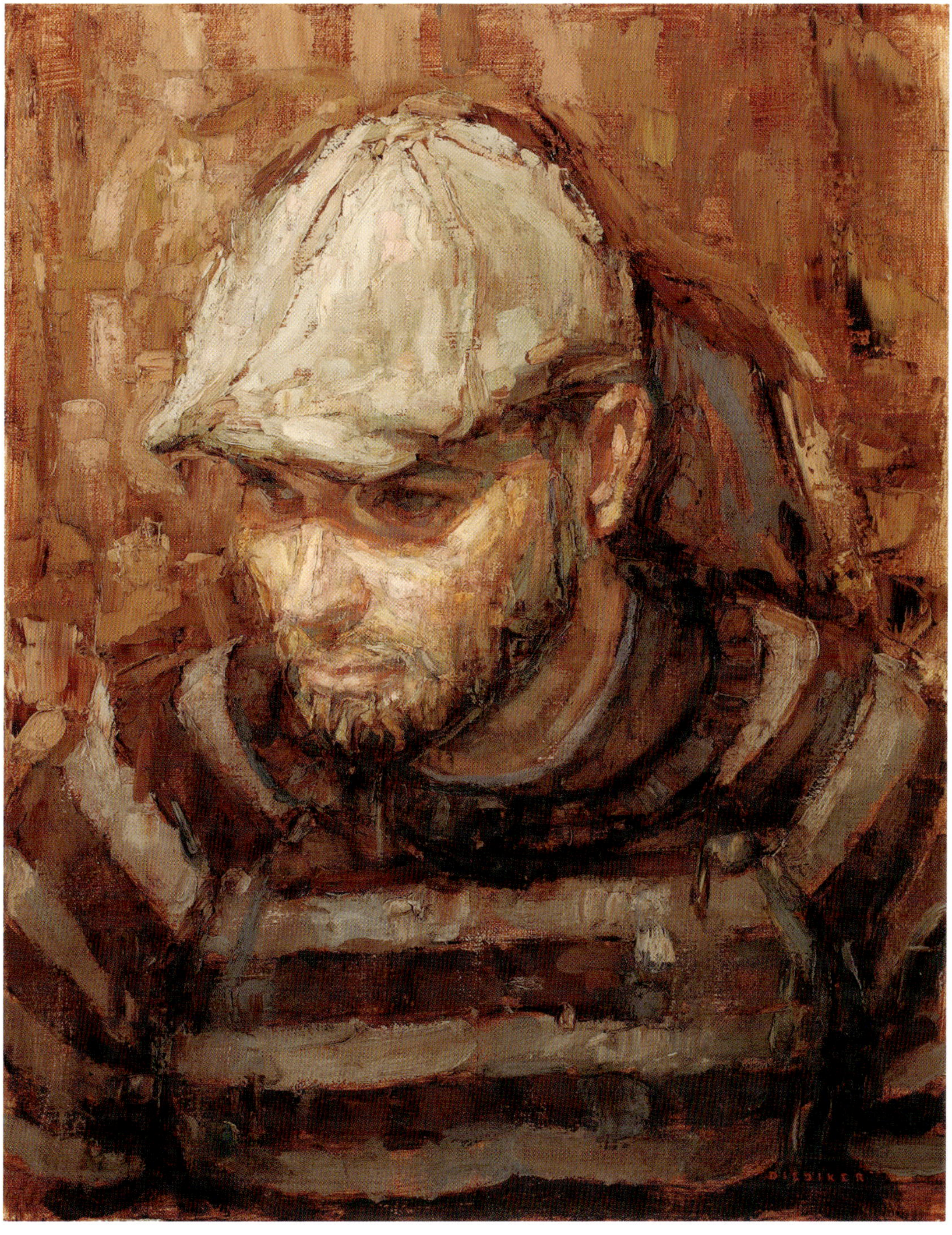

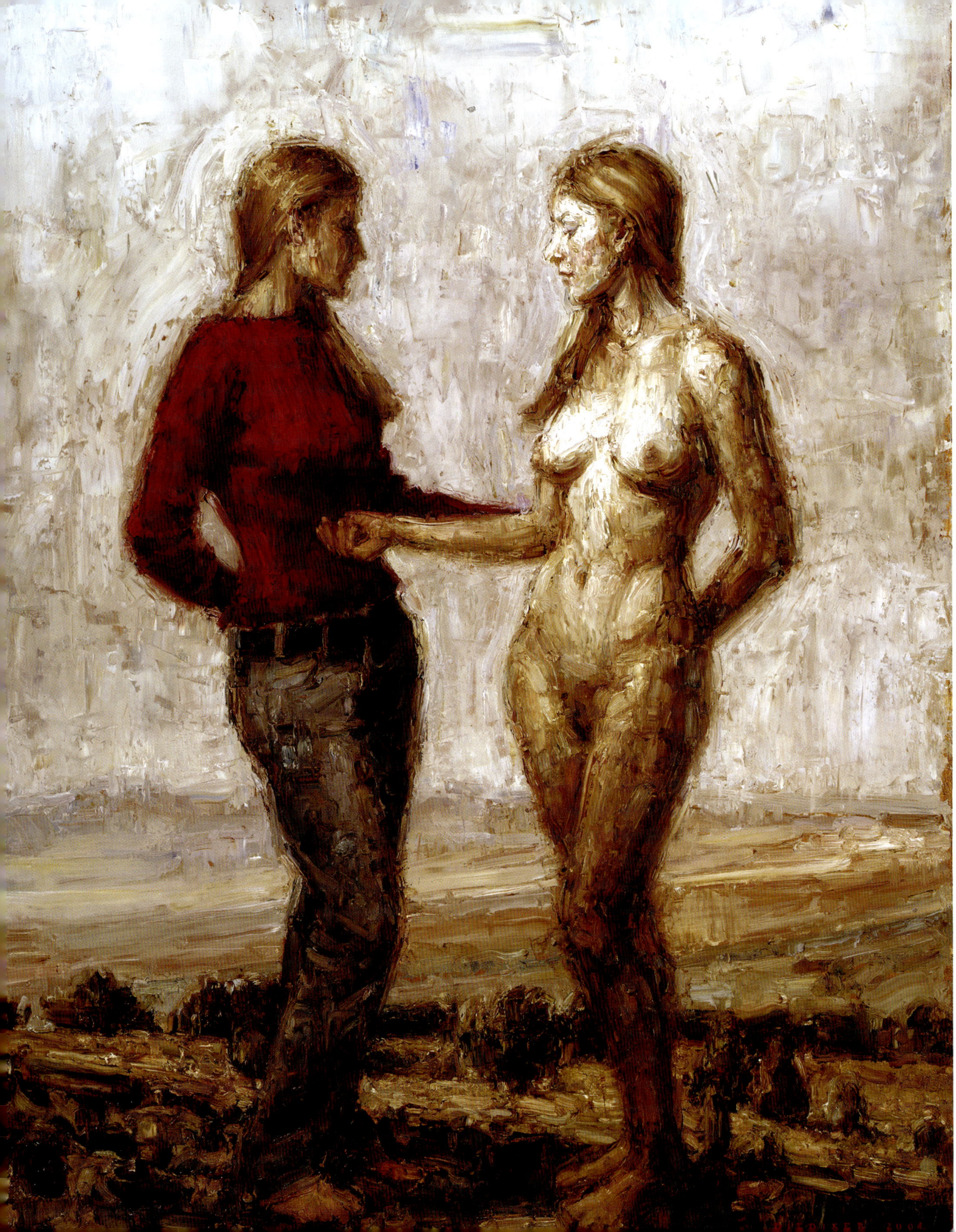

Nanette

Nanette 2004
Oil on Linen
50 x 40 in.

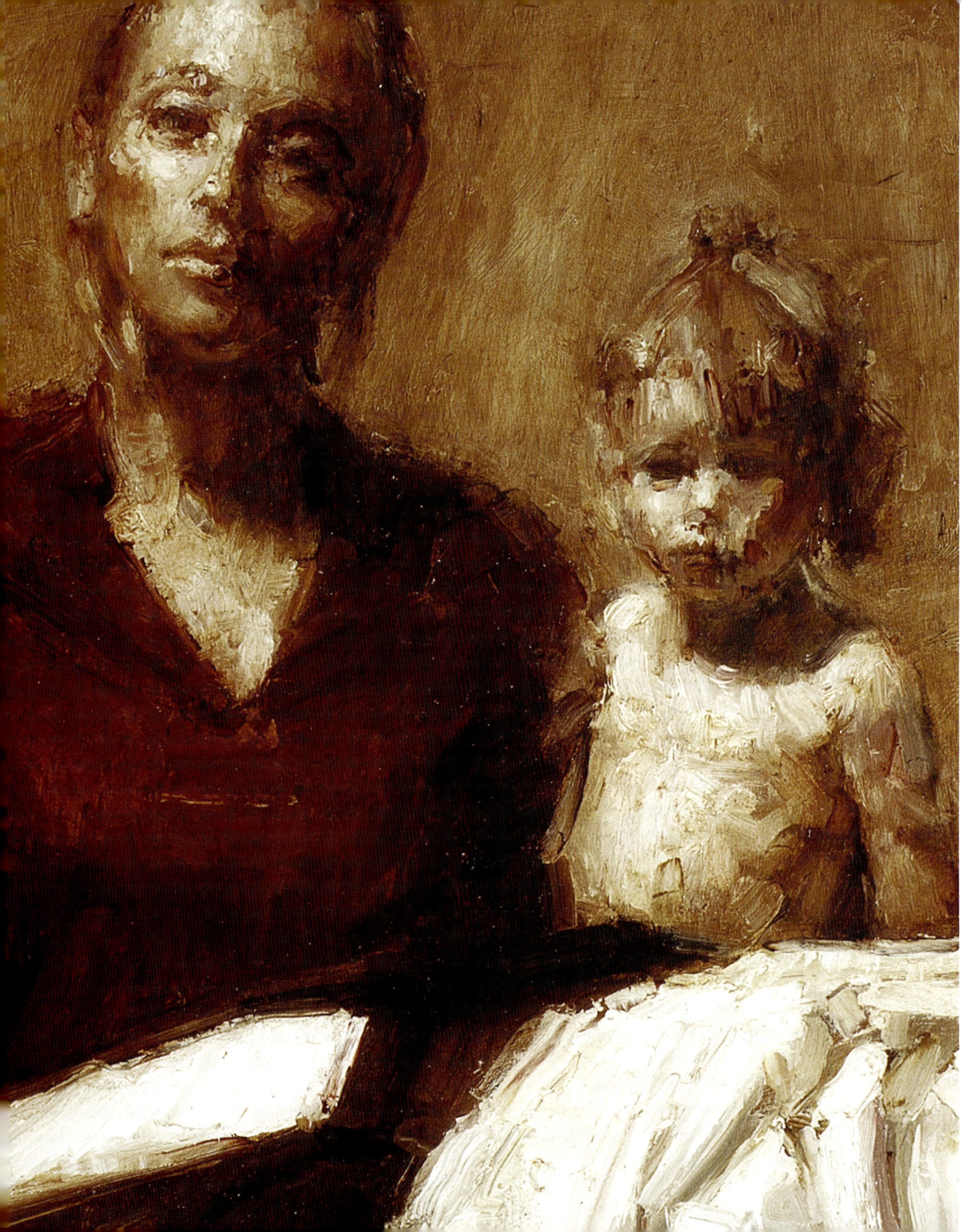

9:20

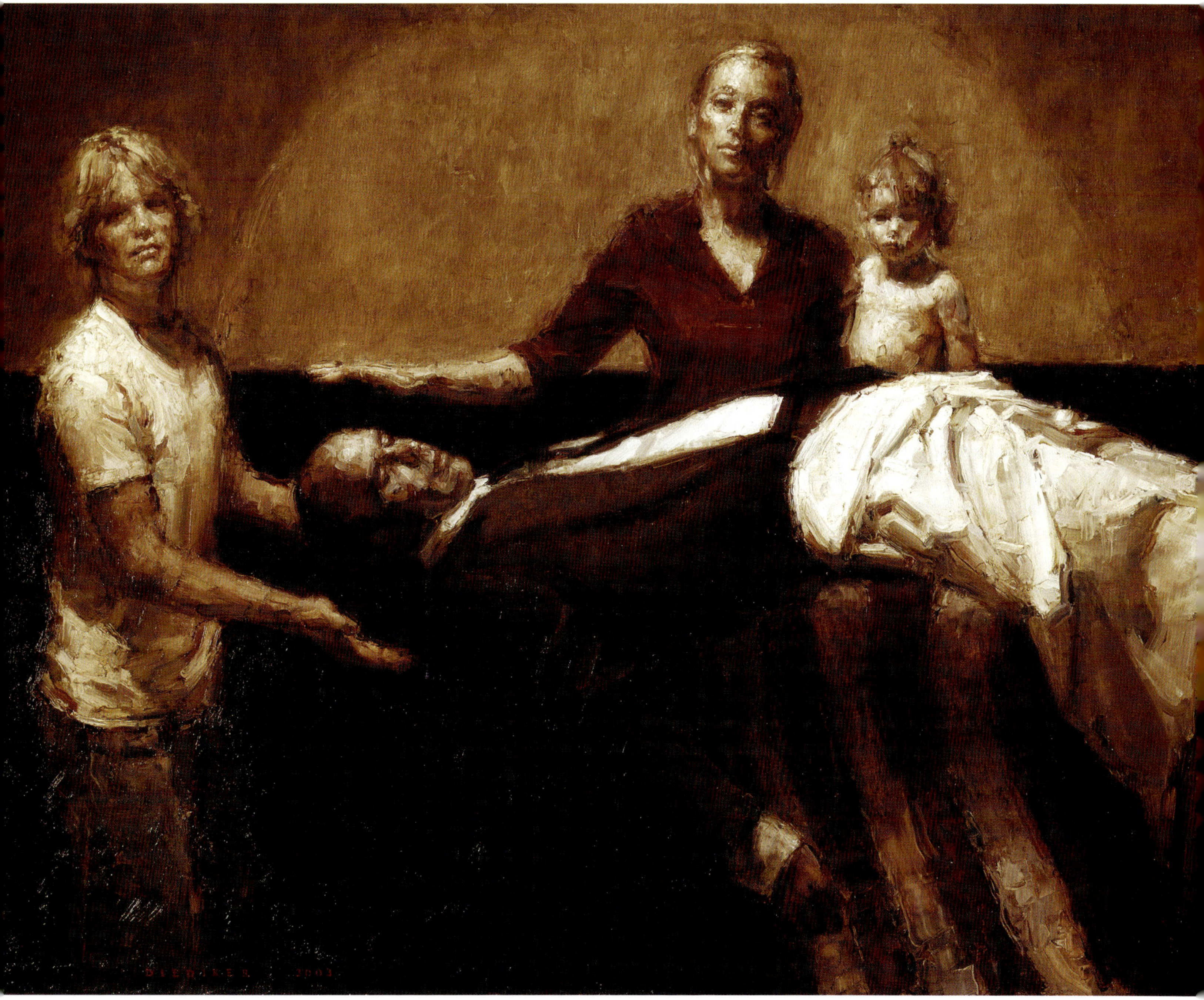

9:20
2003
Oil on Linen
40 x 30 in.

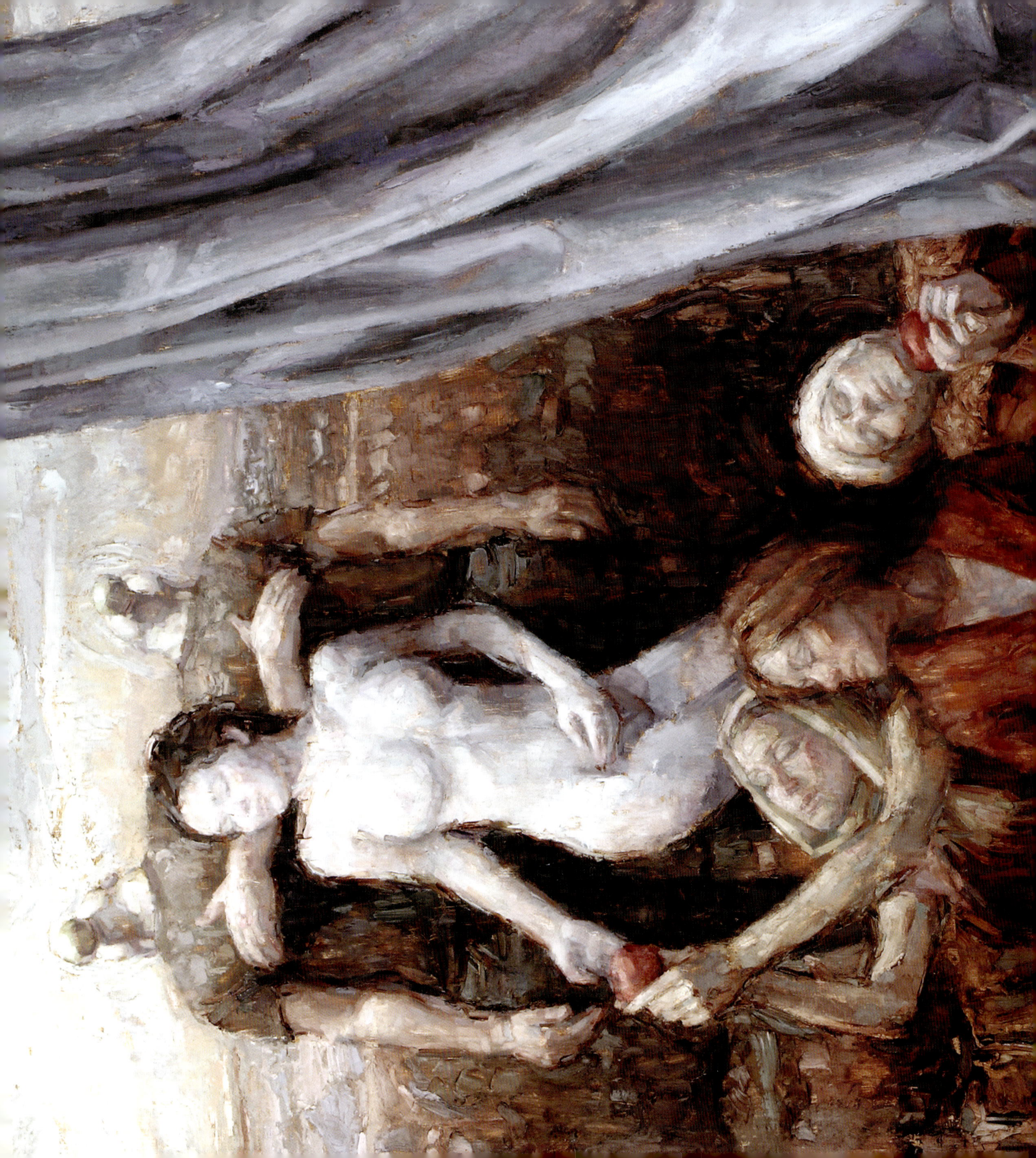

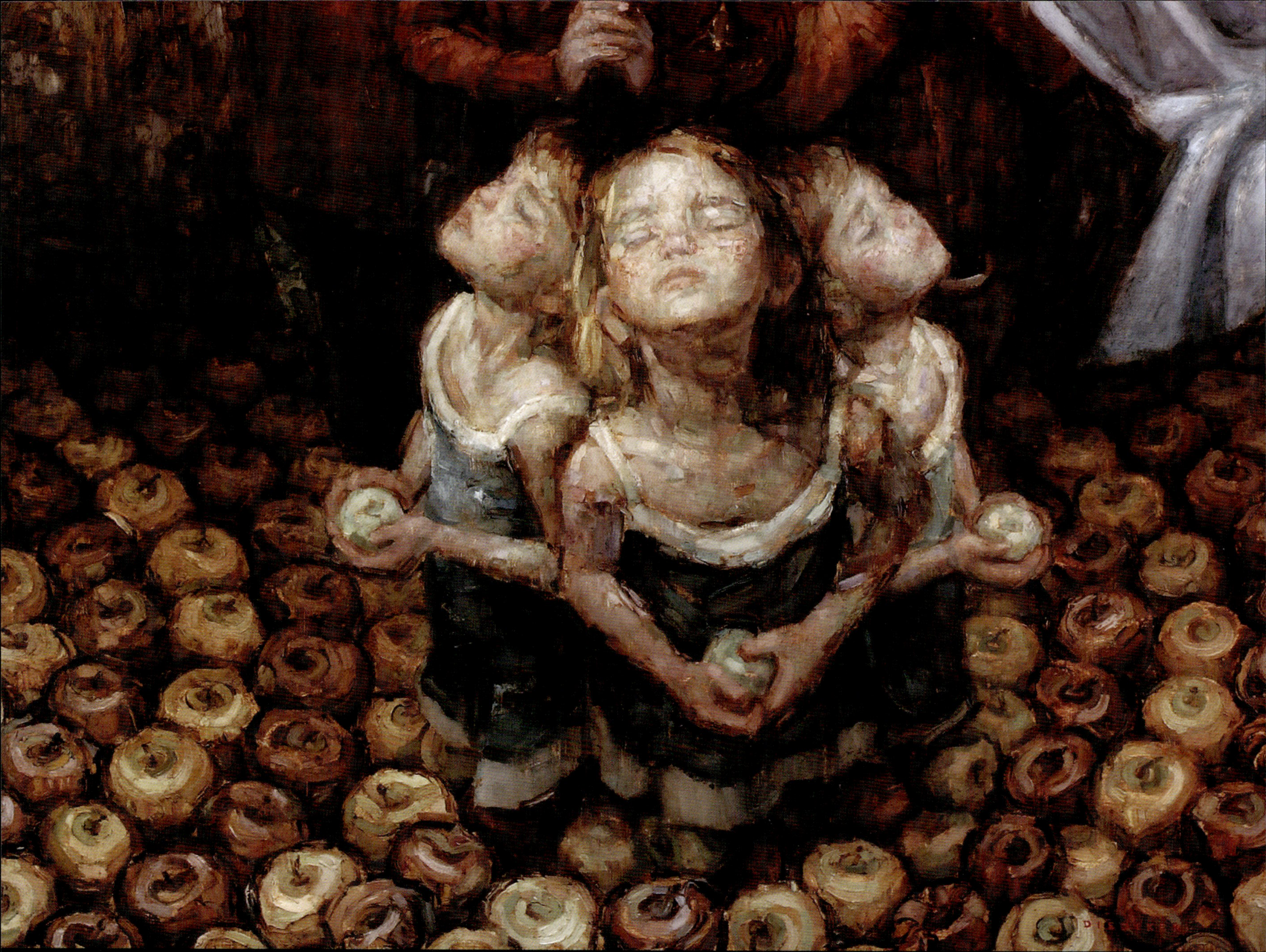

The Condition no. 1
2009
Oil on Linen
70 x 41.5 in.

The Condition no. 2

The Condition no. 2
2009
Oil on Linen
50 x 23 in.

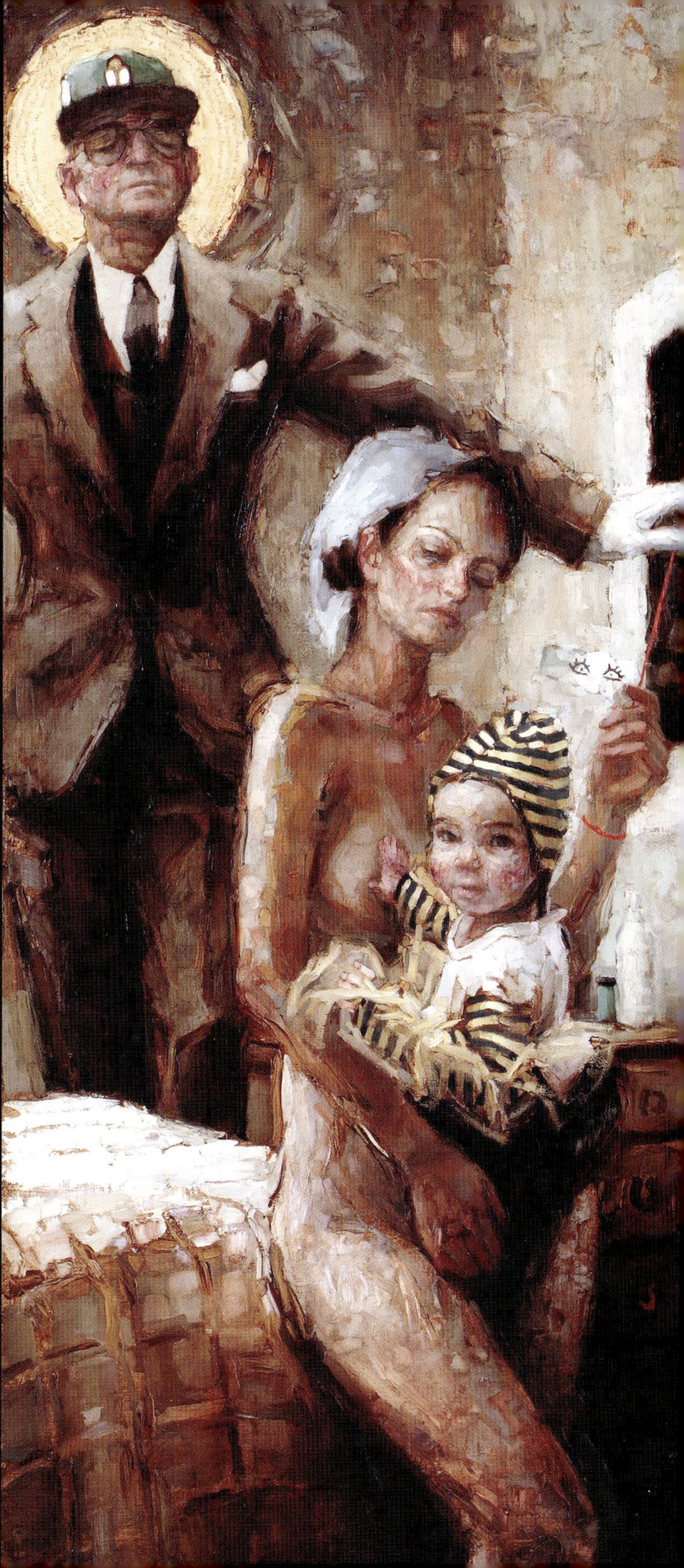

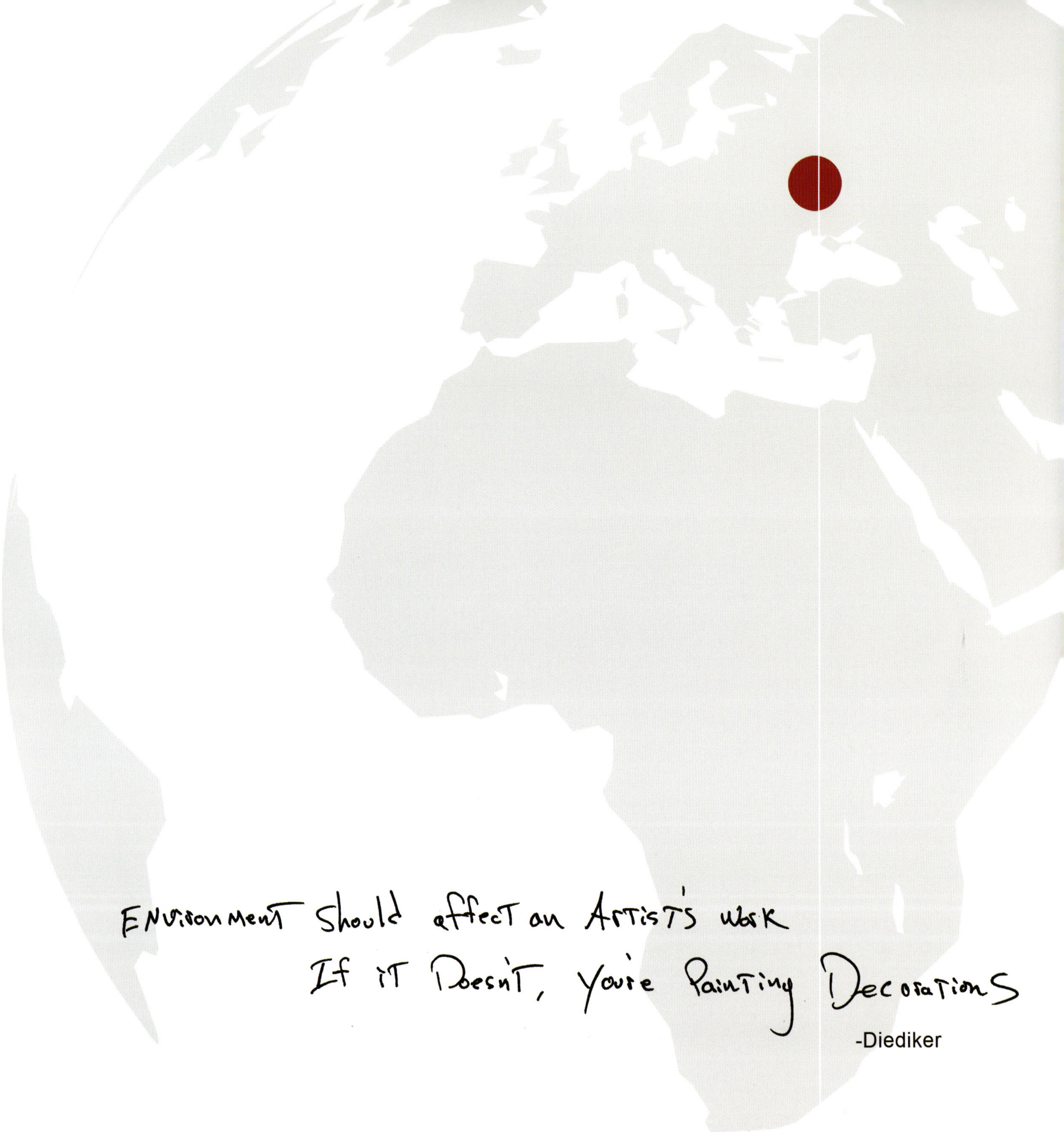

Environment should affect an Artist's work
If it Doesn't, you're Painting Decorations

-Diediker

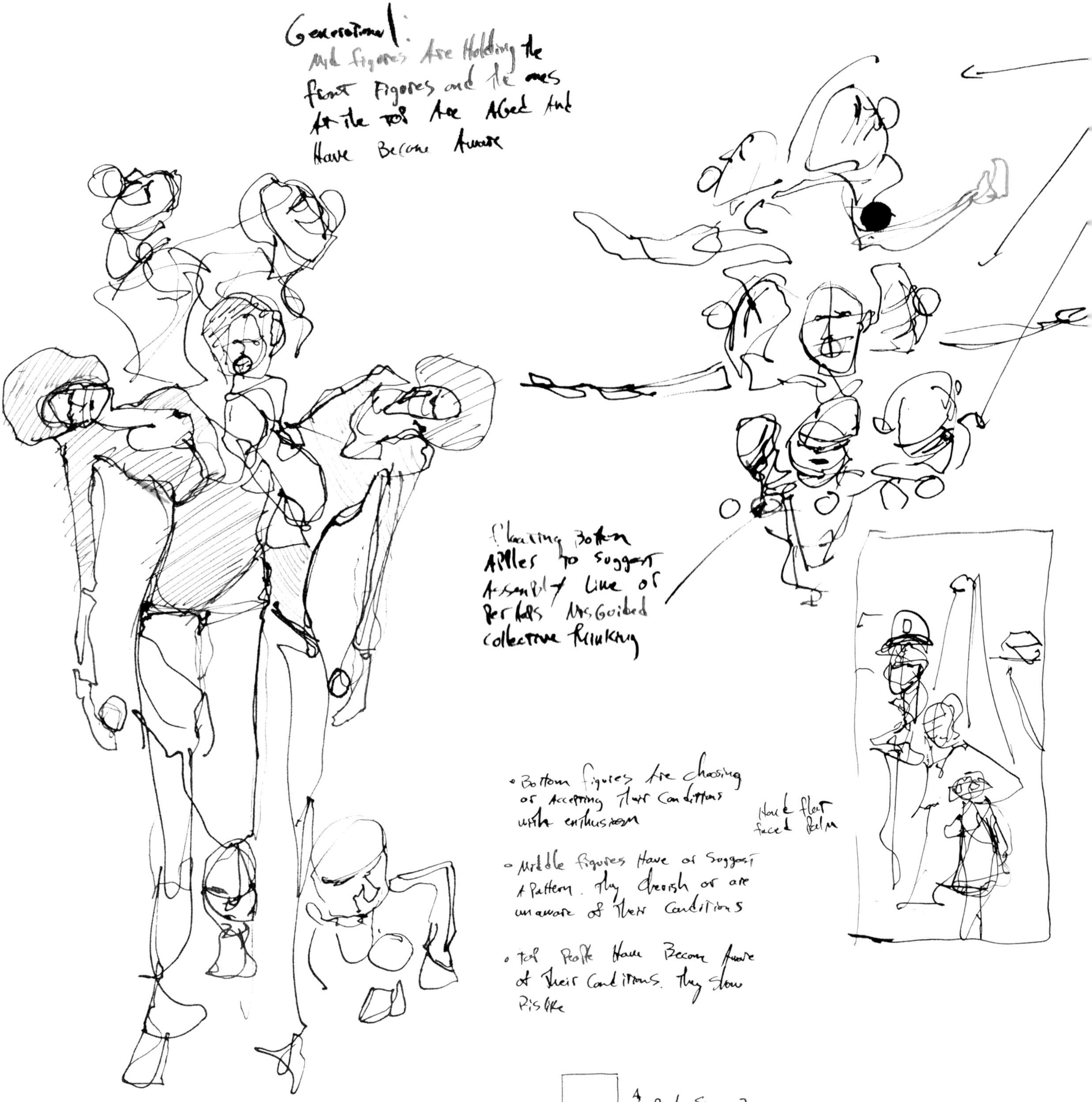

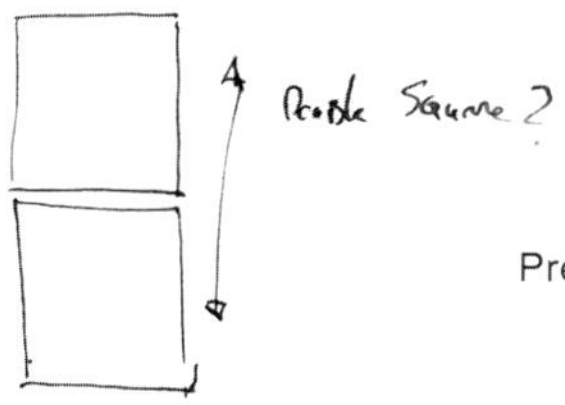

Most of Diediker's paintings start out as abbreviated thoughts and gesture drawings

Preliminary drawings for **The Condition no. 1** and **The Condition no. 2**

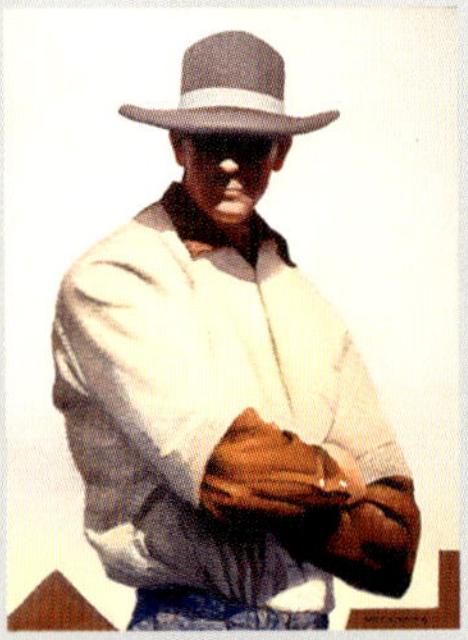

Gary Ernest Smith

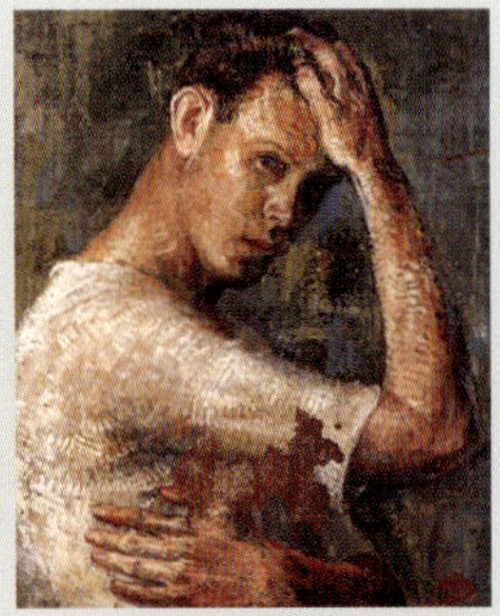

Trevor Southey

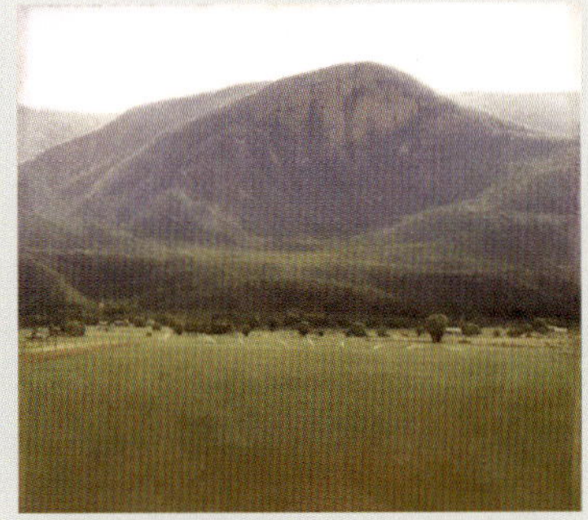

Michael Workman

Smith for His Iconic Approach
To the figure and Impasto
Paint Application

Southey for His Translated
Connection with His Subjects

Workman for Revealing Process
in the finished Work

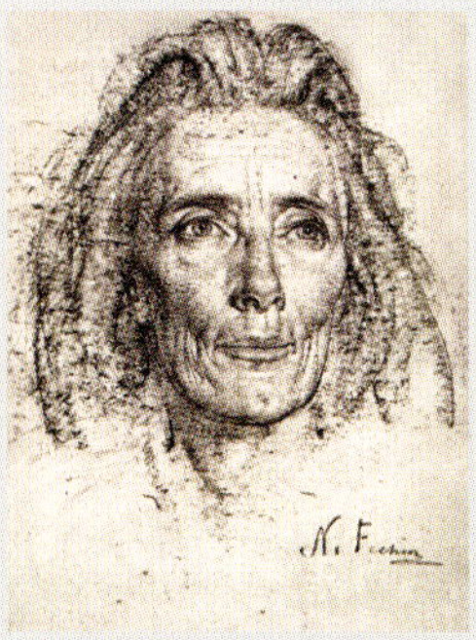

Nicolai Fechin

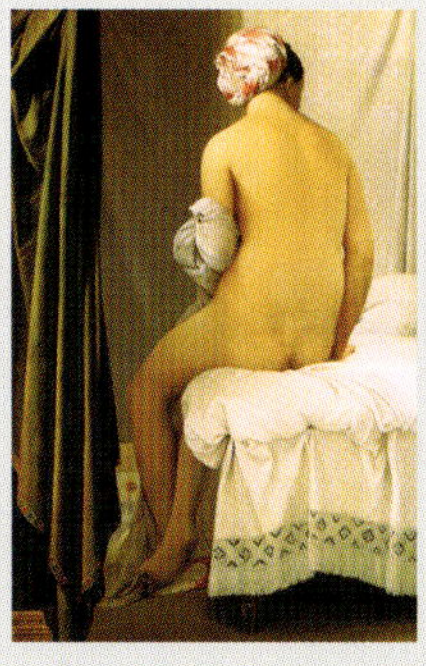

Ingres

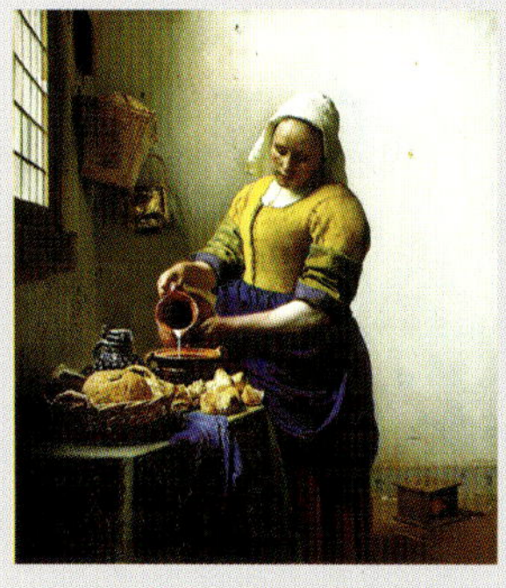

Vermeer

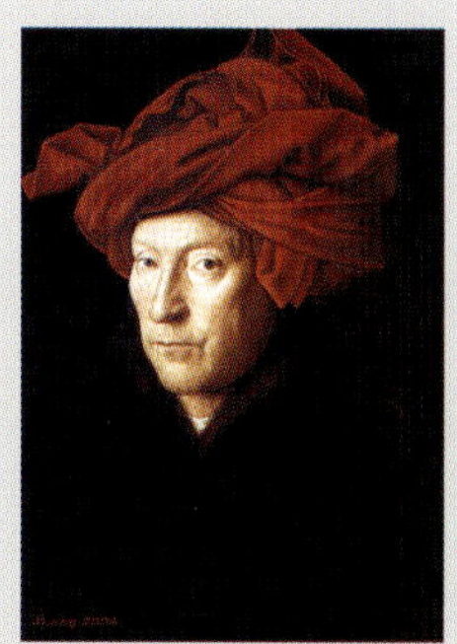

Jan van Eyck

Fechin for His immediacy in Paint application

Ingres for His Seductive Surface Quality And Refined Craftsmanship

Vermeer Composition, Composition
Composition

Van Eyck Color and Value Balance

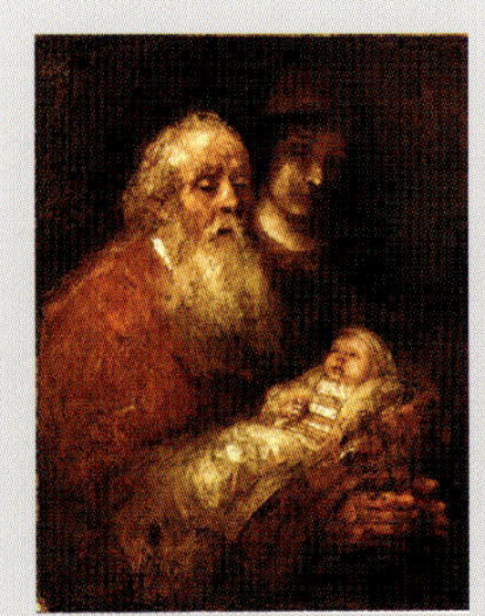

Rembrandt

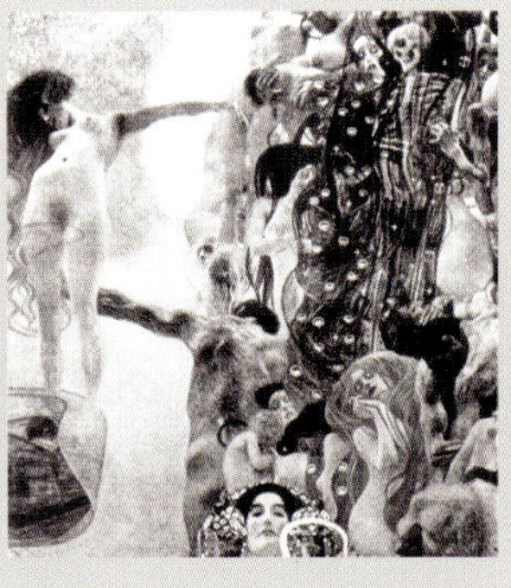

Gustav Klimt

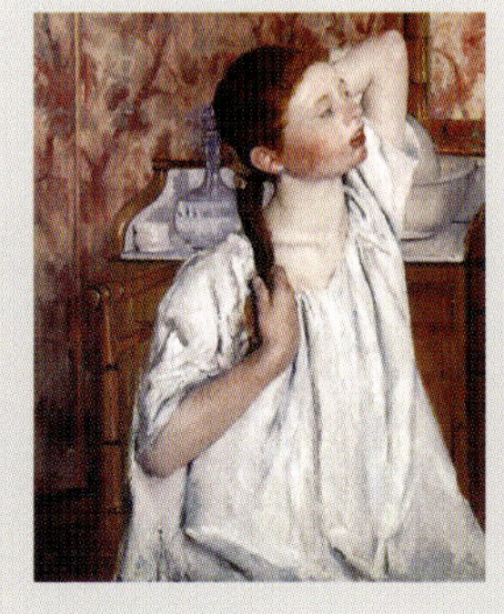

Mary Cassatt

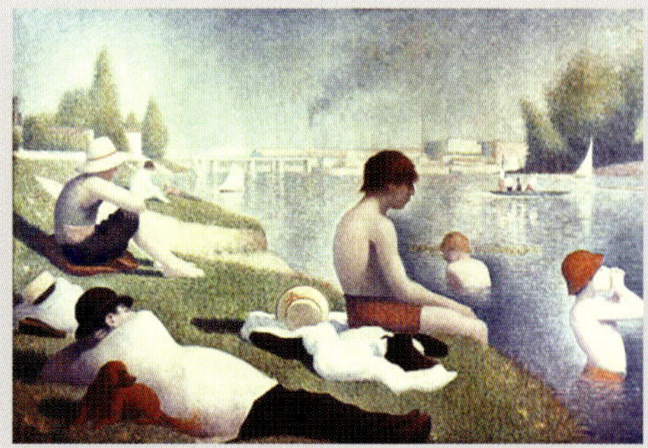

Georges Seurat

Rembrandt Over all Application
and Surface Depth

Klimt Transition from Academic
Classical To The Kiss

Cassatt
Beauty in The Every Day
Through Composition

Seurat for His understanding of
How People see. (couldn't Have Done
The Dollar Bill Pieces without Him)

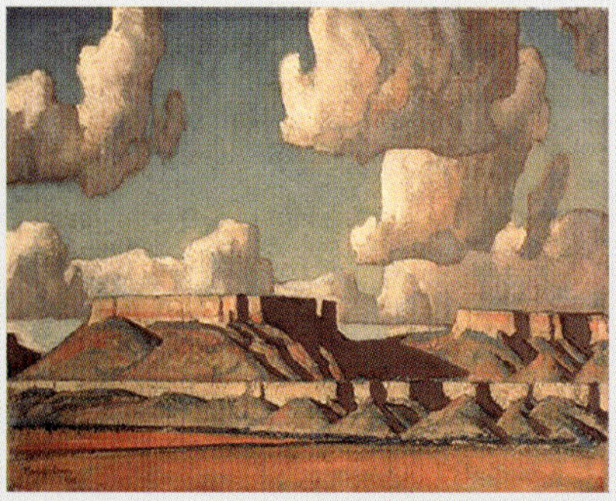

Maynard Dixon

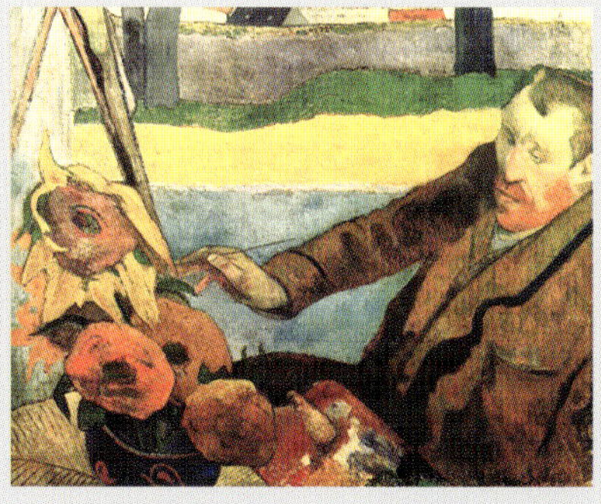

Paul Gauguin

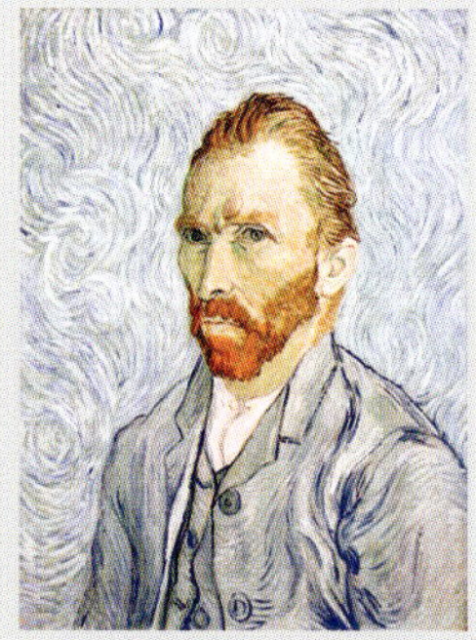

Vincent van Gogh

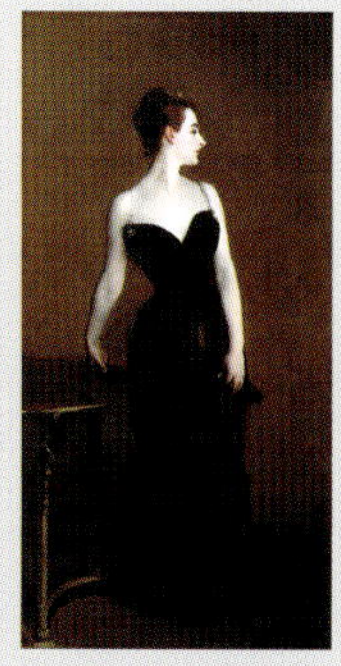

Sargent

Dixon Color and Stylized
interpretation of landscape

Gaugoin Color

Van Gogh for His love of The
Game and original use
of Color

Sargent for His Confidence
in Single Application
Painting

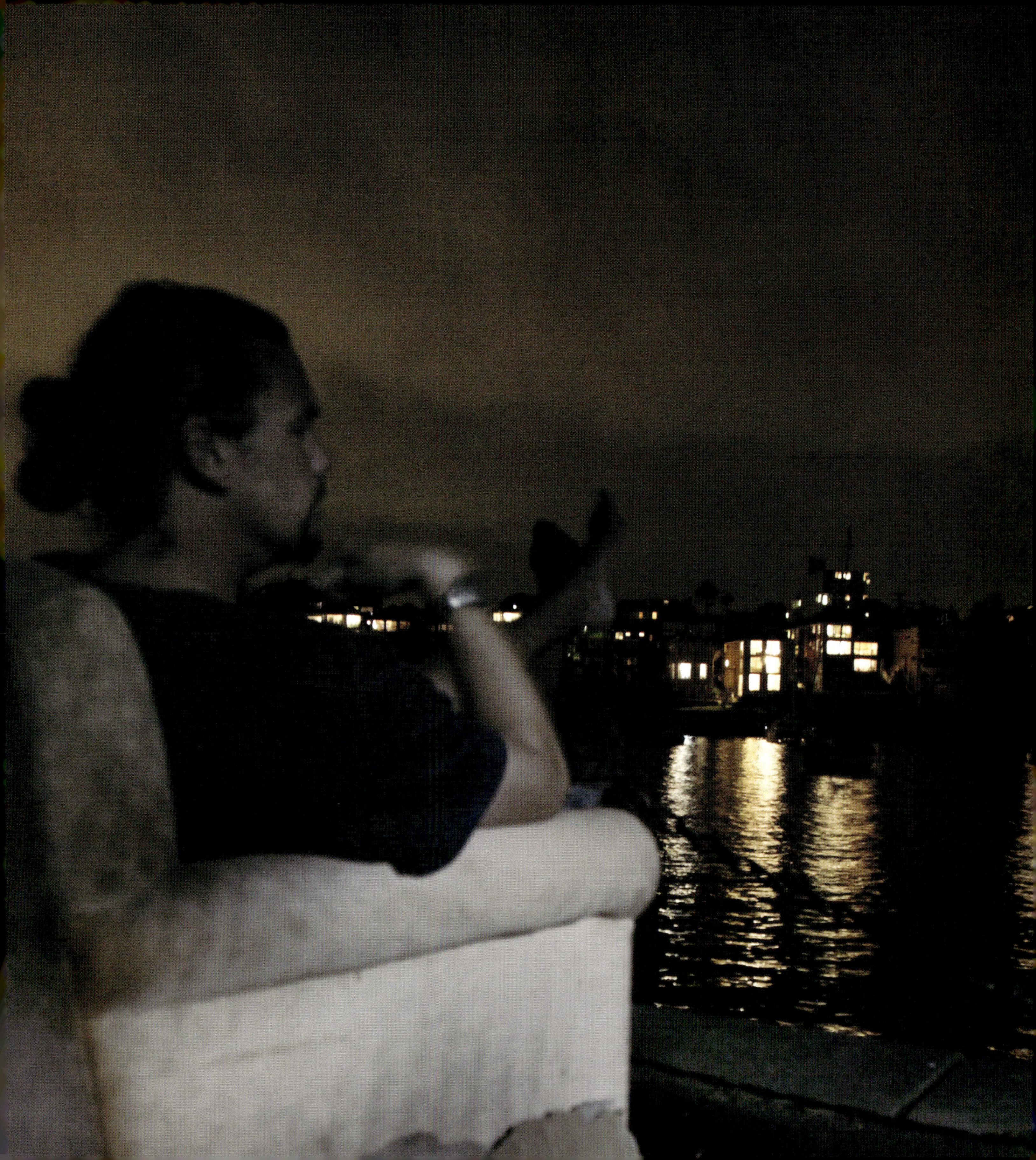

Q&A
with
DIEDIKER

Q: **Why did you take a break from your previous style to immerse yourself in encaustics?**

A: I'm not comparing myself with Picasso in any way, but he comes to mind in answering this question. Picasso got very comfortable with and successful for a certain style of painting, then he went on to experiment in many different styles and mediums. I revel in the idea of opening another door and seeing what might happen. This [encaustic work] is something that I haven't seen before... Encaustics have been done throughout history, and they made a minor comeback with Jasper Johns in the '50s. But I feel like my application, the way I'm laying down the imagery, hasn't been done before in encaustics. If that's the case, it is my artistic responsibility to explore the encaustic medium further to discover its potential.

Q: **You've mentioned that you're more interested in surface than subject. What do you mean by that?**

A: For me, subject is sometimes irrelevant. For some of my work – the 9/11 series and the conditioning series – the subject rests at the crux of my pieces. But, in all honesty, I most enjoy getting lost in the surface of my work... I love what's going on with the paint, all the mark-making. I also love trying to do something that can't be duplicated. In my mind, a good painting has evidence of its creation. While I love Vermeer for composition, you could take that particular style of painting – dry on dry – and duplicate it a thousand times. On the other hand, the way Rembrandt would drag his brush across, say, a piece of lace... That could never be duplicated. He did highly original mark-making. My thought process runs along those same lines. What I'm doing in my paintings, and especially with the encaustics, can't be duplicated.

Q: **In Untitled #24, you posted the piece to the Wax Onion in black and white, asking participants if it helped them better see the imagery. You didn't repeat that again. What did you think of the responses given?**

A: When I'm painting, I usually paint from black and white photos because they allow me to see the imagery and value better, rather than just the emotion of the color. Sometimes when you turn things to black and white, people are better able to see shape and form. In the Wax Onion group, however, I found that the participants needed the color there to provide cues to their subconscious and help them see the imagery better. The color helped them associate their lives and experiences with the imagery in each piece.

Q: **From where do you draw your inspiration?**

A: Primarily with the encaustics, I'm inspired by the natural process that Mother Nature gives us. The patterns and marks that erosion has created over millions of years are truly beautiful to me. In all of my work, I glean most of my inspiration from my environment; I am influenced by where I am and what I see. In my figurative pieces, I'm looking at people and their stories for inspiration. In my encaustic work, I'm looking to nature..

Q & A

Q: **What do you take away from the places you visit? When you go back to snowy Utah and you're working in your studio, what do you take from these places that you've been?**

A: More than anything, traveling provides a much-needed element of change, which then ignites my creativity. For instance, I was inspired to do the dollar bill piece – Washington – in Sydney, where their currency is so different from US currency. It made me look at the American dollar bill in a new light. I started thinking that if I could make a value scale out of folded dollar bills, I could create any image. I did a test project, it worked, and now I've got the Dollar Bill collection

Q: **What do you think your audience will take away from viewing your encaustics? What do you hope to achieve through your encaustic work, which seems like a departure from your traditional work?**

A: I think the most important part of this project is its ability to educate and enlighten. Hopefully, I can still create imagery that's interesting with color, form, and composition.... all of those things that make a painting great on its own. But I also hope that my viewers will want to understand the medium further and educate themselves on the process of how these pieces came about, recognizing that they are a result of the collaboration of many other view points from around the world.

Q: **You're also one of the founders of the Bridge Academy of Art in Provo, Utah. How did that come about?**

A: The Bridge Academy of Art emerged to provide an alternative setting for art education. We are professionals who actually make our livings as artists. We teach our curriculum almost as apprenticeships. We also invite top working artists, galleries, and museum representatives from around the world to our campus, and they forge personal relationships with our students. We believe that each artist holds tremendous individual potential. And we encourage our students to develop their diverse skills and talents in an environment where differing perspectives, skill sets, ability levels, and approaches to technique are equally respected and unique personal

Q: **How does one succeed at being a working professional artist?**

A: The great part about the Bridge is that everyone's formula for success is different. No artist "makes it" exactly the same. Some artists get a lucky break; some take years to earn recognition. Everyone's path is different, and we embrace that at the Academy. In my career, I think I got lucky fairly early. In high school, I wanted to go into medicine, and I excelled in the sciences. I just didn't like the lifestyle that came with medicine. So I decided that I was going to be a painter instead. [Diediker laughs.] From that point forward, I had to succeed at painting. There was no other option. Ten years later, I started getting gallery deals and my career took off

Q: **How do you feel the fans of your traditional work will respond to your encaustics?**

A: In my opinion, abstract work has gotten a bad reputation. Any weekend warrior with a brush and a box of toll paint can call their work 'abstract.' Good abstract work, which includes all the elements of composition, color theory, and concept, has gotten muddled out by the bad... I think I'll go back to painting and realize how much I have learned about letting the paint lie and trying to avoid over-painting and excessive manipulation. If I make a beautiful mark and I decide that's more important than rendering my subject, then I'm going to leave the mark as it is. I hope that viewers recognize that my traditional work and my encaustic work are one and the same: I'm making beautiful marks and exploring the surface quality. There is a subject in both, but with the encaustics, the subject sublimates itself to the surface quality. The final product may look very different, but the work itself is no different in my mind.

Q: **What is the main difference in working with encaustics?**

A: The main difference is my lack of control, which is kind of exciting. With oil paint, I have as much control over the medium as I want. With the encaustic pieces, I start with an absolute abstract first and then worry about imagery, because there is very little I can control in the beeswax medium. I have no idea how an image will turn out, and I submit myself to that uncertainty. The melting of wax is conducive to abstract imagery: it all depends on the heat I apply, how I 'erode' the wax, and the pigment I use. Another significant difference lies in the conception. I enter my traditional work with a subject in mind. With these encaustics, nothing is pre-conceived.

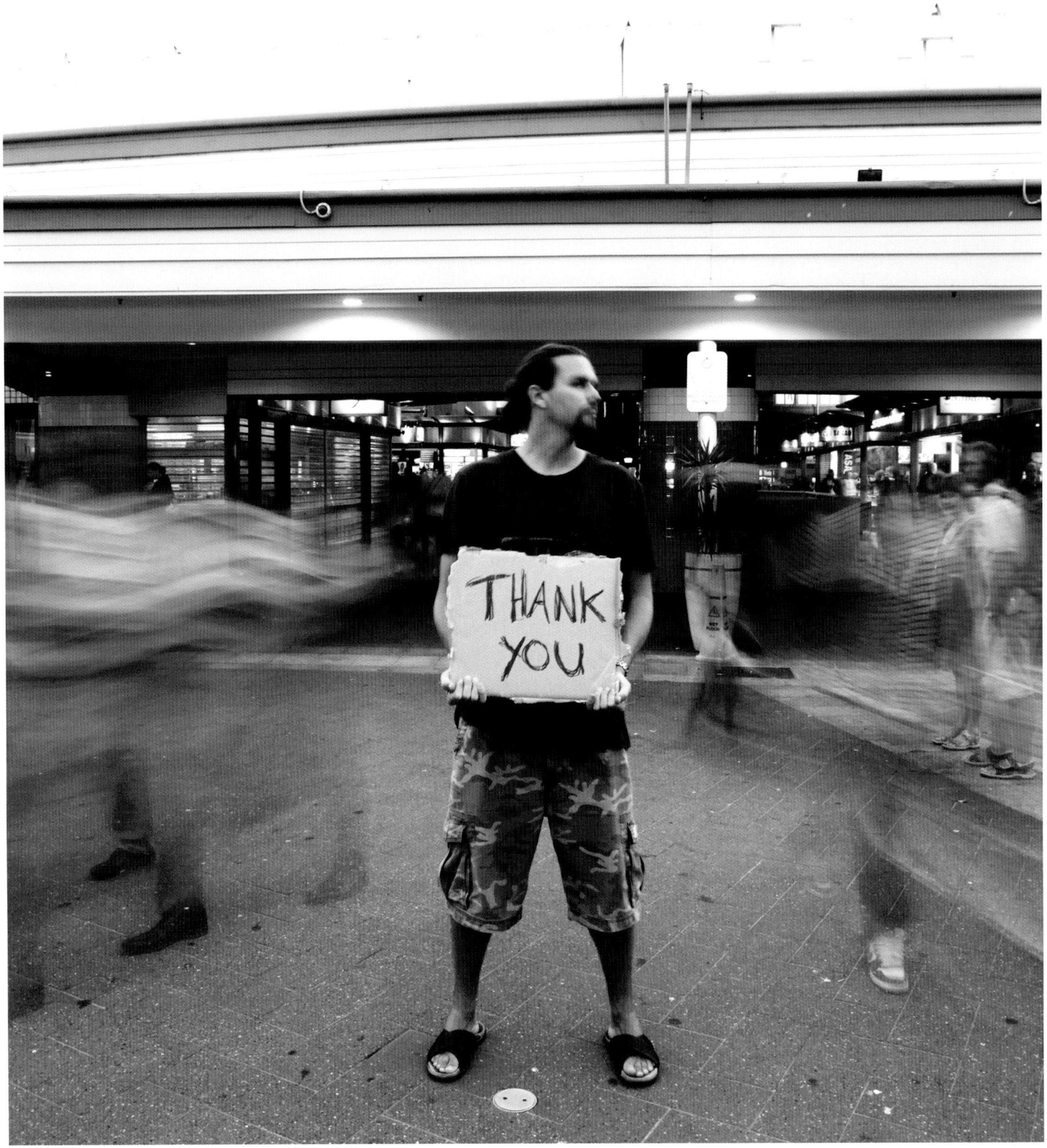
THANK
YOU

Special Thanks

To all those who believed & supported me in my search for Beauty...

Mom and Dad
Jules
Casey
Justin
Ben
Joe
Emily
Verny
Lily
Virginia
David
Roy
Gabe

Dennis
Marilyn
Marc
Mrs. Colell
Virgil
Traci
Kinsi
Bob
Gary
Mike
Karen
LeRoy
Gina ... And Many Many More

All Sincerity
Sean Diediker

Diediker on Manly Wharf in Australia
Photo Courtesy of
Joe Maurer Photography

Bibliography

Anfam, David. *Abstract Expressionism*. New York/London: Thames and Hudson, Ltd., 1990. Page 7.

Cronon, William. *Changes in the Land*: Indians, Colonists, and the Ecology of New England.. New York: Hill & Wang, 1983. Page 12.

DeBuys, William. *Enchantment and Exploitation*. Albuquerque: University of New Mexico Press, 1985. Page 277.

Durham, Michael. *Desert Between the Mountains: Mormons, Miners, Padres, Mountain Men, and the Opening of the Great Basin*, 1772-1869.. New York: Henry Holt and Company, 1997. Pages 149,158.

Finch, Robert. *"Scratching." The Primal Place*. New York: W.W. Norton & Company. 1983. Reprinted in Trimble, Stephen, ed. Words From The Land: Encounters with Natural History Writing. Salt Lake City: Gibbs-Smith Publisher. 1989. Reprinted by Reno: University of Nevada Press, 1995. Pages 186-7, 196.

Gangelhoff, Bonnie, ed. *"An Artist Abroad." Southwest Art (November 2005):* 128-133. Selected excepts of Diediker as quoted in interview with Gangelhoff and reiterated to the author of this book.

Hay, John. *"Homing." The Undiscovered Country*. New York: W.W. Norton & Company. 1981. Reprinted in Trimble, Stephen, ed. Words From The Land: Encounters with Natural History Writing. Salt Lake City: Gibbs-Smith Publisher. 1989. Reprinted by Reno: University of Nevada Press, 1995. Page 159.

Hubbell, Sue. *A Book of Bees*. New York: Ballantine Books, 1988. Pages: 49 (metabolizing clusters); 155 (orbits); 18-23, 72, 81-82 (details about attacked colonies/weak morale).

Kalm, Peter. *Travels, I*. Page 308. As cited by Cronon, William, in Changes in the Land: Indians, Colonists, and the Ecology of New England.. New York: Hill & Wang, 1983. Page 122. (Kalm's work has been translated and appears in several Library of Congress entries and translated versions. I have cited his journal as it was cited in Cronon's bibliography.)

Langston, Nancy. *Forest Dreams, Forest Nightmares: The Paradox of Old Growth in the Inland West*. Seattle: University of Washington Press, 1995. Page 303.

Zervos, Christian. *"Conversation Avec Picasso."* Cahiers d'Art 10 (1935): 173-8. Translated by Myfanwy Evans. Reprinted by Barr, Alfred, ed, in Picasso: Forty Years of His Art. New York: Museum of Modern Art, 1939.

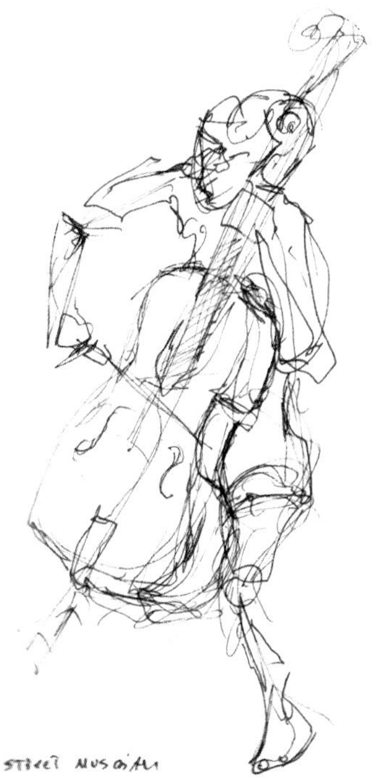

Street musician outside the Van Gogh Museum in Amsterdam.